The Greek-o-File

Volume 4

written & edited by

Sylvia & Terry Cook

The Greek-o-File Volume 4 published in Great Britain by Greek-o-File Ltd 2005

ISBN 0-9543593-3-X

The Greek-o-File Volume 4 is the latest compendium of new articles and anecdotes in paperback format compiled by Sylvia Cook from the work of many writers including Sylvia & Terry Cook and the many contributors acknowledged with their work. Photographs were supplied by authors of the relevant articles except where specified, other illustrations are by Bibby Zinram (BZ) and from free to use 'clipart'.

Edited and set: Sylvia Cook

Acknowledgements

As before, it is the enthusiasm, feedback and contributions from subscribers to our former publications that have ensured a continuation of Greek-o-File in this format. We still depend on and thank those who continue to support us as direct subscribers and contributors. Our thanks especially to the contributors to this fourth volume and to Bibby Zinram for supplying illustrations to fill a few gaps.

We thank our advertisers and supporters, many since the early days of Greek-o-File, who have encouraged us as promoters of the 'real Greece' they believe in, as much as for commercial reasons.

We are indebted to Efstathiadis and Road Editions for their kind permission to reproduce, adapt and use their maps to illustrate and clarify the detail in our travel notes.

We are also very grateful to the London Greek Embassy Press & Communications Office for their continuing support and to the AG Leventis Foundation for theirs.

Printed by: Cox & Wyman Ltd, Reading, Berkshire, UK

Greek-o-File Ltd, UK

Email: mail@greekofile.co.uk

Website: www.greekofile.co.uk

New Tel: 01225 709907

Greek-o-File Volume 4 - Contents

Introduction

The best introduction to this fourth collection of entertaining articles, anecdotes and information would be the previous three volumes - but each volume is also enjoyable on its own. The whole set will allow you to wallow in a feast of Greekness.

How many ways are there to say that The Greek-o-Files will be appreciated by any grecophile? Here is a chance to immerse yourself in the experiences of others, to relive your own memories, plan for future visits to your favourite country, learn more of its background and the psyche of its people.

The articles are from a wide range of people who love Greece. We all have something different we enjoy - the familiarity of our 'special' place and Greek friends, or the joy and uncertainty of searching for new Greek experiences and terrain. Everywhere is different. Everyone is different. But reading the views and experiences of others takes us back to our own Greece or offers ideas for future exploration.

When we are at our little village house in Lesvos, we often wonder at the diversity of our friends and acquaintances spending their days enjoying different lifestyles, each with our own local 'best' friends, all appreciating the same place. We have a common bond in our love of 'our' village, but we each divide our time to suit personal preferences (and resources), coming together here or there to chat or share a common experience.

Multiply that out by the number of villages and resorts in each Greek island and mainland region and you get some idea of how many different Greek experiences there could be ... and yet ... still a common thread of 'Greekness' that we can all relate to.

It is this variety that we try to capture in the pages of The Greek-o-Files, for all grecophiles to relate to.

Read on and enjoy!

Sylvia Cook

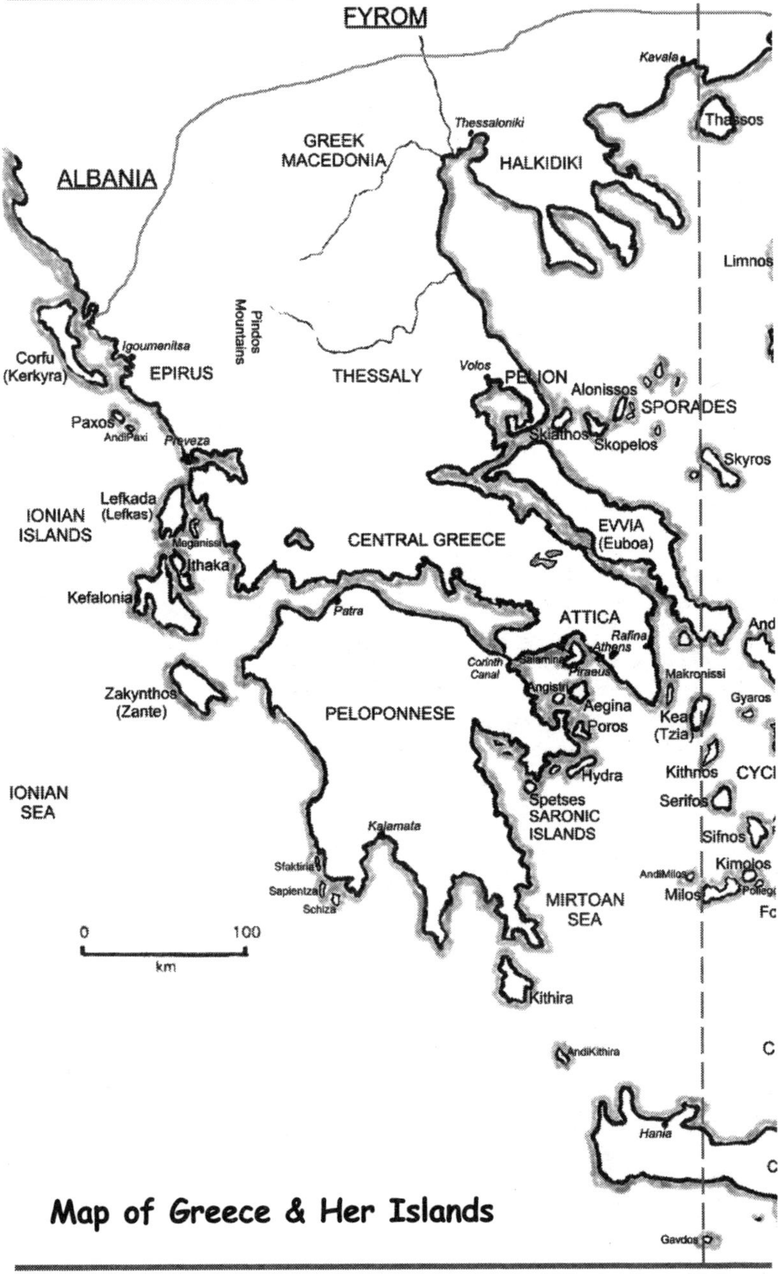

FYROM
Kavala
Thassos
Thessaloniki
GREEK MACEDONIA
HALKIDIKI
ALBANIA
Limnos
Pindos Mountains
Igoumenitsa
Corfu (Kerkyra)
EPIRUS
THESSALY
Volos
PELION
Alonissos
SPORADES
Paxos
AndiPaxi
Preveza
Skiathos
Skopelos
Skyros
Lefkada (Lefkas)
IONIAN ISLANDS
Meganissi
Ithaka
CENTRAL GREECE
EVVIA (Euboa)
Kefalonia
Patra
ATTICA
Rafina
Athens
Corinth Canal
Salamina
Piraeus
Makronissi
Zakynthos (Zante)
Angistri
Aegina
Gyaros
PELOPONNESE
Poros
Kea (Tzia)
Hydra
Kithnos
IONIAN SEA
Spetses
SARONIC ISLANDS
Serifos
Kalamata
Sifnos
Sfaktiria
Kimolos
AndiMilos
Sapientza
Milos
Schiza
MIRTOAN SEA
0 100 km
Kithira
AndiKithira
Hania
Gavdos

Map of Greece & Her Islands

Reference Map

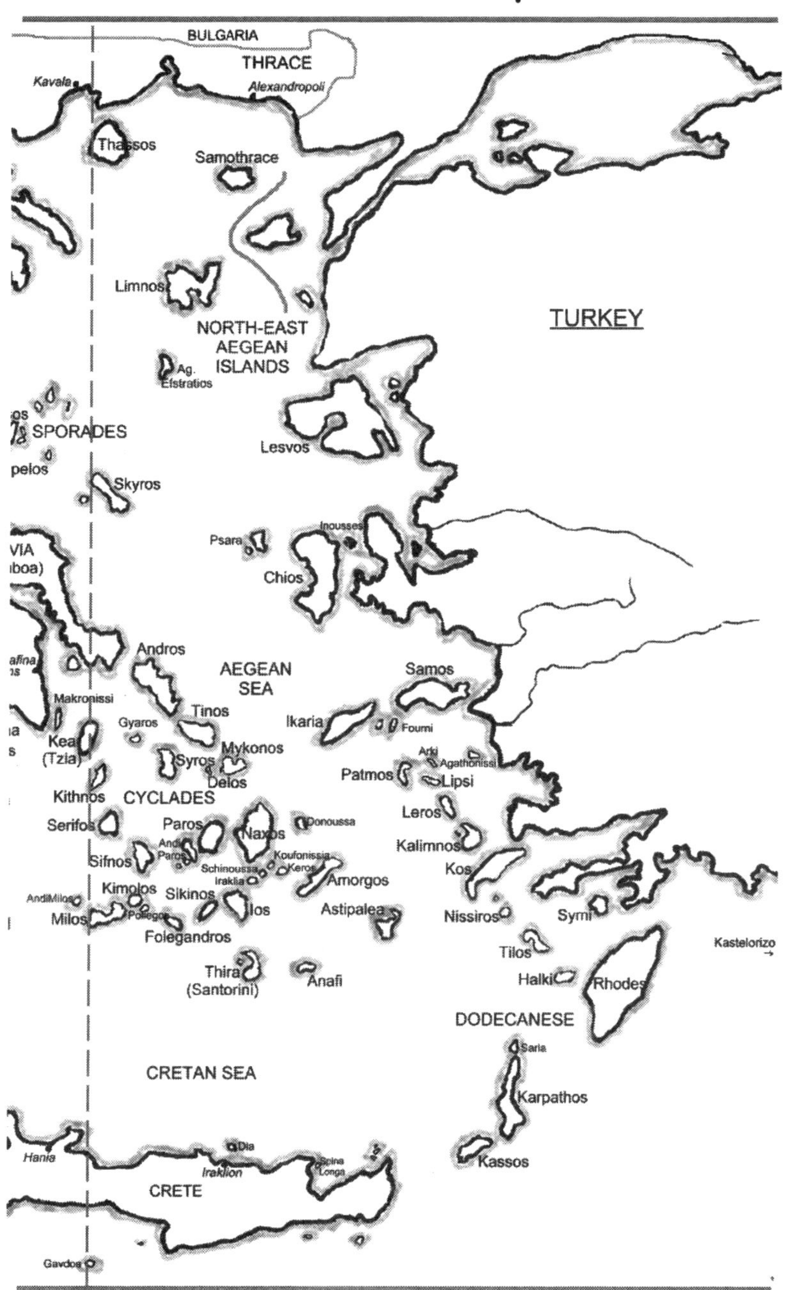

This section includes entertaining and informative articles and anecdotes on 'Life in Greece' from regular travellers to Greece and also those who have made a new life there or have a second home in Greece.

Where There's a Will, There's a Way *by Phil Jones*

During an island hopping holiday a few years ago, there were a number of events which always raise a smile when we look back. In spite of the laid back Greek islanders' way of life, there always seems to be a way to resolve life's little problems.

Due to the vagaries of weather and inconsistencies of Greek ferry timetables, we arrived in Paros at about 7pm one early spring evening. Having researched where we wanted to stay, we immediately enquired as to how we could get to Piso Livadi on the opposite side of the island. We were told there were no more buses today.

We sought solace in a nearby taverna and were sat with two beers trying to decide what to do for the night. We were approached by a Greek gentleman whose only words were *"Piso Livadi?"*. We nodded and agreed *"Piso Livadi."* After some gesturing we got the message to follow him. As we turned the corner, there was a bus. We got in and he drove us to our resort as he was returning home to somewhere nearby.

When we arrived at the resort there was very little open as it was not yet Easter. We asked if there was an apartment where we could stay. Our driver friend led us to a closed taverna and banged on the door until the owner opened up for us. He left us there. We ordered two beers - having left most of the first ones at the main harbour.

Fifteen minutes later he returned with two Greek ladies who encouraged us to follow them to their brand new apartments, which our bus driver had talked them into opening especially for us.

Would this happen in any other country? We think not.

At the end of our holiday we had to get back to Athens for our return flight. We were by then on Santorini and the ferry we had planned to return on either had never existed or just did not sail the day we wanted. The next ferry expected would get us to Piraeus just 12 hours before our flight departure time, so timing would be critical.

We were staying in Santorini Town and the ferry we booked for was due to leave from the New Port at the opposite end of the island. At 6am, along with some other hardy travellers, we boarded the bus down to the new harbour, arriving there about an hour before the ferry was due to arrive.

On cue the large inter island ferry rounded the headland and about 20 travellers stepped forward onto the jetty ...... but the ferry kept on going!

Most of us shouted and waved towards the ferry - but it just kept going towards the Old Port at Santorini Town where we had all been just two hours earlier. Clearly it was not going to come back for us. An excellent holiday was about to be ruined by missing our flight home.

But no ... a caique in the harbour came alongside the jetty and the captain gestured for us all to pile in. With all the speed he could muster, he then chased the large ferry for about 5 miles, miraculously catching up with it when it stopped at the Old Port.

The relative sizes of the boats now became an obvious problem. We could not just step from one deck to the other. Netting was thrown down from the ferry and we climbed up, rucksacks and cases being hauled up by ropes. The day and the holiday were saved.

Why would anyone want to go on holiday to any other country!

Fully Air Conditioned Car *by Jill D'All*

Spotted at Spilia on Meganissi, near where the yachts berth

Retired schoolteacher, Ray Elder, and his wife, Carole, relocated to a small village called Poliani, near Kalamata, Messinia in Feb 2003. He says "we did everything in the wrong way, but luck was with us and it all turned out marvellously. We spent the first year in a childish wonder at the aspects of this wonderful country we discovered." One such unplanned incident is described below.

Ostriches and God *by Ray Elder*

Monday 8th November. An overcast day, the mountains wore the grey-white clouds like scarves. It had rained during the night but the temperature was still only just under twenty degrees. We needed to drive down the mountain into Kalamata to visit a few people.

On our way we called in at a pet shop called the 'Animal Centre'. I had agreed to produce a video for the Kalamata Animal Welfare Society (KAWS) to be used in schools and I wanted to ask them if we could take some footage of the different animals. The owner readily agreed and we left it open as to when we would go back and do this job.

We dropped CDs off for another friend and our next destination was John and Inger's house to deliver a CD of photographs for the KAWS annual calendar. As we drove up to their abode we were greeted by the excited barking of three of their six rescued dogs which in turn set off the squawks and cries of their many caged parrots, mynah birds and other feathered friends. We have never needed to push their doorbell as they always reach their gate before we do, alerted to any visitors by their pets.

John and Inger, as always, greeted us with enthusiasm and overwhelming hospitality. The CD was handed over and John expressed his approval of the pictures. We left with the nice warm feeling of being appreciated.

The time was now just after two pm and we decided to eat at our favourite little pavement café where the food is plentiful, tasty and inexpensive. When we finally finished our meal it was nearly three o'clock. *'"Shall we bother to do the videoing in the pet shop today?'"* we asked ourselves. We were not especially enthusiastic either way and a snap decision as we approached the road junction decided the matter, left was 'no' right was 'yes'. I turned right. *"We might as well get it done now"'* I said.

One of the Calendar pictures chosen

After pulling into the Animal Centre car park I unpacked the video camera and tripod. We were greeted by the shop assistant and then left to our own devices. Carole was looking at pet accessories and prices while I manipulated the camera into the best positions to get clear shots of the animals. I started with the caged birds.

"You like birds?" a heavily accented voice asked.

I explained what I was doing to the interested spectator. He was a man of about fifty in working clothes, stocky and slightly shorter than myself. He seemed a pleasant person, with an easy going smile and he spoke good English.

"What is the biggest bird?" he asked. Was this some sort of test? I wondered. Did he mean the biggest in the shop, or the biggest bird in Greece or the world? I gazed at him blankly. He repeated the question. *"An ostrich?"* I hazarded a guess.

He beamed at me, *"Yes, the ostrich"* he affirmed. *"I have some, would you like to video them?"*

Mmmmm. This could be the Greek version of the 'loony' type of person I seem to attract wherever I go.

"Thanks" I said trying to decline politely, *"but we have to make other visits today."*

"Can't you cancel them? I am on my way now and you can come. It's twelve kilometres towards Messini and I have to feed them. You can help. They play by pecking here and here and here." He indicated various parts of his body, shoulder, arm, waist. Carole was looking very dubious. He indicated a large sack which he had bought from the shop, *"We take them food."* I hesitated and looked towards Carole for help. Carole shrugged. Oh well, I thought, it could be interesting, and Messini is nearly on our way home.'

"I have to finish here first." I said.

"OK" he replied, *"I wait for you. Come down the road, past the Karelia factory, down the hill, past the cemetery…"* I looked blank. I knew the road well but couldn't remember there being a cemetery. *"Where the dead people live"* he elucidated. I nodded. *"...then there is an open area with a car tune-up shop and I will be waiting there."*

The videoing took us just over twenty minutes, and then we set off for our rendezvous with the Ostrich man. We passed the Karelia factory, went down the hill, couldn't see a cemetery, passed a very small open area with a sort of shed with faded Greek writing, then joined with the main Athens road.

"I think we've missed it" I said, *"We'll go back and try once more and if we can't find it then we'll go home."*

We retraced our route, U-turned at the Karelia factory, went down the hill, still couldn't see a cemetery, passed a small open area... *"There's someone waving from the shed"* said Carole. I stopped, reversed and there was our man. I pulled up and got out.

"I have a problem with my car, can we go in yours?" he asked. *"Mmmmmm."* thought I, but *"OK"* I said. He transferred the fodder to the boot of our car and we drove off. It entered my mind, and Carole's mind as she confided later, that we knew nothing about this person and here we were driving off to who knows where with him. He could be violent, a robber, a mugger, a car-jacker, or worse. As it turned out he was worse, much worse.

"I'm Ray and this is my wife Carole" I introduced us.

"I am Dimitris" he responded.

We talked about various things, *"Why do you like living here?"* was one of his questions.

"The weather, the food, the low cost of living, but mostly" trying to be ingratiating *"the friendliness of the people"* I offered.

"Ah, yes the filoxenia" he said. It took a moment to realise that he wasn't talking about the Kalamata hotel of that name, but it was the Greek word for Fellowship, he continued; *"As a born again Christian I understand exactly what you mean. Most people, even the Greeks, do not have this in their personality, but when I go to the Christian meetings we all have this fellowship. Are you a Christian?'"*

DONG! Alarm bells went off - yes it was much worse than being abducted or robbed, we were trapped in a car with an evangelistic Born Again Christian. Quick - distraction tactics! *"How is it that you have ostriches?"* I asked. The explanation took up five kilometres. He had been a seaman and spent a lot of time in Africa where he had developed a fondness for these birds. A few years ago another Greek had imported some in order to start an ostrich meat farm. The business had failed and Dimitris bought the ostriches. He kept them as pets.

"Do you believe in Jesus?"

"Yes, but are ostriches hard to keep?"

Another five kilometres passed while he described their habits and care. *"Just here, on the left, turn now, we nearly there."* he instructed. Phew – saved (or probably not according to Dimitris!)

We went down a narrow track with high growing bamboo. After a few turns and when we were completely enclosed he said *"Stop here a moment and beep horn two, three times....."*

Doubts flooded back and, as we were close to the Albanian gypsy camps, visions of armed brigands bursting from the bamboo sprang to mind.

"..... they hear horn and know I come with food, so they gather at gate" he explained. *"Drive on now."*

I complied and, rounding a corner, we came on a fenced clearing of approximately five hundred square metres containing a dozen bedraggled but impressively large ostriches. He unlatched the makeshift gate and ushered us in. We wandered, cautiously, as he warned us to stay together and close to him, amongst these large powerful creatures, each one towering above us. Seeing them at zoos and on TV is fascinating, but actually being among them and up close is awesome - in the true sense of the word.

He fed them by tipping food into the large bins dotted around the compound and then 'played' with them by catching their beaks and doing a weird form of neck/handshake. He assured us that they liked to play like this. I suppose he must have been right as, after they had been released, they came back for more, if they didn't enjoy it they would have just kept away. Finally he picked some greenery from the field and got Carole to hand feed them.

And then it was time for the return trip. I covered the twelve kilometres in record time, all the while being treated to continual questioning *"Why you no be Born Again?"*

I tried being tactful, *"I think each person's relationship with their God is their own private affair."* No response. He went into the layman's half informed arguments for the existence of God *"No other planet has life, either too hot or too cold so only God created this perfect planet."* Would sarcasm work? *"Really, and how long did it take for you to visit them all, and was it just the planets of this solar system?"*

"No understand..... God give us big brain to be master, not like ostrich which has brain thirty percent of human." I try science and logic. *"That's interesting because they've measured brain activity and discovered that we only*

use ten percent of our brain, so if the ostrich uses all of his brain then, practically, they would be the more intelligent species."

Silence. I dared to hope. Then *"How you know this?"*

"Scientific studies using electrodes and sensors to show human brain activity." "Ahhh, SCIENTISTS!"

It is impossible to express the disdain which he put on the word 'scientists'. I wondered if I should try being offensive. It almost worked once when I was visited by some Jehovah's Witnesses. *"We bring you a message from God."* This was their opening greeting. *"Thank you but I have my religion."* I countered, trying to shut the door. *'Which religion is that?'* They were obviously not going to give up easily. *"Satanism"* I replied and managed to close the door. For weeks afterwards my door was covered in chalked crosses and the letterbox was full of 'Repent' pamphlets.

But Dimitris was basically a nice person and I didn't want to be nasty to him. He tried a different tactic by launching into a story involving a sailor friend who resisted his entreaties to be born again for several years. I felt a lot of sympathy for the friend, imagine being at sea for a lengthy period of time and being constantly badgered about being reborn. But Dimitris seemed genuinely sorry that his friend was heading for eternal damnation.

I asked how long ago he had last seen this friend, it turned out that it was over thirty years ago. I suggested that time may have changed his attitude and that he may now have seen the light. At this Dimitris cheered up considerably, and agreed with me. I suggested he tried to establish contact with his old friend, perhaps using the internet. Dimitris was quite taken with this idea and, thankfully, at that moment we arrived back at his garage.

"You come again soon" he said. *"I'll bring a video for you"* I promised and accelerated off in the best 'Le Mans' tradition.

On the way home Carole said *"That was really interesting, those birds were fabulous, and to think that we almost decided not to bother going back to do the video at all today."*

"Yup." I concurred, *"God works in mysterious ways."*

High Seas & Island Ferries *by Paul Delahunt Rimmer*

Some years ago we had to go from our home on Amorgos to Naxos to the tax office. Naxos is only 35 miles away but takes 5 hours on the local ship, the Skopelitis. This was our first time on the new boat and we were extremely impressed with the lounge. Apart from a few locals we had it to ourselves, with the tourists preferring to stay on deck gathering the last rays of sunshine before returning to rain swept England.

This boat is the life line for the few islands between here and Naxos and usually calls in at Donousa, Koufonnissia, Skhinoussa, Heraklia and then Naxos. It returns to the same islands after a three-hour stay in Naxos to enable people to go and see any officials such as the dreaded tax man, the bank manager or a solicitor. Packages are put on at various islands and the boat is met by the recipients to be taken off at their destination. The grocer was on the quay to put on supplies for some of the smaller islands, the doctor was also meeting it. We have no idea why, but the doctor always seems to be meeting every boat that comes in! The policeman came with us to spend the day on Donousa, presumably to ensure law was all in order there, as they don't have their own 'police force'.

The journey out was uneventful. We dropped the policeman off first, not before he'd had a large scotch on board presumably to steady his nerves to face the vagaries of this tiny island. A few tourists came and went at other islands and some goods changed hands. As the 5-hour trip progressed the sea got rougher and rougher. By the time we got to Naxos and disembarked it was very rough.

We then did our little bit of business involving Greek negotiation tactics, which are always a little lengthy and sometimes extremely noisy, and returned to the ferry completely washed out. The tourists were starting to arrive on the islands and the decks were pretty full but again the lounge was quiet. The steward was busy putting out carrier bags everywhere as makeshift sick bags and made sure that the few tourists down below each had one to hand. He is a pretty surly chap, resembling Igor, but his face lights up as soon as it gets rough. We felt honoured that we were treated like the locals and not offered one. It was a good job we had taken the old pills though. To say it was rough would be an understatement.

The ferry is based in Amorgos so had to get back, but the conditions really were on the limit for it. The movement of the boat was different on every sector between the various islands depending if it was going with, against or across the swell or a combination of all three. The bow was digging deep into the waves and mountains of seawater were being thrown up to either side as the passengers threw up over the side. It was almost impossible to

Calmer Times

walk about and most of the passengers were too ill to do so anyway. They stoically stayed on deck soaking wet and extremely green. We picked up the Greek Orthodox priest at Heraklia and looking at some of the passengers he probably thought his services might very well be needed. Then at every stop he got off to greet and talk to his flock on the quay. On more than one occasion the wind nearly took off his low 'travelling' hat.

Each stop on the return took an inordinate amount of time due to the amount of stores to be off loaded which had come ultimately from Athens via Naxos on a larger ship. At some ports the ferry was rolling so violently that first the left hand side of the stern ramp was two feet off the quay, then it slammed down allowing the right hand side to lift off in a similar manoeuvre. This was quite a challenging movement to work with whilst unloading goods. At Koufonnissi two pallet loads of tiles had to be offloaded but the fork lift truck from the island was only large enough to lift a couple of boxes of lemons. This was solved by three large men hanging on the back of it to counterbalance the weight of the tiles on the front, all precariously managed on a ramp swaying between plus twenty and minus twenty degrees. Usually the unloading is watched by a mass of bemused tourists all straining to get a view of this free pantomime. On this occasion I had no need to fight through hoards of tourists, they were all sitting down very quietly contemplating the lack of content in their stomachs.

We picked up the policeman at Donousa after his day of inspection. I wondered if he ever got beyond the bar on the quay where he was sitting when we came along side. He spent the next hour in a heated discussion with the priest, which involved a lot of finger wagging and poking from both sides. One could only surmise the subjects involved.

In all, the return journey took six hours. For the final sector we went up on deck and stepped over a few prone bodies to go to the flying bridge to watch the sunset over Naxos. It was quite spectacular. No one else on deck seemed interested. Returning inside, and just so the policeman didn't feel bad about drinking alone, we ordered more beer. Sitting opposite was an English couple, two of the very few tourists inside. All I did was to quaff half the can in one large gulp and declare it great and the man made yet another very weaving dash for the gents. They really don't make British tourists like they used to.

There was another occasion when the old Skopelitis was running very late due to a family relocation. Mother, father and two children with all their worldly possessions were on board to be moved to a remote island without even a quay. The ship was anchored off shore and rugs, chairs, kettles, beds, clothes and farming implements were all handed down to a small rowing boat and shuttled to the shore. After a considerable length of time the operation was complete, farewells were exchanged and the ferry eventually set off again. After a few minutes a very observant passenger noticed the rowing boat heading after them at a speed that would do a university boat team proud. Someone was standing in the bows waving and shouting. The captain of the Skopelitis was informed and yet again the ferry came to a halt, the boat pulled alongside, the forgotten toddler was handed over and everyone continued on their way again.

We now have a new service with brand new huge Blue Star ships which are very fast. One service comes here direct in just 5 hours from Piraeus. We do miss the old days though.

Locals Check Out the New Supermarket *by Sylvia Cook*

Orphan Kittens *by Sylvia Cook*

I'd always wanted a pet - a fluffy dog or maybe a cat. But mum was not keen as we lived near the main A4 where cats were regularly squashed, and she felt she would end up looking after it. I even used to take a neighbour's dog for a walk from time to time - whether Pepsi wanted to go with me or not! As I got older work schedules made pet ownership inadvisable as did the more flexible situation when we started working from home with Greek-o-File. What would we do when we were travelling to Greece?

Last summer I finally got my chance to look after some four-legged friends.

We were in Eresos in time for Greek Easter. Friends had arrived a few days earlier to spend 3 weeks at their village house. On their first day they found a plastic carrier bag with two tiny newborn kittens in their garden. Sadly this is a regular occurrence in villages where local cat owners think it wrong to neuter their cats, but not to abandon newborn kittens! Being cat lovers, John and Margy (J&M) could not leave these tiny mites to die, so took them in and asked around about how to feed them. From an eye-dropper at first they fed them 5-6 times a day with diluted warmed baby milk (NOYΛAK) from the local mini-market. Later a small feeder bottle was found. Miraculously they survived, but J&M's trips out and evenings in the kafeneion were often curtailed - *"must go to feed the kittens"*.

We first met Pippa and Squeak soon after their eyes opened. Margy was worried about their future so I found myself volunteering to take them on for the remaining 11+ weeks of our stay. J&M would be back in the summer, but essentially I thought my job was to bring up these kittens to become feral cats. What should I feed them when they moved on from milk? Margy was horrified when I jokingly suggested 'minced mouse'.

They were still very tiny at 3 weeks old when they arrived in their cardboard box. Margy had fed them during the night so far, but we felt that by now I could get away with early morning, twice in the day and last thing at night. They were certainly VERY anxious for their first feed and could be heard mewing as soon as one of us roused from sleep. They had just been introduced to cat litter, so we made them a new bigger box with en-suite toilet. We extended the box sides as they grew and as Pippa especially, became more able to scramble out. With a bit of encouragement, it didn't take them long to use the cat litter for their toilet (they learnt that before they would

eat!) and later when they were outside more they used a patch in the garden strewn with cat litter. They liked sleeping on top of each other beside the comfort-sock we gave them with a warm water bottle inside at night.

When she got back to the UK Margy emailed me information from the Cat Protection Society (CPS) on raising orphan kittens - pointing out that she had not fed them as often as recommended, nor sterilised and refreshed their bottle at every meal and they had survived. These were tough little Eresos kittens from strong local stock. The CPS also recommended special dried milk for kittens, saying that cows milk or human baby preparations were not right for them. We left Pippa and Squeak with cat sitters to handle the midday feed and went to investigate the Kalloni 'Agrotiki' shop over an hour away where we found just the thing - a powdered puppy and kitten milk with vitamins and additives, called 'Weenums'.

Squeak's morning feed

The kittens liked it too. They already had very different characters. Pippa was the most voracious sucker and would down her share of milk in no time. She would suckle on any part of your body she could clamp onto, especially fingers. Squeak, who we thought was a 'he' at that time, was more shy trying to bury his nose in your clothes, didn't suck well and would only take a little milk at a time. Pippa usually had first feed and had to be kept at bay to prevent her getting in on Squeak's share.

The CPS said they should start to lap milk and eat mashed food soon after they were 4 weeks old. These two resolutely ignored dishes of milk or food mashed in milk, attempts at feeding from a spoon end, etc, but Pippa in particular scrabbled at the feeding bottle and chewed the end off making feeding time quite traumatic. I'd started adding mashed cat food into their milk to give them a taste for it. I was becoming quite desperate. I barely had a chance to go to the loo and couldn't touch my own coffee until the kittens had been fed early morning. I wondered if they would ever learn to eat for

themselves. Finally a breakthrough on the day they were 6 weeks old - Pippa started lapping at the milk I'd been putting in their small (soap box) dish. Squeak joined in a day later and took to feeding herself far better than sucking at the bottle.

The CPS had also suggested we weigh them regularly to monitor weight gain. Pippa was just 250 grams and Squeak 200 grams on the first weigh-in at 4 weeks old, gaining slowly until they started eating, until at 8 weeks they equalised, both 550 grams.

It was at this time there was a visiting volunteer vet in Skala Eresos. There are a number who come during the summer giving their mornings to check out local cats and dogs and perform neutering operations. We took the kittens along to find out about vaccinations. The vet didn't have vaccine with her, but checked them over, confirmed they were BOTH female, gave them some worming cream and a dust with flea powder. She said they could not be 8 weeks old, more like 6 weeks she insisted and commented they were 'naked' with very little fur. We knew they had to be within a day of 8 weeks because of when they had been dumped. Because of their size she suggested they should wait another 2 weeks before having their first vaccination, but she could administer it if we bought it at the Kalloni Agrotiki. Although the Kalloni vet would have given the injections free of charge, it would have involved a long bumpy car ride in a box in the Suzuki and all the problems of taking cat litter, etc. Pippa had made it clear she didn't like being in the closed box (their first home) and had travelled the short 4 km drive to Skala on my lap.

Before she left, we returned to the visiting vet with the kittens for their vaccinations. These volunteers really do make a difference as some of the newly enlightened locals as well as many ex-pats with adopted strays took their animals for neutering. She seemed pleased with the kittens' progress and fur now growing on their tummies too. There was much interest in them from other people in the makeshift waiting room/hotel reception. A puppy brought in by a regular ‘friend to the strays’ was the same age as the kittens and seemed very advanced. He was due to be shipped to Austria to a new home. The rules for transferring pets across the rest of Europe are far more relaxed. Even though we now have pet passports for the UK, I understand you have to have puppies and kittens checked, vaccinated and ‘chipped’ for all EU countries, but cannot bring them to the UK until 6 months later.

The kittens had been a little sleepy as predicted after their vaccination, with a touch of diarrhoea, but after a few days Squeak was worse - very lethargic and floppy. She would not eat or drink anything and was probably seriously dehydrated. Neither were keen on water at any time. We were really worried. Terry wrapped her up warm indoors and cuddled her. I prepared some kitten milk to try to force feed her - but had great problems with Pippa who scrabbled and scratched to try to get at her beloved bottle which she had not seen for a while. Terry had to take Pippa outside so that I could try to squirt milk into Squeak. One or other of us stayed with her most of that day, feeding her whenever she would take the milk. We let Pippa in to be with her, when the bottle was not around, as they were very close. I am sure they would not have survived their early weeks if they had not had each other. Squeaky had been equally concerned when Pippa had a little tummy problem after gorging a whole sardine in oil a week or so earlier.

We’re glad to say that Squeak pulled through and started gaining weight rapidly. So much so that by 11 weeks old this weaker kitten became the heavier of the two. Pippa continued to suckle on us at any opportunity. Whilst on the computer I invariably had to type with one hand as Pippa would be on my lap, clamped on to my hand, sucking away. Squeak tried it a few times, but couldn’t see what all the fuss was about. Pippa was always the most affectionate and was happy with almost anyone. Squeak preferred to go to their box and keep out of the way when we had visitors. However she was very happy snuggling up close to either of us when we sat or lay down.

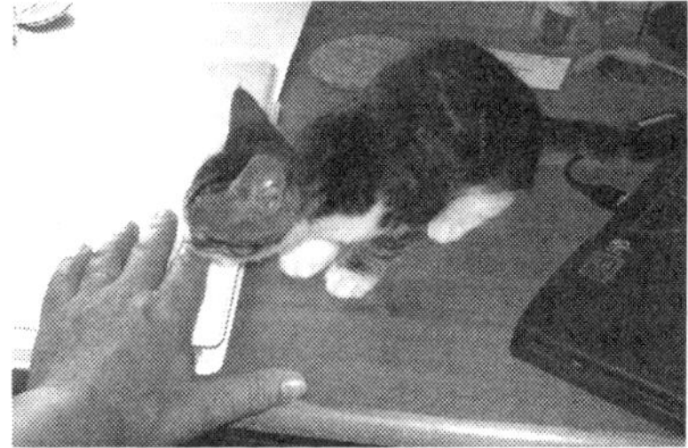

It was great fun having the kittens, especially once they started to run and play, but we needed to keep them ‘contained’ when we were out as they ran around on furniture, up curtains and generally made havoc as kittens do. I probably would have let them sleep in their box in our apothiki at night, but Margy had asked that we didn’t leave them outside alone as this was only

their temporary home. They enjoyed exploring the courtyard daytimes and I was quite surprised they did not get out in the latter weeks. Pippa had tried climbing a tree. Their night-box sides were heightened and, as Pippa became more able, a tall tower lid was added, but the time came when they needed more space and a bigger litter tray at night. The bathroom seemed the place where they could cause least damage so that became their home at night or when we were out. It was quite funny if we visited the toilet at night as they would try to climb onto us as we sat doing our business.

Quite a few nights we stayed in, enjoying the kittens' company, but if we had been out we would let them run about for a while when we got back. As they got older they just wanted to run and play together at first before they would take any notice of us. One night we both fell asleep lying on the sitting room floor waiting for a chance to join in their play - then woke up, each with a kitten sat on top of us!

Many people wondered how we could 'give them back' as we had obviously become very fond of Pippa and Squeak and they of us, but we had always known we were only fostering them for someone else. We sent regular emails and pictures from Pippa & Squeak - John's Cornwall cat Frodo even sent emails with advice back to the kittens! Margy managed to get her Greek class to agree to a lesson at half term so they could return to Eresos a week earlier than planned and be there before we left early in July. They visited them at Spiti Cook first then received delivery the next day and we were able to pop in again before leaving - then it was our turn to receive emails and pictures of their progress during the summer. When originally named Pip and Squeak they were just tiny 'pipsqueaks', but now Squeak is renamed Suki - similar to Squeaky which she seemed to answer to and more befitting her exotic markings.

At the end of summer J&M returned to the UK leaving two normal healthy, well grown, well groomed cats who had a cat flap into a room of their house and were fed every day by friends who live nearby. We visited them a few times around Christmas. They were very affectionate and I'm sure they did miss having owners there, but they seemed well fed, well adjusted, far-from-feral cats, yet perfectly capable of looking after themselves in a Greek village. Now John and Margy are there all year round. They may not have planned to have cats *before* they moved out to Greece, but I am glad they gave life to these two wee mites and that we were able to foster them for a while. We hope they all live happily ever after.

Owning property is always a popular subject with our readers. Here two couples share their thoughts and experiences of building a Greek home - one in the Peloponnese, the other near Chania in Crete.

A Plot in Greece *by Julie Guest*

We had always planned to retire abroad since the early days of our marriage. It was somewhat unusual back in those days, but we dreamed of retiring to a place in the sun, and presumed we would move to Spain. In fact, we considered purchasing an apartment in Ibiza during the 1980s, but didn't follow it through. The Balearic Islands were our usual holiday destination. We also tried Portugal and the Canaries, with our first incursion into the eastern Mediterranean being Cyprus, followed by Rhodes and Crete.

We first visited mainland Greece almost by accident. Well, actually on a very well priced last minute deal to a village in the Mani region. I remembered it being featured in a report by Judith Chalmers on 'Wish you were here' a couple of years earlier, when she said words to the effect *"If you want to experience the* real *Greece, come here now before it changes".* Also the holiday brochure had a two-page spread extolling the virtues of the area, the last line ended *"..... it should be available on the National Health".*

We arrived on an extremely hot Sunday afternoon at the beginning of August, dropped off our suitcases at the apartment, and set off in search of a long refreshing drink. We trundled down a narrow lane, lined with all manner of fruit trees, later nicknamed by us 'the leafy lane', which brought us down onto the beachfront at Stoupa.

We found a bar with comfy deckchairs, ordered some cold drinks and began to absorb our surroundings. We were surprised to see a long curve of sandy beachfront dotted with just an occasional beach brolly. The place seemed almost deserted - a very different scene to our previous experiences of playing 'sardines' along the coastline.

We immediately felt relaxed by the atmosphere. Our rep came rushing past, and we commented on how quiet it was. She looked at us dumb-

founded and replied that she was in a mad rush as it was the busiest week of the year - we still laugh about it now.

We stayed for a fortnight that year, and to this day we can honestly say that it was the first real 'holiday' we had ever experienced. We had been so used to one of us having to get up early to 'get the towels on', then lounging by the pool all day surrounded by concrete and screaming kids. In fairness, at that time our children were in their early teens and we needed to seek out child-friendly accommodation, but we both agreed that we had never felt so relaxed and refreshed by a holiday. That was when the 'love affair' began.

We returned time and time again, firstly for our main holiday, and then for additional breaks in September, and eventually we ventured there out-of-season.

By the summer of 2000 we began to explore the possibilities of purchasing something in Greece. Initially we considered a renovation project, but decided that wasn't for us. However, we came to the decision that if we were to invest in a plot of land it would give us the option of building a house at some time in the future.

We didn't actually plan to purchase anything that summer, but we came across a plot with a view that took our breath away, and knew immediately that if we did not take the opportunity we would regret it forever. At that time

the property market there was fairly stagnant and we didn't know anybody else who was doing the same thing. However, we were fortunate to have made some very good Greek friends in the area, whose help and guidance was invaluable. And so it was that in September 2000 we signed the deeds for our own little piece of Greece.

As with most projects entered into with little or no knowledge, we encountered a number of problems along the way, the first being that we had to pay to change the building permission from two houses to one, because the design had changed, and again later to legalise the basement area. Unfortunately, the date of the original licence remained unchanged on the revisions, which meant that we had to start building almost immediately. This was not only a problem from the point of view of timescale, but also financially. However, we were spurred into making lifestyle changes to enable us to 'follow the dream'.

A team of two local builders were recommended to us. Having studied our plans they agreed to build our house for us. However, a further problem ensued in that they didn't speak English and we don't speak Greek. In some ways, this was fortunate for us. As we obviously needed somebody as a go between as well as somebody local to oversee the project for us, we decided to try to find a local architect who could speak English, and who preferably had an internet connection. Even with the help of our local friends this was not easy, but we were eventually introduced to the perfect person, and he has been worth his weight in gold. Not only has he nurtured our project, but he and his wife have become our very good and trusted friends.

By the time we formally instructed our architect to act as our project manager, discussions had been ongoing directly with the builders (through interpreters) for a number of months, and we found ourselves in a situation where we had been understood to have agreed to a number of things, not least the price. We learned to our cost that had we been in a position to instruct our architect prior to these negotiations, he would have been able to put everything out to tender, which would have undoubtedly provided cost savings.

There is no doubt in our minds that we made the right decision to take on a project manager, even at this late stage. Despite his fees increasing our projected outlay, he quickly made savings that all but matched his fees. His assistance has been invaluable in keeping the project running, consulting with us at all stages, checking progress, purchasing materials, quality management, and in addition keeping us informed of progress by email. He also keeps our accounts in order that we can eventually produce them to acquire our permanent electricity connection.

For anyone thinking of skimping in this respect, take an example where our project manager being able to monitor the work has saved us from disaster. When the shuttering for the stairs was installed, he found the measurements to be wrong and had to make the contractor reinstall it twice before it was done correctly. Had he not done so, the stairs would have blocked the entrance to the main bedroom! Goodness knows what the final outcome would have been if he had not been 'on the spot' to notice their error. With the mathematics involved, we doubt that even if we had been there ourselves we would have discovered the problem until it was too late.

Our house has been built in the traditional manner for the area, in the style of a village house, with ½ metre stone walls, terra-cotta roof tiles and shut-

tered windows, held together by a massive system of reinforced concrete beams so that it won't suffer any damage in an earthquake.

We have been fortunate in that the route we took has allowed us choices - in the plot, the design, the materials, the finishes and in the overall timescale of the project in line with our finances. At the time of writing the structure of our house is complete, and we are now working on the interior. It is an exciting time for us adding the finishing touches. Everybody who has visited the site says what a beautiful house it is.

The last few years have been an enormous learning curve for us, and over this time we have been actively drawing on our experiences to assist other people who have been interested in building their own home in Greece. For this reason we were only too pleased to agree to act as UK representatives for our architect. Now we are working together to make the process easier for others who are considering following the same dream.

Catching Smoke *by Elaine Rhodes*

If we had known more Greek at the time, we would have recognised that what Manolis was trying to say was *"It's as long as a piece of string"*. The question, in rudimentary Greek, had been *"How much does a house cost?"* With the infinite patience of a Greek in the face of a another daydreaming visitor to his Cretan paradise, he took yet another scrap of paper and sketched out the shape of a house on a square of land, added the words and figures for taxes, lawyer, permissions, and costs per square metre. Then he taught us the Greek for 'millions', and produced a sum with an alarming number of zeros on the end. This was in drachma days, fortunately.

We had visited Greece for many years and like many, had become Grecophiles with pipe dreams of a home in this land of filoxenia. Now things had become serious. We had earmarked a sum from our savings and investments, and were determined at last to find a plot of land and build a house, or to renovate an older property.

Several 'holidays' later, after an exhausting round of estate agents, building plots and ruins, we decided to enlist the aid of a friend. David had been living in Crete for several years and spoke Greek so he could listen to the chat in the *kafeneion* and pick up the first hint of our ideal plot of land for sale. A short time later, emails began arriving with pictures of a long abandoned olive grove in a village in the Apokoronas, our favourite area of Crete. The land was large enough for us to share with David, who was volunteered as project manager, and we began the process of purchasing and building.

The chosen architect, Pavlos Papadakis, impressed us on several counts. Early in the search for land he had refused to become involved in building on a piece of land, which had dubious building permission. Others might have made profit a priority and looked for loopholes, but Pavlos' integrity was clear - he would not touch it. When we found our land, he showed immediate empathy for the surroundings and the village during the first site meeting to discuss the house. Further, he demonstrated a uniquely Greek ability to carry on a telephone conversation while simultaneously reading a document, smoking a cigarette, and debating politics - in a foreign language - with the people in the room at the time. The estimated final price, however, was elusive.

Plans were sent by email, adjustments were made, and clearance of the land began on 5th August 2002.

Pavlos had supplied a detailed specification of the methods and materials to be used in the construction and finishing of the villa, and a timescale for completion (later to prove optimistic - but you guessed that).

One of our most important requests was that the ancient olive tree in the centre of the terrace should survive, on pain of death to the murderer. Not something easily understood by the Greek construction workers, who looked as if they might be thinking, *"it's like this Walt, it's an olive grove..."* to paraphrase Bob Newhart. Tobacco leaves...remember?

Another stipulation, was that the plumbing should be British-style and the loos bin-free zones.

As the plan progressed, there ensued a period of intensive, but mainly fruitless research on the internet and in books on the subject of property purchase laws in Greece. At every new step in the process, we tried to assess whether our budget would be adequate. It was like trying to catch smoke. Manolis' wife, Sophia, sounding like Inspector Clouseau, would frequently say, *"there is a low…"*, (or a law, as we eventually translated), and a new set of rules would come to light regarding building sizes, tourist licenses, the need for a swimming pool, or some other bar to our progress. The budget was beginning to look inadequate.

We took another hard look at our savings, took advice on the potential return from letting the house, took a deep breath, and raided the piggy banks. Most of them.

Weekly progress pictures were emailed as the house gradually took shape. The olive tree survived and was given a brand new stone collar.

Adverse weather conditions in the winter delayed the finishing process, but the keys were officially handed over to us early in May 2003. Pavlos proudly presented us with a perfect blend of traditional beamed-roof Greek style with modern conveniences, insulation and central heating. The villagers inspected and approved. We were delighted.

With the indispensable help of Katerina Papadakis the house was furnished, just, in ten days, with the priority of ensuring that the soft furnishing, especially the beds, were sufficiently forgiving for British posteriors. Negotiations with holiday companies began, and we found a tour operator to take on the job of letting. Finally we began to see a way to feed our decimated piggy bank.

Although much remains to be done in the garden and on the overgrown terraces, the house has already proved popular with visitors, and we have spent many out-of-season days getting to know our neighbours and friends

in Crete. The original sketches and costs scribbled by Manolis are framed and displayed in the house as a reminder of all the help given to us en-route, and of all the raki-fuelled hours of encouragement given by Manolis, Sophia, and our friends to make the dream a reality.

Having gone through the experience, and learnt so much on the way, we wrote down all the things that affected the final cost of our furnished house and garden in Greece. Using the records we had kept, and Greek inflation figures freely available on the Web, we devised a calculator so that variables can be entered to produce an end total now, or even a future projection.

Most architects will be unwilling to give this 'bottom line' figure in advance because it is probable that the specification will change as the project progresses. You will add some things, remove some and change the quality of others. These amendments all result in a change to the bottom line that seems to be unpredictable. Not so!

The costs associated with the purchase fall into three basic types: those that are related to (*ie* are a percentage of) the cost of the land/building, those that are purchases whose current prices are simply driven by inflation and those that are optional. These costs can be estimated in advance.

With the benefit of experience, we wrote down our newly acquired knowledge for a book entitled 'The Real Costs of Building a House in Greece - or learning to live with Avrio', which includes the calculator on a CD ROM. Armed with knowledge gained by 'doing the sums', if the answer is beyond budget the design can be revisited, changes made and the estimated final price immediately recalculated. Clearly this iterative process can be continued until an affordable design is determined, with fewer shocks to come in the future. Alternatively, from a personal standpoint, you will be in a position to realise that however you cut your cloth the project is beyond your reach. While you may be very disappointed to be in this latter situation, it is a much better position than one of trying to recover a doomed project. At the very least, you could be saved (as one of our readers was) from the dreaded two-inch toilet waste pipes. (elaineRLR@aol.com & see p.185).

Investing in Greek Property *by Sylvia Cook*

Many Grecophiles dream of owning their own property in Greece, but the dream is beyond their financial means. Others decide to sell up in the UK and move permanently to Greece - but for some of these the reality does not work out for them and they want to come back. For some buying property and sub letting it when they cannot use it themselves is an answer. Those with significant investment cash may even decide that rising property prices in Greece are an opportunity for property investment.

With all investments, you not only need to look at the costs involved to decide if it is worthwhile, but also to understand where you stand from a taxation point of view.

If you are a **UK resident** you will need to declare your investment income (after allowable costs) to the UK Inland Revenue when you complete your annual Self Assessment tax return. There is a separate section you need to request for property income. It is very easy to get information from UK tax authorities and unless things get very complicated you should be able to complete the forms yourself.

As investment income it is only liable to income tax at the appropriate rate depending on your total taxable income - so with no employees' or employers' National Insurance to pay it is a good investment for most of us.

If you become a **Greek resident** or create a **Greek company** to handle your Greek investments then you will need to declare your income to Greek authorities and will be liable to their taxes. In Greece it is not so easy to obtain information from authorities and you will need a Greek accountant to handle tax returns and probably a lawyer to register your company and explain the rules. As a permanent resident all taxable income from any country is payable in Greece, whereas a temporary resident would be liable to tax on Greek income only. Letting income for a property in Greece is deemed as 'earned' in Greece, even if payment is received in the UK.

However, the UK and Greece have a **Double Taxation Agreement** so, in simple terms, you *should* only need to complete tax returns in the country where you spend more of your time (ie over 6 months), where you are 'ordinarily resident'. If you have **dual residency** the Greek authorities will probably insist on you paying tax there on your Greek letting income. UK residents need to declare their worldwide income in the UK. They will get a credit for taxes paid in Greece from their UK tax office. (If you are paid from a Greek company, UK residents only need to declare personal income sent to the UK - ie dividends, interest and/or salary. Income remaining in Greece will be subject to Greek tax.)

Residency in Greece can be a double edged sword. In some places you are still expected to take residency to be able to buy and tax a Greek vehicle, even if you are ordinarily a UK resident.

If you live in Greece (or elsewhere outside the UK) and **rent out your UK home** you will be liable to UK tax on the rental income. You need to complete an annual tax return with details, or your agent or tenant is required to pay standard rate tax to the Inland Revenue for you if the rent is more than £100 per week - obviously it is better if you declare it yourself to set allowable costs against income and take advantage of tax free allowances.

Income from letting is fairly straightforward, but **Capital Gains Tax** on the sale of property can seem more complicated, particularly if you dipped your toe into buying Greek property then changed your mind.

Capital Gains Tax on the profit on the sale of a second or subsequent property owned by you is due in the country where you are resident for tax purposes, if the property sold is in a country such as Greece where we have a Double Taxation Agreement. (The sale of USA properties where there is no DTA, for example, would always be liable to tax there.) In the UK allowances are made for improvement costs, indexation and 'taper' relief as well as your Capital Gains Tax Free allowance - for the tax year 2005/6 this is £8,500 per person - so you may find nothing is due.

If you sold up in the UK and moved to Greece, then fortunately there will be no Capital Gains Tax to pay if things go wrong for you and you decide to sell your Greek property and return to buy one in the UK, or indeed to buy a different home in Greece or any other EU member country. However, if you retained your UK 'bolt hole' there could be taxes to pay if you sell either home or change it for a different property, unless the house you are selling was your only, or main residence throughout the time you owned it.

For further details and latest UK legislation contact your local tax office, or if you are non-resident now call 0845 070 0040 (0044 151 210 2222 from abroad). Leaflets are also available from the Inland Revenue website - www.inlandrevenue.gov.uk. Search for the following documents:

CGT1 - Capital Gains Tax explained & CGT/FS1 Quick Guide to CGT

IR20 - Residents and non-residents

IR138 - Living or retiring abroad

IR139 - Income from abroad

IR140 - Non resident landlords, agents & tenants

IR150 - Property UK & International

More details on **Greek taxation**, employment and self-employment rules are included in an article 'Working in Greece' in The Greek-o-File magazine 2002/1. UK information above was approved by the UK Inland Revenue Press Office.

Memories of Greeks *by Jenny Edwards*

Greece is a country I hold close to my heart, having enjoyed holidays in different parts and met some enchanting Greek people over the years. I've not been able to revisit Greece recently as I took early retirement on a small pension, but my memories remain with me. I still love reading about Greece and often play my many Greek CDs to remind me. In my imagination I am in Greece again.

I remember a visit to Paxos, a lovely small island. En route I had time to spare in Corfu Town. I had imagined the town to be overrun with package tourists (like myself!), but I was very wrong. I went into a small dark shop to look at some lace tablecloths. From the depths emerged an elderly lady completely dressed in black. This was another world to the 'hubbub' of traffic and street sounds outside. Having purchased a small item I told her I was trying to learn Greek. She very patiently wrote down several words for me, completely unhurried. She gave me her undivided attention for an hour or so. Such a lovely lady.

When I went into a nearby music shop the lady there insisted on playing excerpts from many Greek CDs. She said she didn't mind at all if I didn't buy anything. Her face lit up as she listened to the music and, of course, I did buy a few CDs. She was so courteous, so eager to help.

While visiting Petra in Lesvos, I was climbing the steep steps up to the church on the rock, when I noticed a lady carrying some heavy pots of flowers up the steps. I offered to help carry them. She was very grateful and told me the flowers were for her daughter's wedding later that day. She very kindly asked me to come to the wedding, which I did. It was a fascinating experience.

On another holiday I went into Athens on a day trip. After visiting the Parthenon we had a short while to spend in the Plaka district before rejoining our coach. I pottered around some small shops, then just as I realised I had only 5 minutes before I needed to be at the coach, I noticed an interesting shop that didn't seem as 'touristy' as some of the others. I entered and an elderly lady in black offered me a sweet from a bowl on the counter. The outside world seemed to recede into the distance, but I was mindful of my time so I suppose I was rushing and possibly a little agitated. She looked at me very calmly and asked the reason for my rushing. I explained I only had 5 minutes and she gazed at me with a face embodying the ancient wisdom of Athina as she said very quietly *"Five minutes is a long time in your life."*

I have never forgotten those words. Myself rushing from one place to the next - what for? She calm and living in the centre of the present moment.

I hope I can return to Greece one day; but I have many memories of past visits which will always be a part of me.

Donkey Work at Harvest Time *by Paul Delahunt-Rimmer*

The island farmers have a hard time when it comes to harvesting. Where I now live on Amorgos, they grow a combination of wheat and barley in the same fields using mixed seeds. There is evidence that this method of hedging against dry or wet weather has been going on since the fifth century BC. In dry weather the wheat does better than the barley and in wet springs vice versa. This year has been a very dry spring so the wheat is predominant. They cut it all by hand on the terraces that cover the mountainsides. These terraces were built thousands of years ago and are still used today to scrape an existence from the otherwise unfarmable land. The work is extremely labour intensive as everything is still done by hand and using donkeys.

Once the crop is cut using a scythe it is tied into sheaves and piled so high onto donkeys that it looks as if there is no animal underneath. It appears that the harvest is moving down the narrow donkey paths of it's own accord. Only when it gets closer can you see the nose of the donkey as he first turns his head to the left and then to the right chewing for all he is worth in a desperate attempt to lighten his load. As far as he is concerned he is just carrying his own fuel, no different to a car or lorry consuming fuel as it proceeds.

In the next stage the wheat is spread over a threshing circle, which is a stone-floored area, surrounded by a low stone wall about thirty feet in diameter. The grain then has to be separated from the chaff and straw. The well-fuelled donkeys are put to work on this by trampling the crop to break it all up. Four donkeys are tied together in a very neat echelon starboard formation, led by a man standing in the middle of the circle just rotating on the spot. The inside donkey has of course an easy job of it moving relatively slowly but the poor old donkey on the outside knows that he has to move much faster.

They all wear muzzles to prevent them stopping for a further snack but most of them have already eaten their fill whilst transporting the crop. Four stuffed donkeys trampling grain presents further problems as nature takes its course. Donkey droppings mashed into this combination; a) makes it difficult to separate the grain from the chaff and b) affects the taste of the resultant produce, - obviously not popular with the islanders. Here the Greek equivalent to

lacrosse saves the day. They cut the side off an olive oil can and attach a stick to it to fashion a crude lacrosse stick. It is then the catcher's job to walk behind the donkeys and field any droppings lobbing them over his shoulder into the field when caught. Again, it is not too much of a problem fielding from the inside donkey but the catcher also knows the donkeys are moving at different speeds and dreads a performance from the outside one. Of course the donkeys know well what goes on and consider it great fun to all perform at once. Being tied together in this close formation makes communication very easy. They model themselves on their heroes, 'The Red Arrows', and at the appropriate time the leader just bays *'dung on, dung on, and go'* and mayhem rains, along with all the droppings. Now the game plan changes. The catcher transfers his wide range of sporting skills from lacrosse to rugby. He dives across the straw to retrieve the small oblong rugby balls and tries to convert them before being trampled to death by the oncoming team of four, by now with little smirking faces.

With this operation successfully complete the straw is raked from the circle leaving the grain and chaff. A suitable wind is awaited for the winnowing to begin. The wind direction is indicated by a piece of grass tied to a stick at the side of the circle. There are higher-tech models of this indicator, from thin pieces of plastic right up to a proper wind vane. We are just awaiting a cable drive and remote indicator to be installed so the farmer doesn't even need to get out of bed to plan his programme for the day. With a suitable wind the grain and chaff are thrown into the air where the lighter chaff blows out of the circle and the grain lands back in, repeated until only grain remains.

Although no updated methods of winnowing have been spotted yet there is a high-tech version of threshing making headway - called a rotovator. Imported from Athens, these machines designed for tilling soil, have been spotted clawing their way around the stone threshing circles. It is all way beyond the maker's recommendations, as they were never designed to rotovate on stone slabs like large kitchen liquidizers reducing the harvest to its component parts. The one and only local garage is very happy though as they survey the line of machines on their forecourt awaiting repair and another punishing harvest next year. The donkeys are also ecstatic, although it does limit their opportunities for revenge on their owners.

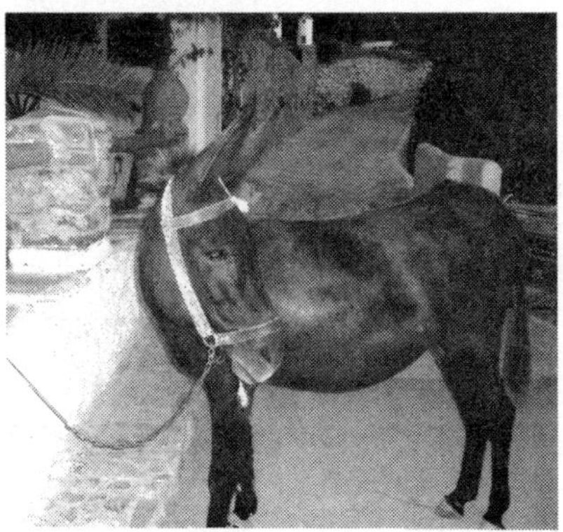

These observations of artist Mary Potter are adapted from her 'Greek Notebook'.

Chapels, Churches & Cemeteries *by Mary Potter*

Small Greek Orthodox chapels may stand dramatically on a rocky headland, a mountain crag, on the crest of a barren hill, at the head of a valley, tucked away in an olive grove or on the edge of a secluded bay where the walls are lapped by the waves.

Examples of popular art they evidence loving care; always simple with the right amount of colour contrasting with the whitewashed walls. The roofs are plum pink, or turquoise blue, or terra-cotta tiled (each island seems to have its preferred colour and style). The bell to call the faithful may be at the top, in a bell-tower, or simply fixed to the wall outside. The simple doors and windows may be outlined in dark blue or green. When seen against a deep blue sky or a backcloth of grey mountains, they form a perfect blend of architecture and landscape.

Inside one finds a miniature church setting; painted icons on the walls, tin trinkets as offerings, fresh flowers (however isolated) and plastic ones, candles, oil in lemonade bottles. Broken windows indicate how these chapels are buffeted by winter storms and mountain winds.

The poorer the country the richer the Church; a necessary compensation for the drabness of a life with very limited opportunities. The poorest village will have its lofty church, decorated from floor to ceiling with wall paintings of the saints, elaborate carvings, silver chandeliers, coloured glass windows designed to send spotlights across the aisle in reds and blues as the bright sun pours through; mosaic marble floors, huge plants and everywhere flowers both plastic and fresh. Add to these surroundings several priests dressed in gorgeous gold trimmed colourful robes, with handsome beards, their highly trained voices blending the chants of the Orthodox liturgy; the incense wafting in clouds throughout the church, bells ringing, chalices raised – one is indeed in another world and at least half way to heaven.

However, in spite of its uplifting nature, the service is not isolated from the surroundings outside. The door is kept open, people drop in, light their candle, kiss the icon, say a prayer, hug their friends with a hushed chat, then go off to feed their animals. Children play on the floor and visitors are welcomed. Notwithstanding the majesty of the visual images, their effect is not awesome; the people feel at home in a church, relaxed. They wear ordinary clothes, even come in their bedroom slippers – they have not come to be seen, but to visit their God.

Every Saint's day is not only an occasion to offer prayers to that saint, but will be combined with all the fun of a day out to visit the saint's particular church, maybe at the top of a mountain. Families set off early. Chapels are built with courtyards edged with stone seats, often round a huge spreading tree for shade. Food is cooked, wine drunk, everyone returning in the evening tired and happy, thanks to St. Constantine or St. Sophia.

On Karpathos the cemetery juts out over the sea, high above the town. Dazzling white marble crosses are silhouetted against the deep blue water, or, in the other direction, against the grey mountains. Each grave is festooned with plastic flowers and has a photograph of its occupant, as well as a permanently burning oil lamp. There are fresh flowers too, and the photographs, often of people in their 80s and 90s, make one fantasize about their - probably hard - lives. At dusk there is a transformation, when everything stands out against a night sky, and the oil lamps glow like iridescent eyes. Who said this was a place of the dead? Not at this time of the evening.

Theophany Traditions *by Sylvia Cook*

The 6th of January is the day of Theophany in the Orthodox Church when throughout Greece, whatever the weather, the Orthodox priests bless the waters. It is a national holiday in Greece.

The word Theophany is from the Greek *theos* (Θεός) meaning God and *phanerono* (φανερώνω) to reveal or show, ie revealing God in a form visible to man. Theophany in the Greek Orthodox church commemorates the baptism of Christ in the River Jordan, hence the ceremonies across the country to bless the waters.

The Epiphany, celebrated on the same day in our churches has a similar meaning *epi* (επι) meaning 'about' or 'upon', but commemorates when the Magi came to acknowledge the divinity of Christ.

A few years ago we watched the Theophany ceremony down on the coast at Skala Eresos. Several orthodox priests from around the area arrived and met up near the platia. They donned beautifully embroidered cloaks on top of their usual attire. They looked quite magnificent, but the cloaks also served to keep out the biting cold wind on this spectacular clear sunny day.

Gradually the villagers gathered and they walked with the priests onto the beach. Prayers were said, readings read, the waters blessed. Then a heavy elaborate metal crucifix was launched out to sea by the senior priest and several of the villagers scrambled, fully clothed into the sea to try to retrieve the cross as it was hauled back. On this occasion the crucifix had been attached to a long strong length of rope - just in case. The one to bring it back was jubilant. Blessed by the priests and said to be lucky for the rest of the year. The two junior priests each had a prayer and a throw too. They seemed to take great delight in seeing who could throw it the furthest.

Sometimes the ceremony takes place further out at sea and a diver goes overboard to retrieve the crucifix. Obviously the local diver was not available the year we watched.

Although on the many islands the ceremony is more often carried out by the sea - it could equally be per-

formed in a river or a lake.

Near our village a dam was built in recent years to harness the winter rains and provide water for the village farms when rain is scarce in the summer. The heavy December rains had filled the new lake in front of the renovated Pithariou monastery. The venue for the blessing of the waters ceremony that year was the lakeside.

It is an idyllic setting and a pleasant spring or summer hike to visit the dam, lake and small monastery. The track to this next valley is rough and after winter rains there are usually sections badly eroded, so not so many villagers went to witness the blessing of the waters at the lake.

On this Theophany we were taken by our friend Alekos with another friend of his from the kafeneion - but we were too late and missed the ceremony. No one ever seems to know what time events are planned for in Eresos, if indeed they are pre-planned. However, we looked around the beautifully renovated monastery church and the incredibly painted chapel and were welcomed into the refectory for a warming 'helleniko metrio' and a chance to sit around the dining table near the blazing log fire and listen whilst Alekos chatted with and quizzed the incumbents. Just two monks live there at present. They carry out their religious duties, grow a few crops and occasionally welcome visitors if they arrive at a convenient time of day, although it is not officially open to the public. Before the dam was built, we had visited the old monastery on a track now underwater and must say its new setting overlooking the vast lake which forms in front of the dam is more beautiful, tranquil and cut off from other human habitation. An ideal place to contemplate whatever it is that monks contemplate.

Summer of '66 *by Collette Hurley*

It all started when I was 18, way back in 1966. My sister, Clare, had gone to teach English on the island of Lesvos, in the main town of Mytilene. She wrote to me saying I should definitely come and that I would love the life there. I was in my very first job and had been there for 10 months, working as a shorthand typist in Southampton's docklands offices. It wasn't a difficult decision to leave although it did infuriate my parents at the time.

We went by boat and train, the three of us, my girlfriend Jane, my boyfriend Pat and me. It took us three days or so to get to Greece and then we took a boat from Piraeus to Lesvos. It was all magical to me as I had never travelled further than Cornwall before.

Clare met us from the boat and took us a short distance to her old, rented, Turkish house in Kyparisia Street. I shared a double bed with my sister and each morning we were awoken by flies dive-bombing our faces. We always referred to it as 'kip 'ere easier' and accepted things as they were.

We stayed for 6 glorious weeks, during which time I picked up a lot of the language, loving languages as I do and being a bit of a parrot. Most of our friends were Greek as there were very few tourists back then. Greek hospitality was second to none. While walking in the street we would be invited into houses just because were *'xenia'*.

My boyfriend Pat became a bit of a mascot in the community as he did the most bizarre things and made the Greeks stare and laugh. One evening at the Parko, where we went to socialise with one and all most nights, he suddenly rose from his chair and tore off into the night. The immediate reaction of the waiters was to drop everything and tear off after him, probably thinking he didn't want to pay for his drinks. My sister had the best Greek language and tried to explain.

Another time we were walking by the harbour and lots of people were staring and talking about us, especially Pat, who wore a wide-brimmed hat and had long hair. He let out a cry and jumped into the harbour fully clothed, hat and all. His white shirt billowed out like a parachute as he went down. "*Trellos*" came the cry, and they were probably right. (Some time later he was to be seen in a glossy magazine, sitting at the Acropolis staring from un-

der the brim of his hat while a model walked up and down in gorgeous clothes.)

That was the most wonderful summer I ever had in my life, those carefree days in Lesvos, with so many lovely friends and a new way of life. It was the custom to swim at the sea wall every day. We all met up there, jumping into the warm water, avoiding the jellyfish, swimming and sunbathing for hours.

Some evenings we would go to the open air cinema where we sat on canvas seats. 'Whatever Happened to Baby Jane', starring Bette Davis, was showing that summer and we saw it three times. I still consider it to be one of the best films I've ever seen, but maybe that's just the rose-coloured glasses I wear whenever I think of that summer in Greece.

Food was extremely cheap and so was the rent on the house. Towards the end of the summer, after a loud storm, Jane and I splashed through the streets, ankle deep in water, to a café where Pat was waiting for us. He was sitting at a table watching the water drip into his food from the roof.

We had some lovely women friends who took us on country walks, showing us the herbs and flowers. We heard about the naïve artist Theophilos and went to the small museum to see his paintings. All the dyes made from local plants by him were carried in small pots on a leather belt around his waist. He, like so many artists, was not famous in his own lifetime. In fact, he traded paintings for food and led a very simple life. Some years later, we rented a room in the house of a very old lady in Mytilene and up on the ceiling, around the rosette in the middle, was a painting by Theophilos.

Ψρίπος Μυτιλήνης - Pêcheurs à Mytilène - Fishermen at Mytiline - Fischer in Mytilene

I travelled extensively in Greece between 1967 and 1979 and had many wonderful times. In 1979 I lived and worked in Crete for 3 months, looking after cucumbers in a greenhouse owned by the baker. A small group of us lived on the beach for the first 5 weeks but then moved into a lovely whitewashed house in the middle of an orange grove '*sto perivoli*' (*περιβόλι = grove, orchard*). This was in a small coastal town called Myrtos. It was still practically untouched by tourism inasmuch as there were no hotels or beach beds.

I spent 5 months in Greece that year - in Athens, Thessaloniki, Rhodes, Lesvos and Crete, all the time studying the language and improving my communication skills. My use of Greek is passable but this year I went back to class to sort out my rather chaotic grammar. I also travelled back to Greece after a gap of 25 years.

Boarding the plane in Heathrow I heard a Greek family talking behind me. I was filled with emotion, tears and excitement. I was on my way back at last.

My partner and I went to Athens for the first night. I spoke only Greek to the hotel manager, which was thrilling in itself. From the bar on the roof there was a magnificent panoramic view of Athens and we arrived just as the sun was going down. *"Have we died and gone to heaven?"* I asked. Then we moved on to a rooftop taverna in Plaka where 4 men sang and played. I requested *'Varka sto Yallo'* an old Theodorakis number and they went into a whole medley of the great composer's songs. I was in heaven again!

From Athens, we travelled down to Kalamata by bus, winding our way through the glorious mountains, over the Corinth canal, on to Tripoli and finally the sea port of Kalamata. Our friends met us at the bus station and as it was evening took us straight out for a meal in Kardamili.

Our friends' house - by the way it's the very same Jane who travelled to Lesvos with me in 1966 who also fell in love forever with Greece and all things Greek - is not yet ready, so they live in a rented accommodation on a hillside overlooking the village where they will eventually live. They warned us about the church clock which strikes every hour on the hour but we found it a pleasant sound.

Spring was just starting, with all the wonderful wild flowers blooming and baby animals being born. The air was scented - a mixture of sage, thyme, marjoram and sheep droppings! Some nights the whole village was a cacophony - a good Greek word - of barking dogs and snorting mules. Then just as suddenly as it had started, it would stop.

We kept hearing a loudspeaker from the village. I asked Jane if it was electioneering. She hooted with laughter and said it was the vegetable sellers.

I couldn't wait to meet the locals and get in some Greek practice. I didn't have to wait long. The very first day a neighbour came out, an old lady dressed in black, very warm and friendly and delighted to meet us. She was soon joined by another woman and together they clucked over us, bringing a small table and some chairs into the street outside their houses. They made us coffee, brought water and cakes and posed for photos with us. They said how they love village life as it's peaceful and simple. I agreed

completely and wished I could stay there for months instead of just days.

The women told us about their children and how they travelled to Germany to see them sometimes. How horrible Germany was - cold, grey and anonymous - but what can one do when one needs to see one's children?

The stark truth about villages such as this one is that the older generation are dying, and with them the old ways of simplicity and hospitality. The young people have had an education and no longer wish to live the village life. Houses become empty, some left to rot and others inevitably sold to people not from the area. These houses become holiday homes and the villages start to die. Our friends have retired there and will live there full time. Jane hopes to run courses from her house and feels she has realised the ambition of a lifetime by buying property in Greece and moving there.

I read about some of the history of the area and realise that the people had a terribly hard life, all through the dictatorship of Metaxas, the Second World War and then the Civil War. So many of them were starved or beaten to death. Their memories of those awful times are still strong but despite this they are friendly and hospitable. The Greek spirit lives on in their large hearts and I always feel completely accepted for who I am, which, let's face it, is a rare and wonderful feeling.

I am planning to go back to the Peloponnese in October to practise my Greek and to enjoy some simple days, which I love more than anything. The area is not yet ruined by overdevelopment, indeed the smaller villages are still, for the moment, like the old Greece I knew and loved.

My sister, Clare, lived and worked in Greece for 7 years. She still has many friends there and often visits. We text each other in phonetic Greek which keeps us amused. We have a secret bond when it comes to the Greece we experienced so many years ago. Only *we* can really understand how we feel and we have old jokes about situations we were in and people we knew in the summer of '66.

A Puppy for Christmas *by Sylvia Cook*

News gets round about soft English people, so when our friend Sam suggested that we go with him to see a friend in Fterounda soon after we'd arrived for Christmas, he must have known what he was doing. We had been sat at a taverna in the afternoon sun sipping a beer and eating fish when he received the telephone call inviting him. We'd not been to this village before, so thought *"why not."* Less than an hour later it was getting dark when we arrived. We parked near the village kafeneion and walked with Sam to his friends' house. They were obviously animal friendly Greeks with a small dog and 2 cats in prime positions in front of the log fire.

Sam asked us if we'd like to look after 2 dogs for a couple of weeks. We said *"No way"* knowing that such arrangements can get out of hand. In the meantime Maria had opened the door and let in two adorable little puppies. One readily let me pick him up and sat on my lap happily being stroked, the other hid under the table, but was eventually persuaded to join his brother on my lap. One of these puppies was for Sam to help him look after his birds - geese, ducks, chickens - but he was due to move into a new house after Christmas and couldn't take his dog until then. He got on the telephone to Michaelis who would take the other one. Michaelis turned up and immediately made friends with the smaller more shy dog - he had said to save the pretty one for him. Sam wanted the stronger one.

As we left to go to a taverna he asked again if we would like to look after his dog but we thought it best to say *"no"*, although tempted. He walked out intending to come back in a few weeks for his puppy. Maria had other ideas and picked up his puppy, followed us to the car and put the dog in! Well, what could we do?

We put puppy number two with his brother in Michaelis' car while we ate at the taverna ... but the decision had been made. *"What do you want to call him?"* we asked Sam. *"The name will come"* was the only reply we could get from him.

As we drove back with the warm puppy cuddled on my lap, I was getting quite excited at having this soft bundle of gentleness for 2 or maybe 3 weeks. He was so good natured and trusting.

They say a puppy is not just for Christmas - well ours would be!

We would give him a good home and life while we could. We must bring him up as a Greek dog, sleeping outside at night and not too much mollycoddling and fancy food as he would have to become a working dog. When we got back we gave him some biscuits crushed in some of the 'Weenums' kitten and puppy milk we still had, put an old dust sheet into a low cardboard box and left him protected from the wind in the apothiki with the door left ajar.

In the morning when we got up I opened the kitchen door. He heard me and poked his little button nose out of the apothiki. *"Ela, ela"* I called and he came running into the kitchen. This became the routine for the next 3 weeks, but he always seemed perfectly happy to sleep in the apothiki, after all his parents and their parents may not have had even that much luxury.

I'd been trying to think of a name for him. Being mostly white reminded me of 'aspro peristeri' the white dove of one of my favourite Dalaras songs, so Peristeris became his name, Perri for short. Calling 'Perri' got more reaction from Terry at first, he thought I was calling him, but it was too late. The puppy had a name and it had stuck. I couldn't change it now. He soon knew his name and also responded to a few basic Greek commands *etho, kato, pano, ela, thelis;* and *ohi* - or maybe just the tone of voice.

Talking to friends about him we were offered a wooden box which had originally been made for carrying 2 kittens. It was perfect size and made a more wind proof box for Perri, made warm and comfortable with a travel blanket we donated to him.

Perri obviously liked the smell and taste of the 'Weenums' milk so I made some up for him each morning. I'm sure the added vitamins were good for him. The people we collected him from did not know how old he was as they were just looking after the puppies until homes could be found, but a friend with similar dogs to watch over his chickens estimated 2.5 to 3 months.

We bought complete food dog biscuits in the mini market (only €1 per kilo) and put them in milk for him. He wolfed them down and ate quite a lot that first day, not so much the next. I suppose he'd been competing for food before then. Friends with animals felt he would still need 2 meals a day for a while. We didn't feed him at regular times, and he usually had a few dry biscuits and water left after a meal if he got hungry later. He had food scraps from our meals too and soon after it was Christmas so there were always scraps for him to have as well as the dog biscuits. He definitely liked real meat best and the tougher lower legs of our locally grown turkey went down a treat. He would sit at my feet while I was preparing food, but was not over excitable.

Perri tried whimpering outside our window the second night, but Terry got up and called *'shush'* without going outside. He trotted off and never tried again. We had worried at first if he knew how to 'woof' - or 'γαβ γαβ' *(gav gav)* as Greek dogs say - which he would need to protect Sam's birds, but on the third night we woke up hearing a dog barking. Our quiet gentle little Perri was actually barking, presumably at a cat who had come to check him out. Most of the local cats are bigger than him so we were impressed. He only barked a couple of other nights and very occasionally in the daytime at sudden unexplained noises. I just hadn't realised that puppies can be SO easily trained. He was just so good and trouble free to look after - especially Greek style with him living mostly outside.

We didn't let having Perri stop us doing whatever we were doing. He obviously liked our company, and preferred to be in the kitchen with us, but would accept his lot and go to his apothiki box or the courtyard when we went out. On our return he always came running when we got to the gate, or was waiting standing on the top step as we came in, then he would run down to us wagging his little tail very excitedly. He loved affection.

For our last week we had glorious sunny day time weather so decided it was time Perri came out with us. I made a makeshift lead from a suitcase strap which he happily let me put on him. He wasn't too sure when I started to walk and it tugged a moment on his neck so I picked him up to take him to the car. By the time we got out at a friend's he realised the lead was no problem at all. In fact it was his passport to freedom. I'd not been able to get him to show any interest in sticks or running after me in the courtyard, but Perri enjoyed trotting alongside me and had his first real run that day.

We also took him to see his new home as Sam had moved in now, although the birds were still at his old home. It seemed a good idea for him to see this place a few times before we left him there and to meet Sam and Mitsos, his kitten. Mitsos had been having a rough time with the birds and had an infected scratch on his nose so Sam had brought him along and made a comfy blanket 'nest' for him on his windowsill. We introduced him

to Perri. The kitten hissed and raised a paw, but soon settled. After I while I put trusting Perri with him on the window ledge. After a little uncertainty it actually looked as if they will become good friends, possibly sharing food and a little warmth on cold nights.

We left Perri in next day. For the first time he peered at us woefully through the gap in the gate as we walked off. He had tasted the outside world and wanted more. The next day we took him to Tavari with Sam. He patiently stayed at my feet on his lead while the tens of cats there competed for fish heads from the diners. Everyone said what a well behaved dog he was.

It was cold on Friday when we went back to Sam's. We'd seen some breeze blocks on his land so used these to build a little house with an 'elonitas' roof to put Perri's box in - no barrel house for our dog!

Saturday dawned. We took Perri to Sam's to have his first meal of the day there, stayed a while, but left him at his new home. He was tied to the table with our suitcase strap to prevent him following us that day, but Sam wants him to be free. He told us later that he cried for a few hours before settling.

We went back to see Perri on our last day. He was very pleased to see us, tail wagging, rolling over. I'd cooked our remaining food for lunch there, with plenty of leftovers for Perri and Mitsos. Perri had missed physical affection so we tried to encourage Sam to pet him. He was impressed with the way Perri went into his box for me as we were leaving - not that he stayed in it. Later we rang to check he hadn't run off. He was comfortably curled in front of the fire, but by our return in May he had a new home (and a new name, Matt) with some dog-friendly taverna owners and customers to make a fuss of him.

Our pet fostering in 2004 was my first taste of sharing my life with animals. Yes, the tiny kittens especially, but also the puppy were a commitment, but so very rewarding. I think they enjoyed their time with us as much as we enjoyed their company. In the summer of 2005 we were adopted by another abandoned kitten. News gets around!

Trees & Woods of Greece *by John Akeroyd*

For The Greek-o-File Vol 1 I wrote of Greece as a land of wild flowers. It is also rich in trees and shrubs, the most barren landscape often covered by spiny Mediterranean scrub or with scattered trees. In more moist, relatively ungrazed or undamaged places, especially up into the mountains, Greece retains considerable native tree cover.

Leaving aside the dark green Mediterranean scrublands that mantle the hills, Greek woodlands are special and scenic places, atmospheric and wildlife-friendly. Even the farmed landscapes, dominated by trees introduced long-term – **olive**, **carob**, **mulberry**, **walnut** and **citrus** – are among the most evocative in Greece.

Olive Grove

Photo by Sylvia Cook

Far too much has been written about the Mediterranean region as a ruined landscape. In fact, as woodland history guru Oliver Rackham has pointed out, woodland survives, fluctuating with cycles of drought, higher rainfall and the economic prosperity or otherwise of the countryside. At the same time, much of the ubiquitous scrub, often regarded as degraded woodland, may never have been proper woodland, especially on poor soils, in windy districts and near the sea. True, there are plenty of stark hills and bare badlands, and some districts (on many islands and some of the countryside around Athens) have a devastated feel. Nevertheless plenty of woods remain, frequently more open in structure than in northern Europe and more like savannah. As people drift away from the countryside, tall scrub or maquis is reverting to woodland. Dwarf hummocky spiny scrub too is being invaded by **pines** and introduced trees such as **acacias** (although sometimes fire clears the ground again).

A magnificent example of open 'savannah' woodland survives in eastern Crete, as one drives up to the Katharo plateau in the Dhikti Mountains above the famous village of Kritsa. The margins of the Lassithi plateau itself have huge evergreen **kermes** or **prickly oak**, usually a shrub but here a subspecies with proper trunk and limbs. You can also see these great trees on and around the Omalos plateau of west-

Kermes/ Prickly Oak

ern Crete. **Ilex** or **holm oak** woods are infrequent in Greece, and in some districts restricted to cliffs. Most Greek oaks, however, are deciduous. The commonest is **downy oak**, which covers large areas in the hills of the Peloponnese and elsewhere, even in barren areas such as the Mani. These trees tend to hold their leaves over the winter and give magnificent shows of autumn colour. I well remember a November bus ride from Sparta to Athens through endless vistas of russet and yellow lit by late autumn afternoon sun – an image omitted from travel posters! A rather similar deciduous tree, **Valonia oak**, has huge acorns in corky cups decorated with great woody scales. For centuries these tannin-rich fruits were the mainstay of the tanning industry, and the trees are widely planted.

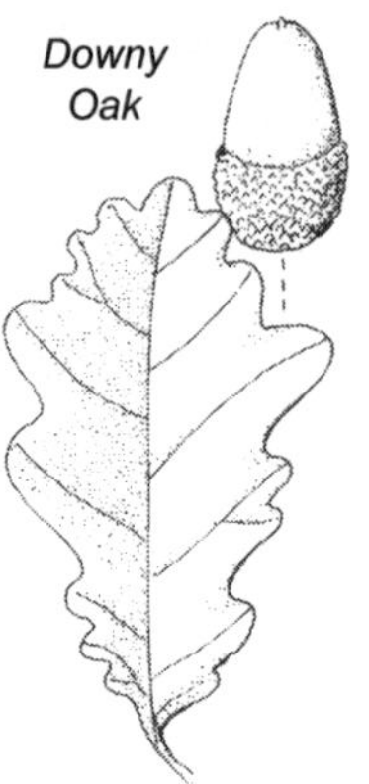

Downy Oak

Probably the first native trees that visitors to Greece notice are evergreens – several species of pine. From sea-level up into the lower hills the commonest is **Aleppo pine**, with slender bright green needles and greyish bark, that forms open woods on rocky ground. Regenerating after fire, it is the natural woodland of the coastal zone. In some places, such as Crete and Thassos, it is replaced by the very similar but more elegant **Calabrian pine** with darker leaves and rather upright cones. Another familiar pine is the parasol-crowned **umbrella** or **stone pine** whose seeds are the pine nuts of Mediterranean cooking. Native in a few places, such as the sandy coast at Schinias-Marathon to the northeast of Athens, it was formerly planted behind beaches and in suburbs as a shade tree. This typical tree of southern Italy gives a distinctly Neopolitan look to some Greek coasts.

Aleppo Pine

Up into the mountains, pines come into their own. On Crete, **Calabrian Pine** occurs up to over 1000 m altitude. The common mountain pine of the mainland is **black** or **Austrian pine**, but on Mt Olympos and other higher mountains one sees the cedar-like **panther pine**,

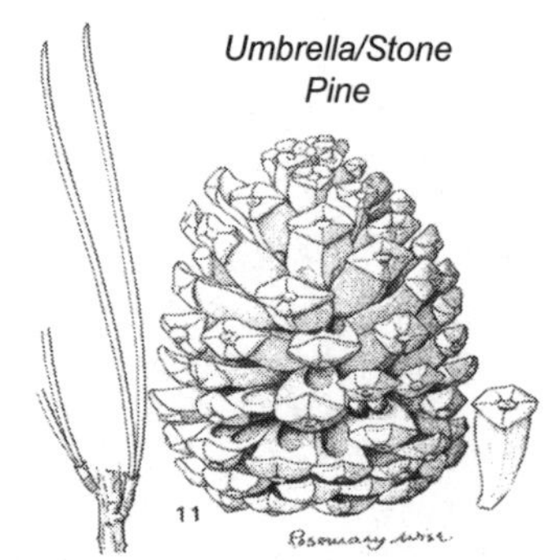

Umbrella/Stone Pine

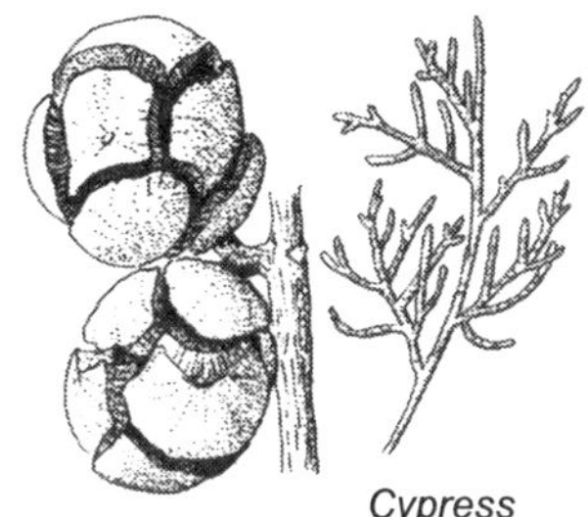
Cypress

with its huge spreading limbs. On Crete and Rhodes, native **cypress** forms a similar zone at high altitudes.

In the mountains, **Greek fir** often accompanies pines – the cones are erect, almost candle-like, and the leaves are shorter, each with a disc-shaped base to the stalk. The ancient Greeks used the strong light wood to build triremes, fast warships with curved hull timbers of **Aleppo pine**.

Junipers too are a feature of mountains, but also coasts. In scrub and on dry hillsides, Mediterranean Juniper replaces Common Juniper (widespread in the higher mountains). On coasts it has a distinct large-fruited subspecies, most notably on Gavdos, south of Crete, where it forms substantial woods – undoubtedly the "large cedars" of Greek-o-File volume 3 (p.76). The most remarkable species is **Syrian juniper**, with plum-like edible fruits, a tree which has its only European station on Mt Parnon in the Peloponnese. All juniper fruits are, of course, a useful embellishment to stock and stews, and an essential flavouring of gin.

Syrian Juniper

A whole range of deciduous trees occurs in Greece, including those we know from the UK. In the north especially you can find **rowan**, **English oak**, **hornbeam**, **maple**, **cherry**, even **birch**. **Hawthorn** is common enough in the hills, and **chestnut** widespread on lime-poor soils. **Beech** is a characteristic deciduous tree of upland valleys and low mountains in northern and central Greece. Greek beechwoods bear an uncanny resemblance to those of the Chilterns and the Downs, although the trees are usually smaller and closer together, often derived from formerly coppiced or grazed scrubland. The ground flora too is similar but richer, with numerous woodland orchids.

Along rivers there is still plenty of **white willow**, and sometimes mixed woods of **willow**, **white** and **black poplar**, **alder**, **elm** and **ash**. Swamp and riverbank woodland is greatly threatened and much has gone. One waterside tree that has survived and prospered is the stately **oriental plane**, icon of village squares throughout Greece. Fine groves and individuals survive: my favourite is a giant at Krasses on the way up to Lassithi from the coast,

and many will know the decayed veteran on Kos under which Hippocrates reputedly taught. Xenophon tells how King Xerxes so loved these great trees that he had one in a Lydian sacred grove adorned with gold ornaments and guarded by one of his 'Immortal' bodyguards!

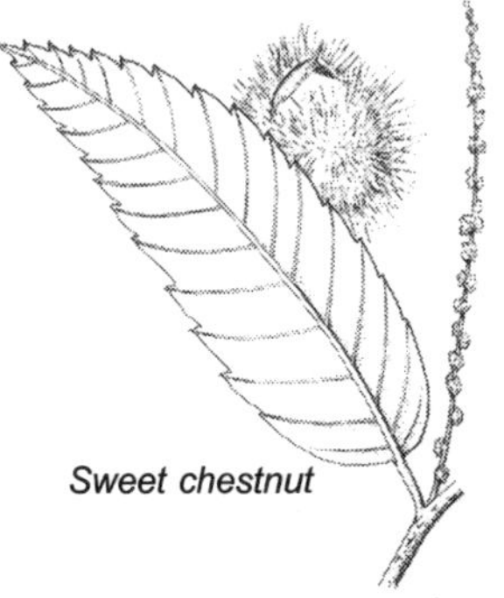
Sweet chestnut

Certainly, trees were special to the ancients, and they preserved many sacred groves, punishing those who damaged them. Dodona in Epirus, site of the first Greek oracle, was established amongst **downy oaks**, some of which still grow nearby. High on Mt Ochi on Evvia is an isolated grove of **chestnut** among huge boulders, surrounded by low spiny scrub, clearly a place of some significance. On a larger scale, the Holy Mountain of Mt Athos has astonishing green woods of **pine**, **oak**, **chestnut** and **hazel**, providing a place of contemplation for the monks. On Patmos, where trees surround the monastery of St John the Theologian, Fr Amphilochos, who died some 35 years ago, would take confession from farmers and make them plant a tree as a penance! *"Do you know?"*, he said, *"that God had one more commandment - Love the Trees!"*

A very special wood occurs on Crete, in a broad, dry stream-bed – effectively a wadi – at Vai at the far eastern end of the island. Here the Greek Forestry Department protects a grove of **palms**, not true date palms but the much rarer **Cretan date palm**. The trees are relics of much wider ancient distribution; you see them here and there on the coast of Crete and in the Dodecanese, and (don't tell the Greeks!) in southwest Turkey. Theophrastus, student of Aristotle and 'Father of Botany', described them in 300 BC and they also featured on ancient Cretan coins. This rather upsets local legend that they were first introduced by 'Saracens' or (a more scholarly hypothesis perhaps) troops of Mithridates, 1st century BC King of Pontus.

Finally, one cannot imagine Greek trees without considering **fig**, which may not be a true native but has certainly been around for a few millennia. A tree of tropical affinity, it is a classic plant of streamsides, damp cliffs and old ruins. Few fruits are so nutritious or easily stored, and the tree is quite a feature of the rural scene.

One of the paradoxes of Greek tree life is that so many familiar trees and shrubs were introduced, often long ago, and more and more are coming in today and being naturalized. The trees and woods of Greece are ever-changing, but fortunately ever-present.

Drawings by Rosemary Wise

Hitching Lifts & Other Gestures *by Sylvia Cook*

A regular subscriber, Ed Prothero, wrote to me some time ago recalling an amusing incident in Eresos some years ago:

"We visited Lesvos in 1986 and stayed at Eresos. As I recall there were 2 settlements, Eresos and Skala Eresos by the sea. Eresos seemed to be mostly deserted but had a petrol station. I drove up there to fill our hire car (a wreck!) and on the way back a little old lady dressed in black stepped into the road in front of me. Much to my surprise the brakes on the car were adequate to avoid a very nasty accident. The little old lady seemed unperturbed and walked to the passenger door, got into the car and pointed down the road towards the sea. As we approached Skala Eresos she screeched at me very loudly and I stopped the car. She leaned over, gave me a very small fig and got out of the car! Geriatric hitch-hiking, Greek-style. I was happy to help the old lady, but I wish she had just stuck her thumb out in the usual fashion."

As the TV advert for an International banking company explains, you need to understand local customs when abroad as the 'usual fashion' in one country may not be seen in quite the same way elsewhere. When we're in Eresos in the summer without transport, particularly in the early years when we holidayed there, we would often hitch down to Skala as do many of the locals.

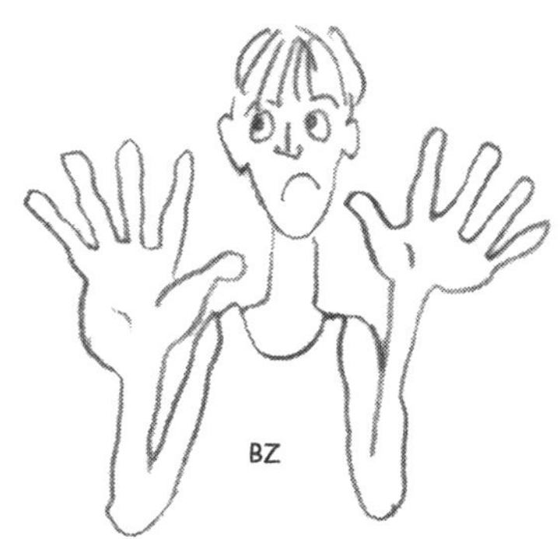

We were told early on that sticking up a thumb English-style would get us nowhere as it is considered a very rude gesture (sexual I believe). It's best to raise your whole hand when you see a likely car or truck approaching and much safer than walking in front of cars! Take care not to have your palm facing them, fingers apart. That's about the rudest Greek gesture - the ***moondza*** (μούντζα) - a very forceful and contemptuous 'go to hell' which is even worse with 2 hands!

We've had some interesting experiences hitching and giving lifts to others over the years. We've been in the back of many trucks, including alongside a tethered donkey, ridden pillion on a moped - *both of us,* with me sandwiched between Terry and Giorgos who we knew quite well. When Giorgos saw us and stopped Terry let me get on the bike and intended to continue walking himself, but Giorgos insisted and didn't (couldn't?) go fast.

We have also had stilted Greek conversations with many villagers who seem to know all about us, but we don't know them. In our Grekovan touring days we would often pick up several people in our converted minibus. The Greeks were always confused by getting in on the other side of the road, but thought our house on wheels - τροχόσπιτο (trohospito) - with fridge, cooker, cupboards and sofa bed, was πολύ ωραίο (*poli oreo*, very nice).

Our Greek communication has improved over the years. We have a bit more vocabulary, but much of the grammar learnt years ago does not come to mind quickly enough. Often we are just getting better at guessing what people are trying to say through understanding a few of their words. This is how most tourists start communicating in Greece and villagers are eager to communicate with visitors, even if they don't speak any Greek. Understanding some of the peculiarly Greek gestures helps.

Rather than nodding their heads up and down for **'yes'** Greeks will tip their head downwards, often closing their eyes at the same time for an affirmative answer.

'No' is indicated by lifting the head up and backwards, with eyebrows raised - often just a quick and subtle movement. If it is an absolute 'NO' they will bite their lower lip at the same time in a more exagerated gesture.

I think she says 'Yes'.

'Come here' can look more like a wave 'goodbye'. It is a wave of the fingers with the palm facing down. If you start retreating they will just wave more agitatedly.

To ask **'What's up?'** or 'How are you?' the enquirer may raise eyebrows inquisitively and slowly rotate his hand to the left with fingers spread upwards as if holding an invisible ball.

'Unbelievable!' is gestured by slowly rotating a hand 2-3 times by the side of the face, pointing upwards - possibly saying *"po po po!"* at the same time.

If someone wants to explain **'a relationship'** between 2 people - family, business or sexual - they may place their hands side by side palm down and rub the forefingers together, as if they were partners in bed together.

One Greek word for beard is also used for lie or fib, μούσι (mousi), so if you see someone stroking an imaginary beard or flexing fingers horizontally under the chin they are saying **'liar'**.

Others are more obvious like sawing the edge of a hand across the stomach for **'hungry'**, or touching the lower lip to indicate they would like to **'tell you something'** and all manner of actions instead of words.

Apart from using their hands and body language to express themselves, Greeks will also raise their voices more than we Brits might and may often seem more agitated than they really are, when just trying to make a point. Personally I find it hard to know when they are discussing and when they are *really* arguing having witnessed both.

In Britain we have started to learn 'continental' ways and woman-to-woman, or man-to-woman people who barely know each other will now greet with a kiss on the cheek - perhaps just an affected 'air' kiss, with hugs and close contact reserved for close friends. In Greece both men and women will greet each other with hugs and affectionate kisses on both cheeks. A man should feel welcomed not wary when a Greek male friend hugs and kisses him on each cheek on meeting.

Believing strongly in 'the family' Greeks are very friendly towards children. One habit hated by most visiting children is that older women will pinch children's cheeks and smilingly say (in Greek) how pretty they are. They might even pretend to spit at your child afterwards, or say *'ftou ftou'*. Believe me, this is not offensive, but merely guarding against the evil eye, because they believe that if a compliment is given, the curse of envy may fall on the envied one.

All Mediterranean people are known to use their hands and gestures more than us 'colder' north Europeans, but the Greeks seem to be the masters. Once you know some of the basic variations, it makes communicating and understanding Greeks more effective.

Tales of Greek Customs *by Bill Harper*

It had been a fraught journey in 1981 towing our 6-metre yacht to Corfu. Sitting sheltering out of the rain under the hull in a breaker's yard in northern Italy while the owner searched the site for a replacement trailer wheel being but one of our travel delights. When we drew up in Gouvia marina I thought our troubles were over. Mind you, I should have been warned when we passed through Greek Customs and our car number and everything inside and on the roof rack was listed in my passport, the final entry being *"1 6-metre boat"* - but not a thing that was inside the boat.

At this point I thought I needed a Transit Log so set off in the car to Corfu Customs - only to find it shut, opening hours being 10am - 2pm. Next morning we drove to Customs again, waited in a queue until 1.30pm to discover they have to *see* the boat. This meant putting the outboard motor on the stern to motor it the few miles to Customs the next day.

Fearful lest I drop it in 15 feet of water, I tied a rope around it and gave the other end to Susan standing on the quayside. As I leant with the motor over the stern I shouted *"Now!"* to Susan - only to see the motor disappear upwards. I looked up to see a giant of a red-haired, red-bearded Bellamy-kind of man holding the motor and smiling encouragingly. This was Ben, our soon-to-be new German guardian-angel-cum-sailor's friend. He thought we'd wanted the motor on the quay and had taken the rope out of Susan's hands to help.

Hearing of our need to take the boat to Customs - every officer of which it seemed was his great friend - and that we were concerned our children would be thoroughly bored with another long wait, he offered to come with me so that Susan could take our children to the beach. What a kind man!

Ben and I arrived at Customs just before 10am and I took my place at the end of a very long queue. On the dot the office door opened. The officer strode out down the queue to where I was sat and beckoned me into his office. When the rest of the queue stared in angry disbelief he obviously felt an explanation was due. *"Him here yesterday,"* he said, and with that they had to be satisfied. That night we bought Ben a meal at his favourite taverna where he waited every night in case his brother from Germany should ring.

We were not yet out of the Customs wood though. Launching our old dinghy in the marina, we discovered the rubber had perished and it was useless. We just wanted to throw it away, but it had been on the roof rack and was listed in my passport. So, back to Customs, where we found our next guardian angel - Greek this time. Solemnly he told us that it was illegal to throw it away, but explained that if I wanted it written out of my passport I could make a gift of it to the Greek people. I can tell you that making a gift of it to the Greek people was very complicated, but under his very patient time-consuming attention we eventually succeeded in making our gift.

For the rest of our holiday there were no problems, but since we wanted to leave the boat in Greece, there was one small problem. Now as you may know, in Greece there are no 'big' problems - only small totally insurmountable ones. If you knew just how, we had heard these could be climbed by making an appropriate gift, though not to the Greek people in the plural! Since we didn't know 'how' I had to rely on unfailing Greek sympathy to smooth my path. The new problem was that we must put the boat into Customs' bond, so back to Customs for the usual wait, only to find at the end that we were not to take the boat to a bonded warehouse. Oh no. We had instead to drive the Customs' officer to where the boat stood (we had found a boat-yard that would winter it), whereupon he wound long lengths of wire around it and the trailer it was standing on and affixed a large number of stamped seals.

The next year we arrived in the evening and rather than finding a hotel we slept on the boat - I may not know how to solve small Greek problems, but I do know how to wield a screw driver! Next morning - back to Customs. After the usual long wait, with only 15 minutes to closing time, we were rather anxious that we hadn't been seen yet. Suddenly we were ushered into an office.

"You want to remove your boat from bond?"

"Please"

"Are the seals still intact?"

"Of course."

"Well I'm sorry but I haven't time to come now, so I'm afraid you'll have to break the seals and take the wire off yourselves." So we did.

We didn't see our former Customs guardian angel - apparently he was in prison - something about fraud. And Ben? We saw his converted caique sunk in 15ft of water at Gouvia. Enquiries revealed he'd been arrested as a very big (everything about Ben was big) international drugs smuggler. That

explained why he sat in the taverna every night in case his 'brother' rang!

The next year we discovered we would have to take the trailer home for Customs reasons. Our boatyard friend suggested we 'import' it ... so, back to Customs early again, towing the trailer, hoping to be near the front of the queue. No guardian angel to 'help out' this time, so we sat there all morning. As two o'clock approached the children had had enough, but things were speeding up. Then from an inner sanctum the Head of Corfu Customs *himself* appeared. Passing, he noticed our small daughter quietly sobbing.

"Why's she crying?" he asked.

"Because she's hungry," her mother replied crossly. *"We've been waiting here since nine o'clock."*

"Oh, that's terrible," he exclaimed and swept out. Five minutes later he was back with a carton of biscuits which he gave to our daughter.

Half an hour later we were ushered into *his* office. To our request to 'import' our boat trailer, he proclaimed *"Impossible!"*

"But what if we pay the import duty?"

"Cost you far too much. How much is it worth?"

"About £50."

He gave a great roar of laughter. *"There's no trailer worth as little as that. Where is it?"*

"Just outside."

"Well, I'll come and look at it," said he, still laughing. We walked outside. He took one look and laughed even louder.

"You'd never get £50 for that" he declared.

So we imported it at an estimated value of £40, paying around £20 import duty *and* saving the cost of two ferries back to the UK.

Many years later in Zakynthos when Customs officers were checking on illegally imported cars, I was stopped and asked for my passport and documents. Since I'd left my passport in my room I could not produce it.

"Bring it to Customs tomorrow morning," they said after prowling round my red Fiesta and noting everything about it. The next morning I went into the cavernous Customs house, walked up to the nearest desk and asked where I had to show my passport.

"Oh," said the officer, *"you must be the man with the red Fiesta. Up those stairs opposite."*

They know all about you on Zakynthos!

More Customs Tales *by Sylvia Cook*

Bill Harper's experiences may have been many years ago, but apart from EU citizens no longer needing to declare items they bring into Greece, much has not changed.

The rules for importing boats and cars are still as quoted in previous Greek-o-File reports. The 'bonding' scheme for boats and cars used in Greece for temporary use less than 6 months of the year is time consuming and unwieldy. We understand it is getting cheaper to import new vehicles, but rates for older vehicles are ridiculously out of proportion to their value.

Until we have harmonisation of taxation across the EU, it seems the Greeks can apply their own disproportionate level of importation tax. The machinations of the European Union will take many years to reach their goal of true freedom of movement, *with their possessions*, for all its citizens.

We reluctantly drove our K-reg Suzuki jeep back to the UK in July 2005, having exhausted all the sensible legal options for leaving it in Greece. The Athens Customs office quoted us €10,000 import duty. We pointed out that its UK value is less than £1,000. *"Why so much?"* we asked. The reply *"We don't want old technology in Greece"* !

A strange excuse when you think of all the endearing sights of old wrecks, 3-wheeler trucks on lawn mower motors, and other 'Heath Robinson' motorised transport you regularly see in Greek villages.

For example, this useful farm truck was put together from a salvaged boat engine, wood and other items found by Nondas in Sigri, Lesvos.

Size Matters *by Dave Rodda*

Over many years of visiting Greece my wife, Linda and I have decided that our ideal place to stay is a small village with a resident Greek population and six or seven tavernas. Any larger and there is too much commercialism, any smaller and there is not enough to interest us in the evenings.

This view started to form when we visited **Skopelos** and stayed in the west coast village of **Elios** (Έλιος) which fitted our ideal. It is a fairly new village, built to house people who had lost their homes in the 1965 earthquake. Many of the concrete block houses that the government provided are still in evidence, but now covered by bougainvillea. The village, though not beautiful, does have character. The town beach is not very exciting but a short ankle deep paddle around the headland brings you to the first of a series of sandy beaches that stretch along the west coast.

What makes Elios special are the people. The old man pottering around the garden of our apartments, who we thought was the odd job man, turned out to be the owner with a finger in a number of other businesses in the village. English was not widely spoken and in some shops it was necessary to communicate in pidgin Greek and sign language, but generally language was not a problem. At the end of one taverna meal my younger daughter decided she fancied baklava and the order was made. Soon after we noticed our waiter riding off on his bike, returning balancing a plate on his handlebars. He must have gone to the bakers for the baklava.

The bakery was 'open all hours'. I never actually saw it closed. Run by a young couple the husband did the baking at night and the wife served in the shop all day while looking after a young family. After our experience we decided we may as well go to the bakery ourselves on the way back from the taverna. The walk was always interesting as the whole of the village seemed to be out wandering about the main street. A common sight was a greengrocery van. It would be there when we went out and on our return, but with a lamp so that the greengrocer could see to weigh his produce.

The next few holidays all had some aspects of what we like but not all. **Kandouni** (καντούνι) on **Kalymnos** is part of a sprawl that extends up the central valley. The beach here is lovely and there are some pleasant walks to be taken around the coast and food in the tavernas is good. Kalymnos is a lovely island and with the bus service and plentiful cheap taxis, visiting other parts of the island is very easy. However, Kandouni feels more beach resort than village. **Nikiana** (Νικιάνα) on **Lefkas** certainly has the village feel and a baker who would only serve me if I asked for the bread in Greek. While we liked Nikiana the food was disappointing - although of good quality, every taverna had the same limited menu. **Old Alikanas** (Αλικανάς) on **Zakynthos** has a beautiful beach but with only two tavernas, choice is very limited.

Realising we needed enough local tavernas to provide variety, our next holiday was to **Loggos** (Λογγός) on **Paxos**. One of the tavernas has tables outside along the quay. As this is also the road, the bus has to squeeze between the diners and the edge of the quay - always an interesting moment. Loggos met most of our requirements but with so many tourists it was difficult to find a table in a taverna after 7pm and we prefer about 9pm, so this was a bit of a problem for us. There are lots of trails around Loggos for walkers and boats can be hired from the harbour so that you can visit remote beaches, but once you have visited Gaios and Lakka there is not a lot left to do.

The island of **Halki** (Χάλκη) had the same problem. Evenings by the harbour were a highlight of this holiday. During the day it would be almost deserted but at night as people came out to dine the place came alive. However, we found even less to do than on Paxos and the number of tourists made the place feel more like a scenic holiday resort than a village.

By now we had fine-tuned our requirements - adding limited tourism and enough to keep us occupied when we want a change from the beach. This quest took us to another winner, **Ag. Evfimia** (Αγ. Ευφημία) on **Kefalonia**. Ag. Evfimia like many towns and villages in Kefalonia suffered in the 1953 earthquake, but the village was rebuilt using the same street plan so many of the old alleys still exist. Although tourism has grown in recent years it has not lost its charm. A bustling harbour provides plenty of interest and the tavernas all sell good local food. Being at the northern end of Sami Bay, Ag. Evfimia is centrally located for visiting other parts of the island. The one drawback is the beaches. If you need a long stretch of sand then Ag. Evfimia

is not for you. The town beach is a narrow strip of sand and shingle and nearby Paradise beach a short stretch of pebbles so you need to head out along the road to Sami for sandy beaches. Friends Barry and Sue came with us on this holiday, their first to Greece. They left as confirmed Grecophiles.

The following year we visited **Alonissos** and stayed in the village of **Votsi** (Βότση), built on a very picturesque horseshoe bay with a small harbour one side, small sandy beach on the other and more pebble beaches not far away. The holiday brochure described Votsi has having several tavernas but there were only three. However, a twenty minute walk along the coast takes you to **Patitiri** (Πατητήρι) and in doing this walk we passed through an area called **Roussoum Yialos**. This is were many Greeks holidayed and as a result the five or six tavernas were all excellent. At night the track was lit so there was no need for a torch. A visit to the old town is a must and boat trips take you to some of the more remote islands and give you the chance to meet Pakis on his restored caique, the Gorgona. He was involved in setting up of the marine wildlife reserve and has a wealth of stories to keep his guests amused.

Our next holiday was the village of **Sigri** (Σίγρι) on the western tip of **Lesvos**. The Rough Guide describes Sigri as having an end-of-the-line feel. Arriving after a two and a half hour journey across the island in drizzle, we had some sympathy with this view, however, Sigri soon works its charm and you start to agree with the Cadogan Guide's view that Sigri is a delight. Many regulars who return year after year, together with Greeks on holiday, create a good atmosphere in the village. Food in Sigri is good and fish very fresh. Our Direct Greece rep, Jan, has lived there many years with her fisherman husband. It was worth the journey to Sigri to hear Jan's highly entertaining welcome talk. Her wealth of information about the area, coupled with the information in Greek-o-File's Introductory Issue meant we had plenty of interesting places to visit. However, although roads in the area are improving, the more interesting places are reached along unmade tracks. The village beach is sandy and can get crowded, but a walk in either direction will lead you to a number of excellent quiet beaches. Our favourite was Sheep Beach, a short walk along the old dirt-track road towards **Eresos**. Even in August we often had the beach to ourselves and friend Sue, a life time nonswimmer, learned to swim. Further along the old Eresos road is the beach of Tsichliodas which has a lagoon at the back. Looking inland with the hills in the background you could imagine yourself in Scotland were it not for the oleanders growing on the bank.

Next we visited **Armenistis** (Αρμενιστής) on **Ikaria**. We flew to Samos where we caught the ferry to Ikaria - surely the slowest boat we have ever been on - it took four and a half hours via **Fourni** to **Aghios Kyrikos** (Άγ. Κήρυκος). A further journey of one hour brought us to Armenistis. The village on paper met our requirements but rather than the quiet village we were expecting, it is busy with tourists of all nationalities and traffic is continually passing through the narrow main road. The beaches nearby are excellent but being on the north coast the seas are often rough. Swimming was normally difficult and sometimes dangerous, snorkelling mostly out of the question. Armenistis does provide you with a base to explore the west of the island. At nearby **Nas** (Νας) a deep gorge meets the sea. Tavernas at the top have spectacular views and steps lead down to a sandy beach with a lagoon at the back. Inland from Armenistis lies **Christos Raches** (Χριστός Ράχες), a sleepy village in the daytime with very little open. However, between 10pm and 2am the place will be buzzing with all the shops open whatever their wares and tavernas in the pedestrianised centre with tables spread so far out that only a narrow passageway is left to walk through. Further inland at **Pezi** (Πεζί) are a couple of small picturesque lakes with a waterfall. At this point the road becomes a dirt track leading to the village of **Langada** (Λαγκάδα), once the capital of Ikaria, now you see just a church and an open area for festivals. In the past, Ikaria suffered from piracy. Their solution was to build far apart, or hidden under slabs of rock, so they could not be eas-

Moni Theoktisti

ily found. On the south west coast is the village of **Karkinagri** (Καρκινάγρι). The road only reached here in the late 1990s and, as in Christos Raches, the villagers live their lives late in the day - so if you arrive in the morning you may find tavernas closed.

Having passed through **Samos** on the way to Ikaria we decided to make this our next visit and avoiding the north coast, we chose the village of **Ormos Marathokambou** (Ορ. Μαραθοκάμπου). Ormos has a resident population of around 200, who were very much in evidence as we walked through the village. Supplemented by just a few tourists, the atmosphere of the village is not lost. Our landlord, Manolis Vourdas made us very welcome plying us with drink and fruit and eggs from his own garden. His wife Patricia even baked us a cake. This friendliness existed throughout the village. On one occasion Barry went to the mini-market for a newspaper to check on the football results. On reaching the till he realised he had left his money behind. Before he could put his papers back on the rack, the lady at the till said *"Just pay me next time you are in."*

We were lucky to be there on 15th August for their Wine Festival. You bought a small commemorative mug for €5 which you could fill as often as you liked. The activities were in the village car park and as the population swelled from the surrounding area, cars were parked in any available space with late arrivals having a substantial walk back. A Greek band and troops of dancers entertained and as the evening wore on the locals had their chance to show their skills - small boys through to old men joined in the dancing. One old gent whom we had seen around the village before had come ill equipped with sandals. He just took them off so that he could move more freely, but inevitably the sandals were kicked all over the place and we doubted he would ever find them again. However, the next day they were back on his feet. On subsequent nights there were other activities until eventually even the locals were saying they had organised too many things!

During our stay we visited more cosmopolitan places like **Pythagorio** (Πυθαγόρειο) and **Kokkari** (Κοκκάρι) which, though picturesque, lacked the Greekness of Ormos with their glossy bars and tavernas lining the sea front. While Ormos also had tavernas and cafes running along the harbour they were clearly Greek rather than international. Ormos main beach is sand and shingle and it can be uncomfortable entering the water. If you can put up without a sandy beach then Ormos meets our criteria perfectly. The right size, typically Greek, friendly locals and Samos has a wealth of places to explore.

You may have different ideals for your Greek holiday, but I hope some of our observations will suggest areas where you would enjoy the real Greece.

Travels with Alexander (age 7 months)

by Sarah Akehurst

Having spent most of the nineties living and working in the Greek Islands, we feel at home there and see ourselves as true Grecophiles. However, this was going to be our first holiday as a family. Paul and I were taking our 7 month old baby, Alexander.

We chose the pretty whitewashed village of Lindos on Rhodes as we already knew that it was the perfect place for little Alexander. Paul and I had met there in 1991 and stayed for a few years, having a marvellous time and making lots of friends. Those friends were all at our wedding in 2000 when we returned to the village to get married. It was only right that we took Alexander to stay in his spiritual home.

Lindos really is one of the most picturesque places in Greece and an excellent choice for families as it has three sandy beaches, all shelving gently into the sea. There are sunbeds, umbrellas, tavernas, bars and a variety of water sports. The sugar-cube whitewashed houses nestle on the hillside under the ancient picturesque Acropolis. The maze of pedestrian streets are full of gorgeous little shops, lovely little bars and restaurants. The only forms of transport allowed in the village are the donkeys that carry people up to the Acropolis and the three wheeled delivery trucks. This is great as you don't have to worry about traffic.

There is a superb atmosphere in Lindos and many people have been returning there for many years. Some we know started going to Lindos as children and are now returning with their own families. Now it was our turn to return with Alexander.

Gone for us are the days of grabbing a bag and a passport and making a dash for the airport. It took Paul and I a whole day to pack this time. Gone too are the times we would spend leisurely lunches at a waterside taverna drinking two or three (small!) bottles of retsina before crashing out on the beach. I could forget about taking a book - I hadn't read one since Alexander was born.

This trip took a lot of preparation. Were my years as a holiday rep in Greece going to help? Probably not as even the most level headed folk get anxious about taking their own baby abroad - it's only natural. You just have to try to remember that women have been having babies in Greece for thousands of years.

We booked a civilised day flight. All went smoothly but we did have to wait nearly two hours for our luggage at Rhodes airport, then the transfer time by coach to Lindos was one hour. When we arrived in the village we were met by our representative and escorted on foot to our accommodation. Our luggage came later by delivery truck.

Lindian accommodation is mostly in traditional village houses so standards can be simpler than at some other Greek resorts. We booked an apartment as opposed to a studio to give us more space with Alexander and all his 'stuff'. Unless you take your own, it is advisable to request a cot before you travel. This is usually payable locally for around £15 per week.

You find yourself thinking more about the local facilities. There are a number of small supermarkets in the village that stock fresh milk, bread, fruit and vegetables, etc. There is a good pharmacy that sells jars of baby food and there is a resident doctor. The nearest hospital is in Rhodes Town. There is a laundry located in the lending library - useful if you are holidaying with a baby.

Eating out is a joy as there is a great choice. Traditional Greek food and fresh fish, of course, but also Italian, Chinese, Indian and Mexican restaurants. Children are welcome in bars and restaurants - some set in pretty courtyards of old sea Captain's houses, or on rooftop terraces overlooking the village. It looks delightful in the evening when the Acropolis is illuminated. The roof terraces are no problem if you have a pushchair as waiters and bar staff will happily carry them up for you. A couple of restaurants have high chairs and children's menus, but if they don't you will find a pocket 'high chair' useful - it is a fabric harness that fits into your handbag and comfortably straps your baby onto almost any chair.

Alexander enjoyed eating out with us and was a great fan of mezes. He was happily tucking into dolmades, gigantes and moussaka. He did find the grilled octopus a bit of a challenge though!

There are some great excursions that will take you to Rhodes Town or around the island to visit for example The Valley of the Butterflies and the ancient city of **Kamiros**. You can also island hop over to the pretty neighbouring islands of **Symi** or **Halki** and even venture over to **Turkey**.

If you are travelling with a baby you may prefer to hire a car as we did, to explore at your own pace. We used our car for short drives to our favourite beaches. **Kiotari** is 20 minutes south of Lindos. It has a pebbly beach which is usually quiet and we enjoy fresh fish from the barbecue at Stefano's Taverna - popular with the locals, AND it had a high chair.

Haraki Bay, 15 minutes north of Lindos, is a crescent shaped bay lined with tavernas. The small family run Haraki Bay Hotel at the north end serves excellent food and the waiters made Alexander feel everso welcome. They kept bringing treats out to him.

We had a fantastic time with Alexander. He was great - he enjoyed playing on the beach and in the sea, although it was a bit cool in May. He certainly loved all the attention that everyone gave him. I think that 7 months was an ideal age to take him away as he was not as vulnerable as a really small baby and had started eating solid foods. At this age babies seem to be very portable and the fact that they are not yet mobile is brilliant. You don't have to worry about them running off.

The trouble starts when they start to walk and run and get close to the 'terrible twos'. Alexander is now 21 months old and we are off to Alonissos in the Sporades soon. I'm already visualizing my next article and am thinking of calling it 'Changing a nappy on the back of a Flying Dolphin' - or perhaps I'll leave that to your imagination.

Sarah's Tips on What to Take With You for Baby

- Pushchair/buggy with parasol.
- Formula milk if required. It's expensive in Lindos and no British brands.
- Nappies can be bought in Lindos, but more expensive. Swim nappies.
- Bottles & cleaning equipment. Disposable sterilised bottles for journey.
- Disposable sterilising bags for sterilising bottles, bowl, spoons, etc. I found these great. Can be bought in Mothercare.
- Wipes. Take some antibacterial hand wipes and some for surfaces.
- First Aid kit to include infant paracetamol (Kalpol) and oral rehydrate.
- Sun lotion factor 30+ and other baby toiletries.
- Mosquito repellent.
- Disposable bibs.
- Baby's cutlery & bowl.
- Favourite soft toy & other small toys.
- Pop up sun shelter for beach.
- Sun hat & baby sunglasses.
- Bedding for cot.
- Cool bag.
- Pocket 'high chair' harness (in picture).

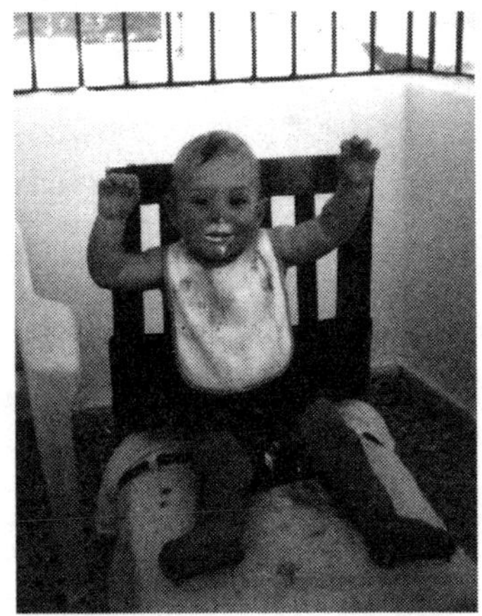

Notes on Travelling With a Baby *by Sylvia Cook*

* A baby up to 2 years old (on date of return flight) flies free, but is not allocated a seat on the aircraft, nor a baggage allowance, other than a collapsible pushchair.
* If you wish you can pay a child seat price for your infant, but will need to bring your own car seat for your baby.
* Holiday companies charge varying amounts for infants under 2 to travel. I've seen prices from £0-£30, more if cot rental and baby care are included. Ask if cot linen is included.
* Infants under 2 are often included free of charge on a parent's travel insurance - check.
* Infants are now required to have their own 5 year passport.

Paros Profile *by Sylvia Cook*

In the heart of the Cyclades, **Paros** (Πάρος) epitomises every traveller's idea of an Aegean island - small (195 sq km), bustling port, picturesque villages with whitewashed houses, sandy beaches by a clear blue sea, fertile valleys between bare hillsides rising to a peak at 771m (Profitis Ilias of course), little churches and monasteries, a wealth of ancient history, a few relics, plus tavernas at fishing harbours for tourists to watch the world go by, or enjoy the lively nightlife particularly in high season. The main port, with regular ferries to most of the Aegean, is often called just Paros, but also **Parikia** (Παροικία). It is a busy, cosmopolitan 'hora' with a maze of narrow streets behind the waterfront tavernas and bars. Within the town is the church of **Ekatondapiliani** (Εκατονταπυλιανή) 'one hundred gated' built from 5th to 7th century AD and adjacent to an archaeological and a Byzantine museum.

Naoussa (Νάουσα) is a smaller port town with a pretty harbour in a sheltered bay. There are several more coastal resorts offering sandy beaches and accommodation (see map). The old capital, **Lefkes** (Λεύκες) is a must to visit, or even to stay.

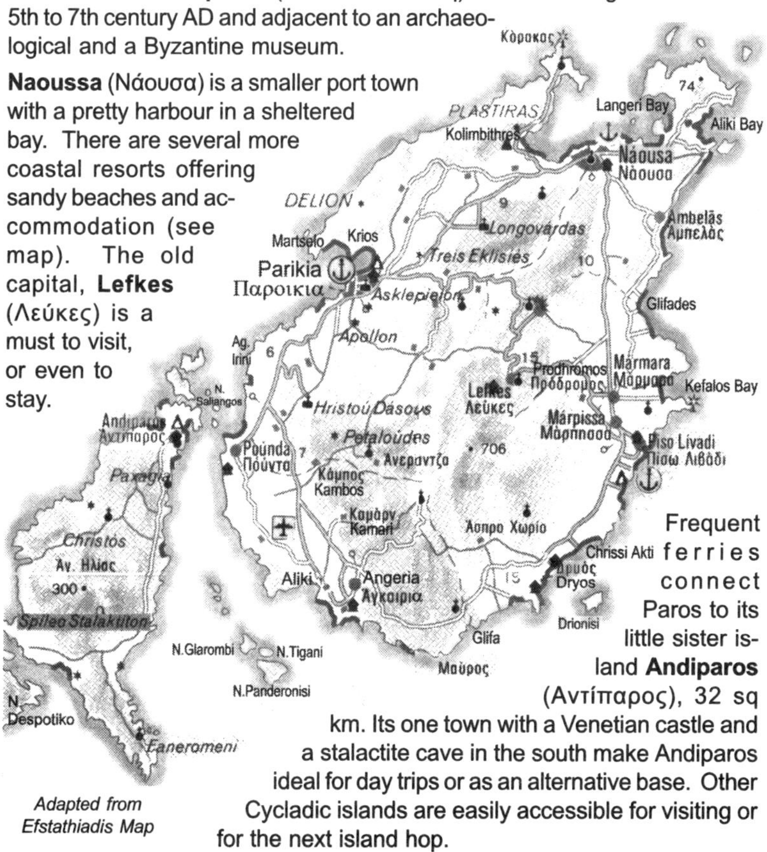

Adapted from Efstathiadis Map

Frequent ferries connect Paros to its little sister island **Andiparos** (Αντίπαρος), 32 sq km. Its one town with a Venetian castle and a stalactite cave in the south make Andiparos ideal for day trips or as an alternative base. Other Cycladic islands are easily accessible for visiting or for the next island hop.

Paros Background

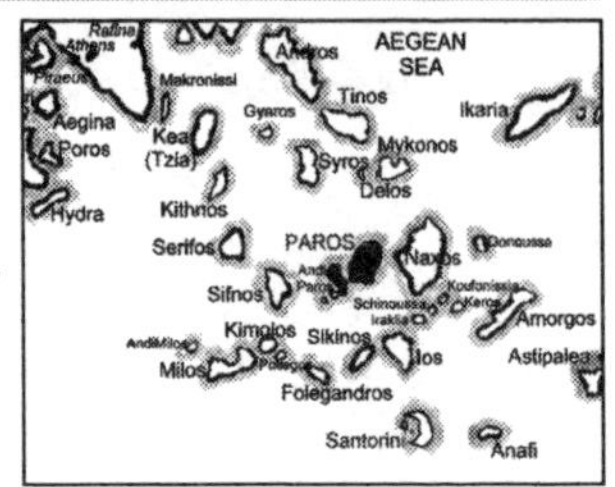

- ❒ *Settled since 5,300-4,500BC (late Neolithic), remains have been found on the tiny island of Saliangos, formerly a narrow isthmus connecting Paros to Andiparos. Many 3rd-2nd millennia BC (Bronze age) sites also found.*
- ❒ *Fertile soil for farming and rich deposits of pure translucent 'lychnites' marble made Paros prosperous in ancient times. Both are still important to the economy, but modern tourism probably ranks higher.*
- ❒ *Paros followed the fortunes of its neighbours through more modern history - Byzantine, Crusaders, Venetians and Turks before reunification with the rest of Greece in the 19th century.*

Paros Perambulations *by Jenny Booth*

Having been to most of the island groups we decided it was time for a further venture to the Cyclades. Santorini was something of a one off with the spectacular scenery of the caldera, so we felt we should try another more typical Cycladic island. Paros was chosen because although it has no international airport, you can still get there on a reasonably priced package holiday from Manchester. (Don't be put off if 'package holidays' don't usually appeal, the numbers are very small).

A couple of spare hours were spent on Mykonos after we landed, but we were not sorry to be moving on. We had heard various horror stories of the boat crossing from Mykonos, but although the sea was quite choppy at no time was there any cause for concern. Our reward nearly 14 hours after we had left our beds in Bewdley was the arrival at the small port of **Naoussa**. It

has a real 'wow' factor and we hadn't seen the best bits yet.

Naoussa is lovely at any time but particularly so at night when all the fish tavernas around the old harbour come to life. Although we are not great fish eaters, a stroll around the harbour, often squeezing between the tables that spill out onto the pavement, became part of our evening ritual. This must be the place of a million photographs - typical Cycladic architecture, colourful little fishing boats, octopus hanging up, whitewashed churches and of course very satisfied cats.

Eating around the old harbour is quite expensive but it was always very busy even though we were there towards the end of the season. The island does seem to 'close down' in early October. However there was a good choice of traditional reasonably priced tavernas elsewhere in the village. In fact we were pleasantly surprised by the prices and even brought some euros home with us (a nice start for next year). We couldn't beat last year's €1 euro for a large Mythos in Samos though, the best we managed was €1.40. As an aside, our relatively modest breakfast on Mykonos on our homeward journey cost more than any evening meal on Paros. We like to stick to traditional tavernas but we did notice 2 or 3 more up-market restaurants in the village that I'm sure would cater for those who prefer something a little different.

Behind the harbour area the streets are something of a maze. Designed as such to outwit the invading pirates of times past. Again it is all very picturesque and you reach for your camera frequently. There are few tacky shops and many selling quality fashion, jewellery and craft items. After the best part of a week we reckoned we knew our way around - but not so. Even on our last but one day we got lost again. Skopelos was a bit like this but at least it is on a hill so you have the direction of up or down to rely on!

There's a traditional kafeneion in the back streets. Open all year and frequented by locals and visitors. It is very popular and the owner can always produce extra seats for customers with the result that the street (which is thankfully vehicle free) can often fill up as the evening wears on. We were

there one Sunday lunchtime for a Greek salad and 'kalamari' (squid). It was the best kalamari I have ever had but the bread .....well! I thought maybe it was because it was Sunday that we had bread resembling house bricks (I'm not exaggerating) but discovered later that it was normal for this establishment. It seemed as if it had been sliced from a loaf and dried out rather than toasted. We then saw these bricks (I mean bread) for sale in a bakery in another part of the island so realised it was 'normal' after all. (Ed's note. known as *paximadia* (παξιμάδια) these rusks are made in most parts of Greece from unsold bread, for dipping in soups or maybe coffee, but also for making breadcrumbs mixed in meat or vegetable keftedes). However I have to question how normal is a shop that was playing a tape of the carol 'Silent Night' in September when it was too hot to stand outside and wait for the bus.

The bus service on Paros appears to be a very well run operation. We used the buses a lot. They were cheap, frequent and always ran on time. It was end of season so you had to ensure you had a current timetable but most of the island was accessible by bus and the service ran through the evening for anyone wishing to go into the capital **Parikia**.

The buzz and air of excitement when a big ferry was in with all the coming and going that entailed made us want to visit Parikia a few times. However we had the feeling that it was more of a place people passed through for a few nights and preferred the intimacy of Naoussa. Referring to my Toilet Talk article in Volume 3 there are some very high scoring public toilets in Parikia and I say that even though some are the dreaded footpad type!

When in Greece we like to walk most days, although a walk of 6-7 miles can often be enough in the heat. The classic walk on Paros is the Old Byzantine Road (like a cobbled track) leading from **Lefkes**, a beautiful inland village,

downhill to **Prodhromos** near the coast. It is then possible to walk to **Piso Livadi** another pretty coastal village. Buses to Lefkes and from Piso Livadi are quite frequent.

We followed the route from 'Walking The Aegean Islands by Dieter Graf' and thoroughly enjoyed it. At the start of the walk we only had time for a drink at the lovely taverna in Lefkes with it's panoramic views down towards the coast. It was so enjoyable that we decided to do it again another day. This time we caught the bus to Prodhromos then walked uphill along the Old Byzantine Road to Lefkes where we were well rewarded with lunch at the taverna. A walk back down to Prodhromos for the bus back home made for a good day out.

Usually we would not spend all day on the beach but find a couple of hours during or after a walk is most enjoyable. On Paros the beaches are sandy and very pleasant, in our opinion second only to Skiathos. There are many secluded beaches if you want to get off the beaten track but at the quiet time of year we were there the popular beaches were most agreeable (uncrowded and with sunbeds, parasols and a handy taverna). We were reminded again that Greek people don't understand our love of walking - it was not unusual for a local to stop and offer us a lift to the beach.

The capacity in season seems enormous. One of our favourite beaches **Aliki Bay** (not to be confused with the village of Aliki in the south of the island) had an enormous campsite behind it and I certainly don't think it would have been our favourite a few weeks earlier.

Another beach we walked by (there are lots of informal coastal paths linking the beaches which do not appear on maps) had a bar which had closed down for the season. It looked as if it could have catered for the entire population of the island!

There is talk of the small domestic airport expanding to take international flights within a few years. I don't know whether this is one of those ongoing stories I have heard elsewhere in Greece or whether it will actually materialise. If it does it is certain to increase tourism so I would recommend anyone thinking of going ought to do it sooner rather than later.

If you enjoy trips to other islands there are plenty from Paros. **Santorini** is one of the popular ones and a trip would be a good way to see the sights if you did not fancy a full holiday there. I believe Santorini is a must for anyone who loves Greece. **Naxos** is possible by scheduled ferry service but we decided to put it on the list for a future holiday (you know the list – the one that keeps growing even though you keep ticking places off!).

Two delightful and unspoilt islands we enjoyed visiting were the 'Smaller Cyclades' of **Iraklia** and **Koufonisi**. The trip to **Delos** was highly recom-

mended by people we spoke to who enjoy history and ruins which are in abundance. **Anti Paros** is easily accessible by a fairly regular dedicated ferry service costing only €2 each way from Parikia, less from Pounda. We also met some people who had hopped to **Tinos** for a few nights but I don't think you could have done this on a day trip.

The weather was lovely for the last 2 weeks in September we were there. The Cyclades can be very windy as it was on our arrival. This can upset the travel arrangements but we had no problems. At least the wind was warm and died down after a few days. We learned that the weather stays good until well into December but that winters can be horrid - wet, windy and cold. In fact last winter brought snow for the first time in many years. We were also told of the 'short summer' which often occurs for about 3 weeks in February. Apparently the wind changes direction, coming from the south, and the temperatures rise into the 70's before the wind changes direction again.

There were many nationalities holidaying on the island, with British in the minority.

Overall Paros ticked all our boxes for an enjoyable fortnight. We usually like to try new places but could certainly see ourselves returning to Paros.

Paros On The Buses *by Anne Cox*

We recently had a very enjoyable holiday in Paros, staying in **Naoussa**, where we hardly heard another English voice the whole time we were there. Everything was still very Greek. No English bars, restaurants, karioke or even English people working there. The people were lovely, restaurants fabulous and very reasonable, the public transport excellent.

We toured the whole island using the service bus. The most expensive fare was €1. The water taxis to the other beaches in the bay left every 30 minutes so you could go to a different one every day until you found your favourite - which we did. Twice we took the ferry over to **Anti Paros** from **Pounda** which cost €1.20 each way for <u>both</u> of us. The second time we just popped over to kill some time whilst waiting for a bus at Pounda, and to buy an ice cream at a small shop we had found on Anti Paros. It was better than standing around in the hot sun without any shade and the ice cream was the best I've ever had in Greece!

Several amusing things happened during our stay, many of them on the public transport. Where do the old Greek women come from when the bus pulls in? They seem to appear from nowhere with shopping bags brimming over. Determined to get on the bus before anyone else, they use sharp elbows and anything else they have to hand to ensure they do. We just stood back and watched (like many others) with much amusement and still managed to get on the bus.

Another time we had just left Naoussa when the young conductor reached over the head of the driver to get the 'shoebox' containing the bus tickets just as we went round the first bend. He dropped the shoebox, which bounced off the drivers' head, tipping the tickets and what seemed like hundreds of elastic bands out of the open window. The driver slammed the brakes on to stop the bus, shouting at the young conductor (only some of which I managed to translate). They both had to get off the bus and pick up the tickets while everyone on the bus was in hysterics. I was still laughing when we reached Parikia.

Next year we'll go back again to do and see all the things we didn't have time to do this year - the first time we have gone back to another place straight away.

How to get to Paros

By Air - Scheduled flights via Athens to Paros, Charter flights to nearby Mykonos or Santorini then ferry

By Ferry - links with Pireaus, well connected with most Cycladic & many Dodecanese islands, plus Crete, Ikaria & Samos

Tour Operators - Actual Holidays, Elysian, Freedom of Greece, Greece & Cyprus Travel, Greek Sun, Hidden Greece, Island Wandering, Islands of Greece, Kosmar, Best of Greece, Sunvil, Travel Lounge

Won Over by the Greeks *by Denise Offord*

It took my husband a long time to persuade me to go to Greece. I'd heard about the plumbing and it just didn't appeal to me. Having spoken to people who went there I finally agreed to give it a try and for my first Greek experience we went to Rhodes.

We stayed in Lindos and had a great holiday. At that time once the boat and coach trippers had departed it was relatively quiet at night. There was even a bar playing classical music in the evenings. We were hooked.

Since then we've visited Skiathos, Corfu, Kefalonia (twice), Crete, Kos and the Peloponnese.

Whilst in Corfu we met a rather scruffy looking great character called Spyros (of course) in Corfu bus station. We were waiting for the bus back to Paleokastritsa when we got chatting, and he asked where we were staying, was it our first time in Greece, etc, and went on to inform us we were waiting in the wrong place. Being typical Brits we weren't convinced as the sign definitely said Paleokastritsa and that's where we wanted to go. However, he beckoned us over to a bus which was about to leave from the other side and, yes, it was going to Paleokastritsa. We had to admit that the locals do know best.

We met Spyros a couple more times on the bus and he told us how he had worked all over the world, learnt his trade and now had a taverna in Corfu town. He gave us his 'card' - just a printed piece of paper, but at least he had fixed the spelling mistake. The taverna used to be on the direct route to the bus station, but the bus station was moved so his trade had been badly affected. At one time he said he had even played a part as an extra in the James Bond film 'For your eyes only.'

The day before we went home we decided out of curiosity that with the help of a local map we'd try to find Spyros' taverna, but as we had to go on a plane early the next day I decided that I definitely wasn't going in. The taverna was down a back street, had a 'coffee sack' theme and Spyros was really smart in his hemp apron. He saw us and welcomed us like old friends, so we decided that a drink couldn't harm and we might even risk a snack. Spyros said *"How about a meze"* and on the basis that I didn't have to eat anything I didn't like the look of, we agreed.

He brought the wine and when the meze came out I just couldn't resist. There were anchovies, stew, meatballs - it was wonderful. It just goes to show you should keep an open mind.

When we left, Spyros asked that when we got home if we bumped into Lenny Henry - whose photo he had pinned up on a wall - we should tell him that Spyro said "HELLO". So, Lenny, if you're reading this ....

This is just one of those small incidents which makes Greece so special and has meant that for the last 2 years we've only holidayed in Greece, going twice a year now. There always seems to be some small incident like this, which sticks in the memory and makes Greece and the Greeks so special. Yes, I must admit that I have definitely been won over by the Greeks.

If It's September This Must be Finikounda - *More Last of the Summer Retsina Tales by Arthur Deeks*

A spectacular (but sober) cartwheel down the stairs early one January morning followed by a short period in hospital, gave me an opportunity to rewrite my new year resolution. Out went 'eat and drink less' and in came 'visit Greece more often'.

The problem is that, as Harry is genetically modified to take only two holidays each year, it meant entering the singleton market, or finding other companions. In the end I did manage four trips but as a consequence this year is a kaleidoscope of impressions.

May saw us back in the **Pelion** (Πήλιον) with Harry's new pacemaker - and it loomed large on our trip. At Birmingham he waved his 'international excused electronic scanning multi-language document' and made an enthusiastic bee line towards an attractive blonde airport security guard, only to be headed off by a very burly and shaven headed male who firmly carried out the necessary groping. The Volos airport (small and apparently part time staffed) experience on the return journey was more bizarre. Harry, again exercising his international pacemaker rights, was ushered around the permanent scanner (which I had already gone through and set off, but nobody seemed concerned) and sauntered towards me. The policeman, who was busy chatting up female airport staff at the other end of the hand luggage scanner, suddenly noticed him, immediately grabbed his hand held electronic scanner and approached us - pointing it like excalibur. As the policeman advanced, we retreated backwards in tandem, like some demented tango routine, me protesting volubly - Harry waving his papers. Eventually the policeman came to the end of his cable (or patience), shrugged and gave up.

We really don't do very well on our trips to the Pelion. Perhaps it's something about it being the magical land of the centaurs. Two years ago we were re-routed via Mykonos - a 25-hour journey including overnight ferry to Rafina and a coach journey. This year there were three changes of flight times and carrier and a challenging return flight. Low season consolidation seems the name of the game. The tiny airport at Volos improves, slightly, and there was a lot of building work nearby, but it's still pretty laid back.

On arrival Harry noticed the colourful display of international flags outside - with the UK flag upside down.

"I want to see the airport manager."

"Harry, the minibus is waiting."

The manager arrives.

"The Union Flag is upside down, are you in distress?"

"Ah, the Union Jack."

"No, it's only the Union Jack when it's on one of Her Majesty's ships."

"Harry! We have to go."

The manager shrugged, *"Endaxi, put it down to ignorance."*

I dragged Harry away grumbling,

"How would they like it if we put their flag upside down?"

It was still upside down when we returned on the way home.

We liked the west side of the Pelion last time, but the journey across the mountains to the east side is a lovely overture to a holiday with terrific views back to the calm waters of the **Pagasitikos Gulf** (Παγασητικός Κόλπος), wooded slopes, ravines, picturesque villages of distinctive traditional architecture plus some apprehension as the minibus driver spent the whole journey driving with one hand while answering his mobile phone. The room in **Agios Ioannis** (Αγ. Ιωάνης) was yet another triumph of Greek micro technology but adequate for our modest needs.

What a difference a month makes - June last time to May this time. Thriving bars are echoing empty spaces, deserted tavernas, closed shops. But in compensation the wild flowers are truly amazing, as are the walks (try Lance Chilton's 'Walks in the Pelion' and the coloured map that accompanies it). Our particular favourite was the kalderimi along the coast to **Damouhari** (Νταμούχαρη), A couple of eating places here worth mentioning: In the Taverna Ramona, you order in Greek and the waiter will translate it into

Damouhari

English for you. Greek salads big enough to fulfil government fresh vegetable targets five fold and beautifully cooked calamares. It was clearly loved by Greeks, particularly those on what appear to be church outings, (ie loads of elderly Greek ladies accompanied by a Papas), but avoid an evening meal if they've been in the afternoon - locusts come to mind. The Akrogiali was really pleasant with local bouzouki talent twice a week, very atmospheric and enthusiastic - even if slightly off key.

If you're going into **Volos** (Βόλος), and have a driver, try a 'tspouradiko', the food and little bottles of tsipouro (sort of high octane ouzo) just keeps on coming - Mezetzidiko to Dixto - in a back street was pretty good but I am told that there are some even better ones around the harbour of Volos.

The return flight sort of summed up our travel arrangements. The half empty plane had no sooner taken off when the rather camp and sibilant steward announced that they had been unable to load sufficient meals for the return flight. *"Ever so sorry, just press your call buttons only if you really, really must have a meal."* Everybody pressed their buttons! *"Ooh, you're my favourite"* the steward said as he passed Harry. He looked puzzled. *"Why me, I pressed the button like everybody else?" "You pressed your light button"* I said as he ungraciously received a complimentary can of Pringles, bar of chocolate and cup of coffee to the value of £3.10. *"And that's 10p more than it should be"* said his new found 'favourite' friend.

By late June I was beginning to get Greek withdrawal symptoms so dipped my toe into the last minute singleton market. There is a reluctance, apparently, for many travel companies to dish out singles until the very last minute, presumably even with the dreaded single person supplements they find it's financially worth hanging on for a more rewarding pair.

After three weeks of the, *"Could you go tomorrow?"* conversations I was ready for them, not quite sprinting through the departure lounge and picking up the tickets for Crete like an Olympic relay runner, but pretty close. This trip involved a delayed night flight to Heraklion with what appeared to be the local chapter of Club 18-30. Fuelled up, revved up, loud, flatulent, matching T-shirts with logos that left little to the imagination and a lot of, what my psychology lecturer once called 'free floating libido' - and that's nothing to do with swimming pools. I felt very old and judgmental and uttered a silent prayer of thanks for places like Kavos, Faliraki and in particular Malia, which, as it turned out was where they were all heading.

The early morning journey from the airport did make me wonder if **Makrigialos** (Μακρύγιαλος) (long shore) had been a wise choice as there seemed to be a disproportionate number of half built houses and endless polythene greenhouses. A nap and an ouzo or two later and the place took on a different complexion. Accommodation right on the beach, a room big

enough to hold a dance in, air-conditioning and a shower curtain (in my price range a Greek rarity). Makrigialos has a very fine gently shelving sandy beach facing the Libyan Sea and you really do get the feeling you have to walk to Africa to get out of your depth. You are well placed to explore the south east end of Crete: **Ag Nikolaos, Sitia**, Minoan burial ground and palace at **Zakros** and **Ierapetra** (if you must), and off shore islands of **Chrissi** and **Koufonisi**.

Sitia (Σητεία) can be reached by bus via Ierapetra and has a sort of north African feel about it with a palm tree lined promenade and loads of French and Italian tourists. It's quite charming and seems to have a lot to offer, a beach, fishing and ferry port, interesting architecture, an old town and lots of tavernas. Unfortunately I was too early for the Sultana festival which is at the end of August and where allegedly the wine flows and Cretan dancing is performed.

There are some pleasant walks from Makrigialos particularly the one up the Pefki Gorge to **Pefki** (Πεύκοι) and **Agios Stephanos** (Αγ. Στέφανος). OK, it's not exactly in the Samaria Gorge league, but very attractive with spectacular views of the bay. Above Pefki is a charming folklore museum run by a little old lady who has little English but is extremely hospitable. The museum speaks for itself, with rooms furnished traditionally and a schoolroom with portraits of national heroes. With any luck the sweet old lady, who is very enthusiastic about the whole project, will give you a sweet on the way out. It seemed totally a local initiative so do pop in and

make a donation. There is a pleasant little bar down in the village called 'The Pepper Tree' and a tree outside from which it's supposed to take its name - but does pepper grow on trees? This is where I miss Harry with his Rural Studies background.

Back to Makrigialos. For a small place it does have plenty of tavernas mostly, along the beach path and all serving very good food. Walking along this, if the tavernas aren't busy, is a bit daunting for a sensitive soul like me. There is no excessive hassle but once you've been in once they seem to have a proprietorial interest in your custom. I began taking the main road and diving down a back street to the small harbour at the end of the beach for my ouzo. The cheapest ouzo in town - and it's pleasant to sit and watch the fishing boats coming and going. Among the many very good tavernas I particularly liked the Tzivaeri, in the corner by the harbour, the Botsalo and the Petra Bay - outstanding. The highlight of my visit was undoubtedly the European Nations Football Final. To sit in Greece in a Greek crowd watching them win was a truly, amazingly, joyful experience devoid of any unpleasant behavioural excess.

The return flight was serene and peaceful with the majority of my fellow passengers comatose presumably with headaches, nursing broken hearts, or promises, or empty wallets.

In September Harry, the 'carers' (Zeb and Bear) and myself went to **Finikounda** (Φοινικούντα), in the south west of the Messinia region of the Peloponnese. Harry took against it from the start, *"it's too flat"*. Now that's an exaggeration, but I suppose if your last two visits have been to the Pelion, and up against the Taigetos mountains in the Mani, then it doesn't quite measure up, but flat it ain't as we found on our walks into the hills. At our digs the ablution department arrangements left a bit to be desired, and many unanswered design questions. Why build a big kitchen next to a minute bathroom and not plan in a shower space? To use it required careful planning. First remove all toilet rolls, then build a dam by the door of surplus mats and towels to stop the water running into the bedroom, then position yourself carefully in the one square foot of space between the toilet and the wall so that you're looking out of the meshed toilet window. (A few conversational gambits for passing locals are useful). Then, if you're lucky AND the day hasn't been overcast, you will get a hot shower. Harry cheered up once it was clear that a little light maintenance was required, descaling the kettle and unblocking the tap which unerringly directed a jet of water down the front of your trousers. He cheered up even more when he realised that the Greek Air Force used one of the off shore islands for target practice, not that you could see them but you could hear them on most days.

In early history Finikounda was a port used by the Phoenicians (who traded

the *murex frunculus* shell - used to make Tyrian purple dye) and Finikous Limin was mentioned by Pausanias the 2nd c. AD Greek geographer and historian. In the mid 19th century a fishing community was started by people from Crete who called it Taverna - because it had one and they hadn't read Pausanias. By the 1930's they presumably learnt to read again, studied Pausanias and changed the name - or something like that.

It's a pleasant village with a sandy (blue flag) beach backed by tavernas and accommodation stretching back to an impressive 300 yards of dual carriageway (the only bit) on the road between **Methoni** (Μεθώνη) and **Koroni** (Κορώνη). Looking out to sea is the offshore island of **Schiza** (Σχίζα), and to your right past the harbour, up through the old village and over the headland past the churchyard with panoramic views is another blue flag beach, Anemomilos, very long and backed by camp sites, water activities etc. To the left, past the village school on another little headland is a small beach with a 'watersports' hotel. It also flew the Union flag upside down. I tried to shepherd Harry past the flagpole before he noticed, but only just managed to restrain him from climbing the pole to put it right. Beyond is **Loutsa** (Λούτσα) beach backed by a camp site with a handy little taverna.

There are some reasonable walks. The most interesting we found was past Loutsa to an old tower and a small beach where there have been turtles. One of the serendipitous things about Finikounda is the sunset and the orange glow it bestows on rocks and buildings at the east end of the bay. The afore-mentioned tower disappeared in the daytime, invisible against the trees but stood out in the reflected light of the sunset. We did ask a number of locals what it was. Replies varied from a shrug to *"It was built by my great great grandfather"*, and *"It was a pirate tower"*

Sunset Tower & hills

to *"It's named after this taverna"*. The 'carers' thought that it looked like 'Tracy Island from Thunderbirds' - and they're supposed to be looking after us!

There was plenty of choice for tavernas and bars. We tried them all. The Elena, with wonderful views of the harbour and seafront is described as being built 'amphitheatrically' and 'placed into the green of the plants' an accurate description, if odd. They also have Greek music twice a week. The Five F's (Pente Fi) serves beautiful fish. We tried to work out what it meant but our ideas always ended in hysterical laughter. In the end we asked the waiter what it meant and he said *"Friend of a friend of a friend of a friend who frequent your taverna"*. *(Alternative explanation in book review p164.)* To Kyma was good. Dionysos seemed to roast a pig nightly and served huge portions. They also had a waitress with a model's hour glass figure - not that Harry or I noticed. Best scrabble venue was the Medusa zaxharoplasteio, although if you sit in the roadside part it's a bit like a youth club. To Karavi served excellent meals ('A mother cooked with traditional Greek style'). In the Omega the starters come after the main course and the waitress is likely to take your lunch order and then go for a paddle. O Antonis at the back of town with views over the rooftops had a very good if limited menu (including 'drunk chicken' and 'drunk pork' - chicken or pork in wine) and a very select clientele - just us.

One thing that struck me about Finikounda was the number of abandoned cars with no number plates, left on patches of land with grass growing through them. One of the most sinister was a black prewar Mercedes. For a few days we thought Herr Flick was keeping observation behind some apartments because it never moved. A more sophisticated abandonment was next to the taverna Psykos - two cars, one on top of another, the top car quietly rusting away but with pretty fairy lights draped over it.

To get to or from Finikounda (as explained in the local guide book), by the Kalamata-Methoni-Pylos road, I can only agree that 'if you choose this road you will have the company of the sea' and 'the scenery becomes rough and

lonely' - don't worry, the road is quite good. The buses are absolutely beautiful, brand new and luxurious but if you discount the early 7am buses, a tad infrequent - three to Pylos and two back, and one to Kalamata (presumably you stay the night) but mostly running on GMT (Greek Maybe Time). The good news is that the taxis back from Methoni and Pylos are reasonable. The bus routes often take you up to the villages en route and it's amazing the way the drivers thread these large, state of the art, buses through seemingly impassable village streets.

We revisited **Methoni** and **Pylos** (Πύλος), which are musts if you are into castles, but on this occasion noticed things we had missed on our last visit, like the hibiscus lined main street in Methoni. We spent time in the lively and picturesque Platia Trion Navarhonin Pylos, refreshing ourselves under the shade of the plane and lime trees, and the watchful gaze of Admiral Codrington. This time in the castle we visited a sad little memorial to 44 men killed on 27th September 1944, many of them professional people, doctors, accountants, bankers, lawyers, etc. The guide books gave no indication why they died but I assume it was during the strife between the various political factions once the Germans withdrew.

Finally in late September I went to **Rhodes** staying in one of the many Captain's Houses with Gwyn Harris (former readers will remember - Welsh, preschool playgroup XV and serial hypochondriac) and Gill, this time with their extended family. The house had fantastic ambience but, oh those pebble floored bedrooms. It's a shame that **Lindos** pays for being spectacularly pretty and is invariably overwhelmed by tourists. I tried to avoid the narrow main thoroughfares, particularly when the buses from the cruise ships arrived. It could be a bit like facing The Light Brigade with the tour guide, holding his numbered wand aloft like a sabre, leading the charge.

Captain's House - Lindos

I don't know whether it's because it's a busy tourist place or not but there did seem to be a lot of helpful and highly educated waiters intent on putting me right with regard to gender, case and other grammatical shortcomings, so much so that I was tempted to lapse into the imperative, *"ere tosh gis a beer!"* - but I struggled on with my 'greeklish'. There were also some very friendly ones, like Aris the Albanian.

"What's your name?" said my Welsh mate. *"Aris, what's yours?"*

"Same as yours - 'Arris, Gwyn 'Arris from Ponypridd. Where you from boyo?"

"Albania" *"'I've been to Albania"* I said helpfully, *"twice."*

"Why," said Aris, *"were you a spy?"*

Having previously only used Rhodes as a stopping place en route to somewhere else, I was surprised how attractive the island is. It's not just sun, beaches and booze, it's the contradictions that get you; the charming back streets of the medieval parts of Rhodes Town alongside the tourist tat shops and predatory shopkeepers. Away from Rhodes Town there are some pretty barren parts but also forests, mountains, verdant valleys, impressive castles, ancient sites and delightful small villages, particularly in the south, which compensate for the appalling tourist development in the north.

Rhodes gave us a rare anthropomorphic moment. It was unseasonably hot for October. We had stopped in a quiet village and retreated to a shady taverna in a hot and dusty square, deserted apart from our car parked outside the church. Into the square loped an unkempt pack of dogs led by the strangest dog you ever saw, front half short haired, rear half dreadlocks, a sort of Rastafarian Just William. They moved with a nonchalance which indicated that they had not read Sofka Zinovieff's article on 'Street Dogs' (Vol 2). They deserved background music, perhaps Peggy Lee singing from Lady and the Tramp. They sat in a line across the square but nothing moved, nothing to chase, nobody to beg from and finally bored they arose at William's command, sauntered over to our car and flopped in its shade. *"That's torn it"* said Nick, *"how are we going to get in our car?"*

"No rush" said Julia, *"just don't tell the girls or they'll want to take him home."*

Did I miss Harry? You bet. No scrabble, no tea in bed, and I miss those discussions where he thinks that my opinions, although interesting, are irrelevant. So we're now planning next year's trips - assuming I can keep up with the bionic man.

Profile of Leros *by Anne Buchanan*

Leros (Λέρος) lies in the Aegean, part of the Dodecanese group of islands, with Kalymnos to the south, Lipsi to the north, Patmos northwest and the coast of Turkey 40km to the east. The island is just 15km long, northwest to southeast, 1.2 - 6.5km wide. It has a highly indented coastline with four main peninsulas joined by two narrow isthmuses. Covering 54 sq.km, the gently mountainous island rises to a peak at **Mount Klidi** (Κλίδι) (320m) in the northern mountain range. Although the mountains are generally barren, there is plenty of water. The valleys have some trees and produce olives, carobs, figs and other fruit, tobacco and wine. The extensive network of military roads constructed by the Italians is well maintained.

Leros is a diverse island. Starting in the north of the island, **Blefouti** (Μπλεφούτη) has a beautiful quiet bay with one (excellent) taverna, not far from the airport at **Partheni** (Παρθένι) and the site of the Temple of Artemis; to the west are **Gourna** (Γούρνα) and **Ag. Isidoros** (Αγ. Ισίδωρος) with its panoramic little church on a promontory (only accessible in fair weather). On the east side of this isthmus is the tourist resort of **Alinda** (Άλιντα). It offers unbelievable views across the bay and is especially spectacular at night when the magnificent Kastro is lit up. Just below the castle is the island's capital of **Platanos** (Πλάτανος) which sits between the peaks of two hills and merges down the north side with the port of **Aghia Marina** (Αγ. Μαρίνα) and down the other side with **Pandeli** (Παντέλι). Pandeli is a picturesque small fishing harbour lined by beachside tavernas, popular with visiting sailing boats and small yachts but retaining an old fashioned Greek feel. Here it is popular to celebrate wedding feasts (we witnessed a particularly beautiful one under a magical full moon) and young children can safely play and run around on the beach. Around from Pandeli nestles the bay of **Vromolithos** (Βρομόλιθος), views over which are stunning. Heading south takes you to **Lakki** (Λακκί) which has lost some of its former elegance and beauty due to war time bombing and subsequent neglect, but there is still evidence of its Italian architectural influence. Lakki has a hospital, large hyper-market and the majority of the island's shops and offices. A few miles on is the southernmost tip of Leros and the fishing village of

Street in Platanos

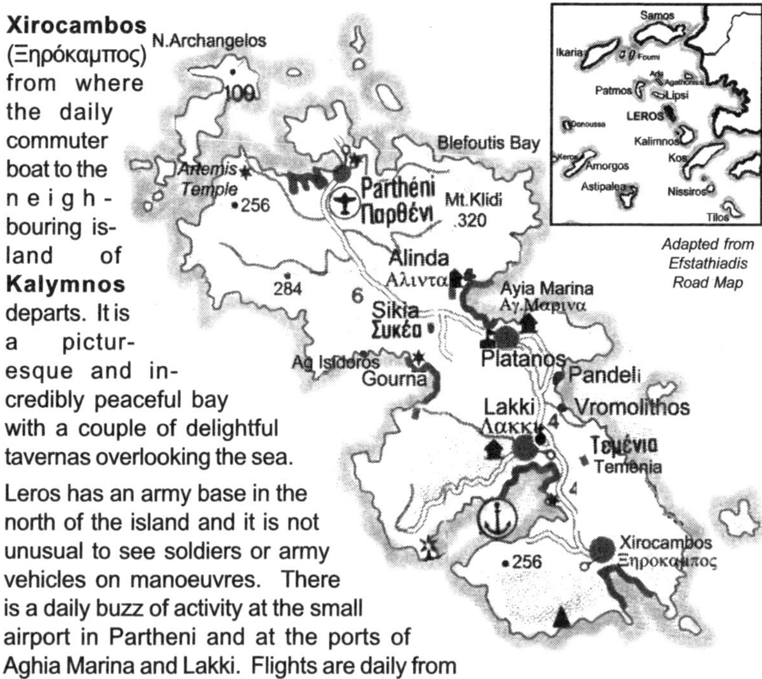

Adapted from Efstathiadis Road Map

Xirocambos (Ξηρόκαμπος) from where the daily commuter boat to the neighbouring island of **Kalymnos** departs. It is a picturesque and incredibly peaceful bay with a couple of delightful tavernas overlooking the sea.

Leros has an army base in the north of the island and it is not unusual to see soldiers or army vehicles on manoeuvres. There is a daily buzz of activity at the small airport in Partheni and at the ports of Aghia Marina and Lakki. Flights are daily from Athens (except Tuesdays in winter) and now also to and from Kos and Rhodes. The recently renovated and extended terminal building, now with air conditioning, is adjacent to the car park which is bustling with waiting taxis, cars and a truck selling fish. The daily arrival and departure of the Dodecanese Express catamaran at Aghia Marina harbour provides a fascinating spectacle. Larger ferries use the main port of Lakki.

Leros Background

- *In mythology Artemis, the virgin goddess of the moon and hunting, chose Leros as her island. Actaeon, son of King Cadmus, unwittingly came across her naked and weaponless in her sacred wood. She turned him into a stag and he was hunted down by his own pack.*
- *The first human inhabitants of Leros date back to the Neolithic period 8000 to 3000 BC. After the Trojan and Persian wars, the islanders of Leros joined the Athenian Alliance in 600BC.*
- *Many magnificent Christian churches were built in the Byzantine period as well as the famous Kastro. In 1306 Leros was occupied by the Knights of St John. Initially the island's fortifications were extended but then the island was offered to its Governor and its fortunes reversed.*

- *From 1455 a series of raids and invasions left the island economy in ruins and in 1522 it fell to the Turks. Leros reverted to Greece in 1821 but the Turks returned 9 years later and held control until 1912 when the Italians invaded. They modernised and built roads, schools, hospitals and a naval base for their Mediterranean fleet in the huge natural harbour.*
- *The British took over when Italy capitulated only to lose out to a German invasion in 1943. After the war Leros was under British rule until 1948 when it and other Dodecanese islands were reunited with Greece.*
- *In more recent years Leros housed exiled opponents of the Greek military dictatorship, then Leros psychiatric hospitals were scandalised in a TV documentary in 1989 resulting in the tourist trade avoiding the island for many years. Although still low key, tourism run mostly by Lerians is now on the increase.*

Leros, the Island of Artemis *by Anne Buchanan*

Graham and I first came to Leros in 1997. I had been looking for a small island within reach of the larger, tourist island of Kos. I found Leros in the Thomson brochure and a gorgeous studio, Angelika, in Alinda. For once, the reality lived up to the brochure and our expectations! It was covered in bougainvillea, the view down to the bay was breathtaking, the accommodation spotless and the owners incredibly Greek, welcoming and friendly. After 7 years and nine visits, we consider Markos and Areti some of our dearest friends.

Our first few visits to the island had us believing that little happened in the way of nightlife. We were under the impression that the whole island shut down around 10.30pm, the time we usually strolled back from a delicious dinner at one of the many beachside tavernas. The whole pace of life in Leros was slow and laid back, so much so that days just seemed to drift by and the peace and calming effect was magnetic to us. Days were spent on quiet beaches (pebbly on the whole, but beautiful clear water), followed by restful siesta times with only the odd sound of a goat to disturb, then a lazy meal and early night.

Year 3 and our friend Giorgios asked us if we wanted to go with him to the Greek bars in Aghia Marina. We agreed, but we didn't know where they were. He said he would pick us up 11.30 - midnight and then we would go! (We had to snatch an evening nap first to ensure our ability to stay awake through to the early hours!). To our amazement 3 fantastic Greek cafe-bars appeared as if by magic. There was music (mainly Greek - we are now huge fans and have a respectable collection), lots of young people and an amazing convivial atmosphere. Needless to say we frequented those bars on several more occasions AND have returned to Leros every year since then.

View from Alinda

In 2004 we returned with our 17 month-old daughter Grace and nightlife reverted back to much as it was in the former years. We had booked a 2 week holiday in mid September to introduce Grace to Leros and our friends. However, only a few days into the holiday I kept saying to my husband *"Do we have to go home?"* and one warm evening after a few glasses of local wine in a beachside taverna we decided *"No ... let's stay a while longer!"*. His recent misfortune of redundancy led to our being able to stay for two months on our favourite island.

Anyone who has looked for longer stay accommodation on a Greek island will know the trials and tribulations involved. Word soon got about and friends and strangers alike approached us with offers of apartments and houses to rent. Some of their definitions of a 'fully fitted kitchen' were certainly different from mine! We were strongly advised to ensure that the chosen accommodation had heating as we would be there into November. It was hard to imagine cold weather on a hot September's day, but we heeded the advice.

The time went so quickly. We felt that we gained a new respect from the locals, being there out of season. We joined in local commemorative days such as the 'War never again' parades (end September) and the 'Οχι' day celebrations on 28th October, commemorating the day that Greece said *"NO!"* to the Italian command to surrender. The pride for their country and island was overflowing and we felt honoured to witness this.

I always admired the Greeks for their love and acceptance of children plus their respect for the elderly. However I truly experienced the first of these with our daughter Grace last year. Nothing is too much trouble for them. Not only did they prepare her special food if I wished, they also entertained her while

we ate - supplying her with biscuits (when I wasn't looking), playing, smiling and generally showing her a lot of love. She thoroughly enjoyed it and has grown in confidence enormously (both physically and emotionally).

If I were to write of the memorable characters or experiences, where would I begin? There are so many I could write about: the time we trespassed onto an interesting property and instead of being shooed off were invited in to spend the evening with the Deputy Mayor and his wife; the family Baptism we were invited to where we shared their joy of the new child with all the guests wandering in and out of the tiny church during the baptism; the many occasions old friends just happen to return to the island the same time as us; the time I ordered 'aghori' (αγόρι - boy) instead of some 'a**n**ghori' (αγγούρι - cucumber); the strangers who walked up to us offering us places to stay when we decided to extend our stay; getting to the bakers before the shop was open and being ushered round to the kitchen for hot fresh bread; not having the right change in a shop, and being told to bring it 'avrio' - the trust! We frequently seemed to leave things in taxis or restaurants, to have them returned to our apartment or carefully looked after until we caught up with them. The one bus driver on the island is also a fisherman, which occasionally results in a bus service being cancelled without notice. We bumped into a primary school outing and all the children in turn wanted to practise their English with us. For those readers who know and love the Greek isles, I know these anecdotes will bring smiles and sighs of remembrance to you.

We love Leros. It is an island of sudden and surprising beauty. It is welcoming and remembers its visitors. The people are like a family and many true friendships have been made. Each part of its funny little shape has a character of its own. Watching the fishing boats bob up and down from our balcony window puts a smile on my face and calm in my heart. The underlying all-encompassing love that the Greeks have for life and God is conveyed here. Many people return year after year to this hidden little-known gem. We hope it remains this way, and doesn't get spoiled by the masses. Leros will always be the place that revives my soul.

Coincidentally Ray Fordham ended up in the same studios at the same resort a few years earlier - coinciding with a special commemoration.

Leros Memories *by Ray Fordham*

In company with my son Jonathan, I visited Leros for the first time back in 1993 when we had a couple of spare days on our way back to Kos from Samos and Patmos to catch our flight home.

We arrived at **Aghia Marina** and adjourned to a kafeneion to decide where to stay. On carefully perusing our guidebook, we decided on **Pandeli.** We hailed a taxi and, on telling the driver our proposed destination, he responded *"Why Pandeli? Why not* ***Alinda****? - Much nicer."* With a shrug of the shoulders we gave in and minutes later arrived at the rather attractive hamlet with a long narrow beach stretching alongside the road.

Our taxi driver asked *"You want accommodation by the beach, or up there?"* pointing to the top of the resort. *"Up there,"* I indicated. In next to no time we arrived at the Angelika Studios, set in beautiful, picturesque gardens. We were made most welcome, served a super breakfast for the 2 days of our stay and, (what a coincidence !), the owner was the taxi driver's uncle.

Our first evening we chose what appeared to be the busiest taverna on the front for our evening meal. Replete after an excellent meal, we were enjoying an after dinner brandy when the taverna was invaded by a large Greek family, accompanied by two rather elderly English gentlemen. Before long two of the younger members of the family were setting up amplifiers and tuning guitars to entertain us with an impromptu 'Country & Western' concert. It transpired that our entertainers were professionals, two brothers who lived in the USA and were on their home island for a summer break.

I was of course intrigued by the presence of the two English gentlemen. Sponsored by the British Legion they had come to Leros to participate the previous day in the 50th anniversary commemoration of the bitter battle that took place in 1943 when German paratroopers invaded the island. They told me that 10 veterans had planned to take part but most had cried off leaving just these two. No sooner had they arrived than they had been 'adopted' by this Greek family who extended the usual Greek hospitality.

One of the gentlemen in The Royal Navy had been amongst just a handful of survivors from a British destroyer that had hit a mine and immediately sank just outside Leros harbour. Its resting place is officially designated a war grave. The British Army unit in the battle was a company of the East Kent Regiment known as 'The Buffs'. They were more or less wiped out in the battle.

All this prompted a visit the next morning to the Service Cemetery situated beside the road and beach at the entrance to Alinda. The wreaths and

flowers were still in place and an examination of the graves indicated that the East Kent Regiment were in the majority. One in particular caught my attention. It was that of a Lieutenant Colonel who was obviously the Allied Commander. On his grave had been placed a letter which read *"This is from one of your junior subalterns, just to show that after 50 years your memory has not been forgotten."* A truly touching tribute which could not but bring a tear to the eye. Needless to say, the cemetery is extremely well maintained and in one of the entrance doorposts is a visitors' book signed by visitors of many nationalities.

Our short stay on Leros could not have been more memorable and for this we had to thank our taxi driver for changing our minds.

The following year I paid a brief return visit to Leros, this time with my wife. On arrival at the Angelika Studios the owner's wife came running down the drive to greet me and immediately enquired *"Where your son?"* *"No son"* I replied *"wife"* pointing behind me. Needless to say we were made most welcome again and thoroughly enjoyed our short visit.

How to get to Leros

By Air - Scheduled flights via Athens to Leros,
Charter flights to Kos, Rhodes or Samos then ferry

By Ferry - links with Agathonisi, Fourni, Ikaria, Kalymnos, Kos, Lipsi, Patmos, Piraeus, Rhodes, Samos, Symi, Tilos

Tour Operators - Actual Holidays, Freedom of Greece, Greece & Cyprus Travel, Hidden Greece, Island Wandering, Laskarina, Ramblers, Travel Lounge

Trips with Greek Friends *by Pat Fitton*

Over the years we have forged several long lasting friendships with Greek people. I try to meet up with them from time to time and we have had some of our most memorable trips in Greece when we travel with Greek friends.

In September I went to stay with my good friend Persephone in **Thassos**, to practise speaking only Greek. I managed this in the main, although our vocabulary was more concerned with shopping, preparing vegetables, domestic disasters and the shortcomings of husbands rather than life, the universe and higher things. Persephone's helper in her small hotel, Olia, arrived in Thassos at the age of 12 from a Greek community fleeing the civil war in Georgia in the early nineties. She was very patient with me and her seven year old daughter Albina was an excellent teacher.

Persephone works very hard and rarely has a break, so I was amazed when she suggested a weekend trip to the mainland. Olia was left in charge as the hotel was not very busy.

At 7.15am Persephone and I were on the ferry to **Keramoti** (Κεραμωτή), We then took the bus to **Hrissoupoli** (Χρυσσούπολη), changing there onto the **Xanthi** (Ξάνθη) bus. The driver dropped us off on the main road and we walked the kilometre or so up into the village of **Toxotes** (Τοξότες). Our idea was to take the train through the river **Nestos** (Νέστος) gorge to **Stavroupoli**

Persephone at Toxotes Station

(Σταυρούπολη) further along the line. We soon established that the train would not leave until 11am so we explored the village, falling into conversation whilst admiring vegetable gardens and acquiring samples of lettuce and basil.

The train journey was marvellous, clattering alongside the **Nestos river**; often high above, then going through tunnels cut through rocks - it was rather like a rail journey in the Scottish Highlands but with better weather.

At **Stavroupoli**, where there is a large military base, we walked about a kilometre into the town and stopped at the first guest house, a traditional house built around a courtyard. The young manager was very hospitable and offered us coffee and sweets, but he had no vacant rooms. He telephoned the only other hotel and fortunately they could accommodate us.

We found lunch, then visited the folk museum - a marvellous collection of household goods and agricultural implements mainly collected by one family. After a rest at the hotel we explored the town and walked out a little into the countryside. By 5pm it was already cooling down. The panoramic view of mountains from our balcony was wonderful, but we needed the extra blankets provided to be cosy as it was very cold overnight.

Next day found us walking along the river, watching canoeists and horse riders. The area is being developed for ecological tourism and is popular with Germans, Austrians, Dutch and Scandinavian tourists who enjoy the walking and water activities on offer.

We chatted with an elderly man we met on the bridge across the Nestos. It was the feast day for **Stavros** (Σταύρος) which means 'cross', and he told us how the young men used to jump into the river from where we were standing to try to be the first to retrieve the cross thrown into the water by the priest. However, so many drowned over the years that they had to move the ceremony to a calmer spot further downstream.

At midday we caught the train back to **Toxotes** and inquired about buses. The station master told us there were none on Sundays. Taxis? Not really.

We walked the kilometre down to the main Kavala-Xanthi road. By now it was very hot. Persephone is ample and I am skinny - both in our sixties. So far only one car had stopped, to ask directions to a village. Hot and thirsty, we were wondering if we should continue walking, when a battered pick-up truck stopped. Piling our packs into the back, we gratefully squeezed into the cab.

The driver's name was Ali, from Turkey. He was driving from Izmir to Vienna. There was a little battery fan on his dashboard, but no sign of any cargo that might make this trip worthwhile. We tried Greek, English and French - no go. My few words of Turkish did not get us far, but smiles and mime enabled us to let him know where we wanted to be set down. By incredible luck, at that moment, a bus to Hrissoupoli appeared and we were soon en route to Keramoti and the ferry back to Thassos.

"Good trip, eh, Pat?" said Persephone. *"We go again next year?"*

In **Athens** for a few days last October, we took the opportunity to meet up with our young friend Angeliki. We first met when I was in hospital in Athens during another holiday and she was in the next bed. She helped me with translations for the doctors and nurses and chatted to me in excellent English, which she was perfecting along with her business studies course. We kept in touch by email and letter and she told us about her life and studies in **Kastoria** (Καστοριά) in northern Greece.

After she graduated she came to spend a week with us (February 2004), on her first trip abroad. It snowed and was very cold. We did the London tourist scene and Cambridge, but the trip she most enjoyed was to the shops in our local town of Kettering.

In Athens on a Friday we met up for a meal with Angeliki, her sister Vaso and Vaso's boyfriend Apostolis, enjoying good food and lively conversation about music and world events.

On Saturday Angeliki's mother joined us for a day at the seaside, **Halkida** (Χαλκίδα) on **Evia** (Εύβοια), about 80 km north east of Athens. We enjoyed our train ride from Athens on a clean, modern train, arriving at Halkida with other Athenian day trippers, but no other foreign tourists in sight.

First we walked up to **Karababa** (Καράμπαμπα) castle, a Turkish fortress designed by a Venetian architect. We were the only visitors and the custodian was only too pleased to explain the history of the castle and to have a good chat with Angeliki and her mother.

After coffee and ice cream on a terrace above the town, we wandered slowly down, stopping at the bridge over the **Evripos** (Έυριπος) to remark on the notorious alternating currents which change direction suddenly several times a day and give the appearance of water flowing in opposite directions, side by side. The cause of this phenomenon has been studied since ancient times and

is still not properly understood. According to popular belief, Aristotle, frustrated by his inability to solve the problem, threw himself in the water!

We spent a proper amount of time choosing the perfect restaurant by the water's edge and enjoyed excellent seafood, chicken and vegetables. Angeliki's mother had learned some English for the occasion and was very patient with my attempts to converse with her in Greek.

Later we walked around the bay and events began to take a surreal turn. A party of scouts was marching and exercising on the beach. Some were in costume for a play, including a lad dressed as executioner, whose axe was not cardboard but the real thing. He popped up solemn and silent in front of us during our walk - quite startling at the time.

On the beach a small girl stood on the concrete shower platform fully clothed, turned on the shower and proceeded to scrub the platform with a broom. Then walking back into town we stopped to read at an advertisement in a bar window, translated as - *'Wanted, a young woman to work here. Not a blonde!"* (Οχι ξανθή)

By the time we got back on the train we were feeling as if we had stumbled into a Bunel or Almodovar film! This seemed to be confirmed when a tiny elderly man sitting across the aisle began to complain drunkenly that he had no money left, turning out all his pockets one after the other to prove the point. He seemed confused about which station he needed. Angeliki's mum tried to help, asking where he wanted to get off. He replied *"Off the earth!"* and eventually disembarked at a little station in the middle of nowhere.

All these strange events only added to our enjoyment of a lovely day. We told Angeliki she was an excellent tour guide.

Profile of Santorini *by Sylvia Cook*

Often known as **Thira** (Θήρα), but more commonly in UK holiday brochures by its Italian given name of **Santorini** (Σαντορίνη) after its patron Saint Irini, this most southerly of the Cycladic islands is one of the most photographed destinations of the Aegean Sea. Just 73 sq kms (28 sq.m) of land is all that remains of the ancient volcanic island split asunder around 15th c.BC. The land rises majestically from the sea at the crater's edge and slopes more gently to the eastern coast.

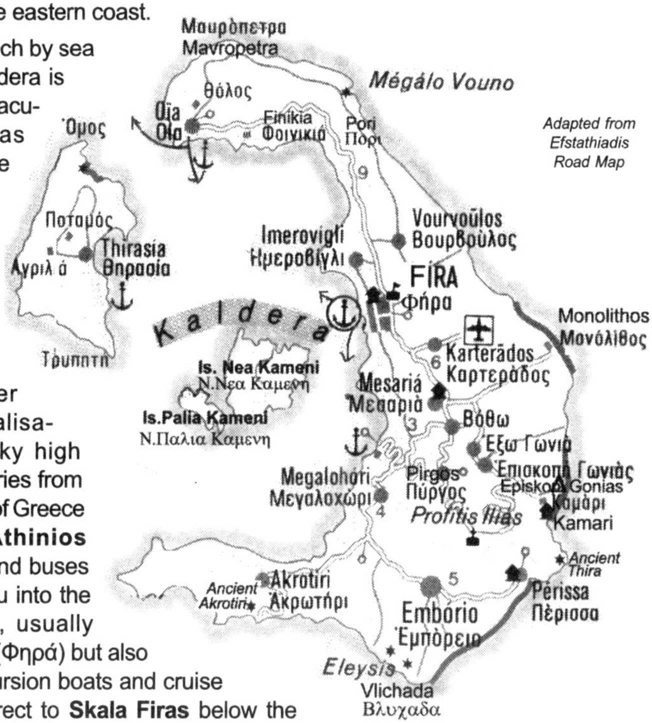

Adapted from Efstathiadis Road Map

The approach by sea into the caldera is quite spectacular and has made Santorini one of the 'must see' sights of Greece, sadly leading to over commercialisation and sky high prices. Ferries from other parts of Greece dock at **Athinios** (Αθηνιός) and buses will take you into the main town, usually called Fira (Φηρά) but also Thira. Excursion boats and cruise ships go direct to **Skala Firas** below the town where passengers disembark on day trips. The energetic walk up the 580 steps, or in the summer the cable car takes the strain from the often overloaded mules and donkeys. Visitors also arrive at **Karterados** (Καρτεράδος) airport on domestic or charter flights.

Inland villages and coastal resorts show a different perspective, set in fertile land which produces grapes for the well known Santorini white wines and other agricultural products. The other side of the caldera is now the inhabited island of **Thirasia** (Ν.Θηρασία) and in the middle the volcanic **Kameni** (Καμένη) islands, some formed in quite recent centuries as a result of eruptions.

Santorini Background

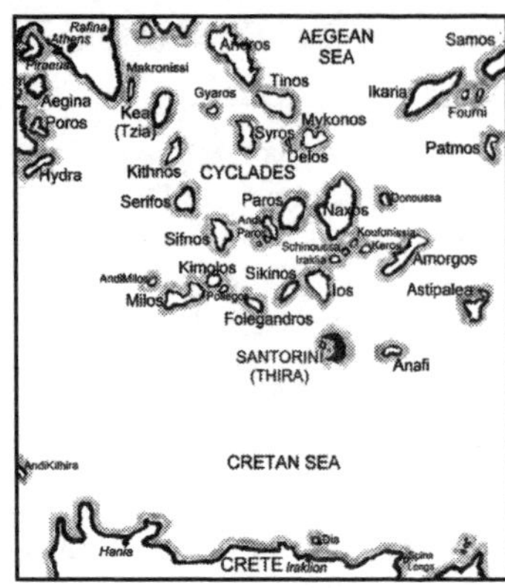

❒ *Inhabited before 3000 BC and an important Minoan settlement, the conical volcanic island of* ***Kallisti*** *erupted violently around 1470 BC, (possibly destroying the entire Minoan civilisation) leaving just a ring of islands, of which Santorini is the largest. It was resettled by Dorians and renamed* ***Thira****. It was allied with Sparta at the start of the Peloponnesian War and later paid tribute to Athens until Roman rule.*

❒ *After the 4th Crusade in 1207 it was conquered by the Italians and then Turks in 1539 and finally reunited with Greece in 1830.*

❒ *It was an important wine-growing area thriving on the rich volcanic soils. Water is limited but the vines flourish as they are coiled into a ground-hugging spiral which catches all the dew and moisture. Santorini wines were exported in quantity to Russia in the period before the Second World War.*

❒ *The decline in markets for Santorini's wine and agricultural produce led to depopulation after the war. In 1956 a devastating earthquake demolished 2000 buildings and killed 50 people, injuring many more, with the result that many people left the island. Only in recent years has the population increased to over 7,000.*

Photograph by Tony Lambell

Santorini - 20 years on *by Tony Lambell*

In 1984 we had just watched the TV series 'Greek Language and People' with Chris Searle being taught Greek by the delectable Katia Dandoulakis, filmed on Andros and Sifnos. We decided we must go soon before the quintessential Greekness was submerged by a flood of tourism. That was prophetic as since then we have been striving to find places that have survived the onslaught!

We landed at Santorini airport in a temperature of 40°C in August 1984. It was a military airport so photos were banned, though the only secret was that there was no evidence of military activity at all. There were no re-fuelling facilities and the terminal building was a small hut that could only cope with either departing or incoming passengers. The departing passengers were 'processed' through the building into a chain-link fenced compound, and incoming passengers were treated to the sight of a 'Tenko' type camp with passengers striving to cope in the intense sun. Luggage was unloaded onto a trolley which was wheeled from the plane 100 yards to the waiting travellers who unloaded it themselves. Though our studio was only a half mile from the runway, there was no noise problem as there were few flights on only one or two days a week.

How different now! Returning in 2004 we landed on a smart long runway with a proper taxiway, a glossy new terminal and planes leaving and arriving throughout the day - with Tuesday the day for UK charter flights. The air-conditioned departure lounge has a large shady upstairs terrace where passengers can wait in cool airy comfort.

On that first holiday we certainly met more unique Greek characters than on any subsequent holiday. Arriving at our studio apartment, we introduced ourselves to our host, a gnarled wizened old Greek - or so we thought. *"Hi!"*. he said *"I'm Bob, from Los Angeles"*. An American, he had married a Greek emigrant, Anna, from Santorini, and on retirement they had moved back there. Despite living for years in the States she was not fluent in English, and he knew no Greek. When Anna's friends come round he said, *"I can't understand a word they are saying"*. During breakfast one day two Greek young men called asking for accommodation. Mary, who can speak modern Greek fairly well, had to translate for him. *"No rooms"*, he replied (which we knew to be untrue). *"Don't want any Greeks staying here"* he explained after they had left.

Our studio was set a little way out of the village of **Kamari** (Καμάρι). On the walk down to the beach we passed other accommodation where the owner Katerina also sold refreshments. In view of the heat we would stop off there on the way down. We experienced for the first time some of the no non-

sense directness of the Greek character. *"Why are you staying with that Americano?"* she would expostulate, *"why not stay here with me?" "I like your dress"* she said one day to Mary *"I will buy it for 3000 drachmas"!*

The village of **Mesa Gonia** (Μέσα Γωνιά) (or Episkopi Gonias), built a little way from the coast as a defence against pirates, used the beach of Kamari as its harbour. The village was virtually destroyed by the 1950 earthquake. The surviving inhabitants moved down to Kamari where they tended their small vineyards, and vegetable plots. As the tourist trade developed a few villas and studios were built scattered among the plots, retaining the village atmosphere. This was the situation in 1984. The beach was lined with tamarisk trees and there were some 15 or so tavernas along the shoreline. Today the whole area is covered with buildings devoted to the holiday trade, with few of the small vineyards left. The tamarisk trees are gone and the whole shoreline is built up. There are innumerable tavernas, though it has to be said that they are well laid out with a traffic free road in front of them, and very few noisy bars. In 1984 the Santorinians were turning their hand to tourism to supplement their other activities. Now people come from the mainland to work just for the summer season.

Kamari 2004

So the economy of the island tourism has been a life-giving boost but the characteristic life of Greek village communities is less evident. However the underlying elements of traditional Greek hospitality can still be experienced. The Greek welcome to children made eating out in the evening with our grandchildren a particularly enjoyable experience.

Back in 1984 I needed to cash a giro cheque and in the main town of **Fira** (Φηρά) the notice outside the PO clearly said - in brass - that it closed at 2.30 pm, so at just after 2pm it must be OK. Wrong! Inside we found the cash window was blocked up, though a queue was waiting at it expectantly. A Dutch back-packer at the front of the queue rapped boldly on the partition - which shattered under his fist. Immediately a short red-faced man jumped out and expostulated vigorously with the man, shouted to an assistant to close the doors and call the police. Shortly in came three policemen - all with side arms. The red-faced man harangued the Dutchman in Greek who looked on in bland incomprehension while the police listened inattentively.

We were allowed to leave and shortly after we saw the policemen wander off - presumably having placated the postmaster and released the Dutchman. (Next day there was a piece of sticky paper on the brass notice board modifying the closing time to 2pm.)

We caught the bus to the hilltop town of **Pyrgos** (Πύργος), and sitting in the taverna in the platia, closely observed by the usual row of senior male citizens, we observed a *tachidromeio* sign. Following it we found a perfectly efficient, open and 'unbusy' PO where we had no trouble getting our cash.

There is a problem with brass notices. They have an air of permanence and authority - but they are inflexible and the information they give may have long since changed but is too difficult to alter. On a hill not far from our accommodation in Kamari lay **Ancient Thira**, a Greco-Roman town, built high up to escape the pirates and roughly excavated in the 19th century by a German archaeologist. The engraved notice at the bottom said that the site opened at 9am on public holidays, so we started to walk up from the bottom around 8am to miss the heat of the day. At the top was an identical notice except for one point, the opening time was now 10am. Fortunately the view was good, there was a breeze, so we enjoyed the ambience for that hour. Another basic lesson on the Greek character - things will happen maybe sometime, meanwhile just relax and feel the surroundings.

On our recent trip with our daughter and grandchildren, we stayed in a converted winery in the small non-touristy village of **Vourvoulos** (Βουρβούλος) set on a hill with fine views to the sea a mile away. While they enjoyed the pool we made nostalgic tours around the island.

Rather than travelling by bus as we did in 1984 - there were very few to our village - we had a hire car. 'Our' village of Kamari, so sadly built over, was ideal for our grandchildren. We ate at the same taverna each evening because they were so welcoming and the children felt at home. We even persuaded them that chicken souvlakia were Greek chicken nuggets!

The towns of **Fira** and **Oia** (Οία) still showing many signs of earthquake damage in 1984, are now very smart. Oia, once virtually derelict, is now the resort of choice for the well-to-do and artistic.

Sadly, like many, we have a 'rip-off' horror story from Fira - a bill for €200 for five of us. Nothing special or excessive had been ordered, so we paid €70, walked out and did not return to Fira after that.

Akrotiri (Ακρωτήρι), the Minoan town buried by the volcanic eruption of 1500BC and discovered in the 1950s was better for visitors in 1984. Then we could wander through streets lined with buildings three stories high and see the rooms with storage jars still in place. Now they have European funding to improve the structure covering the archaeological remains, but

progress is slow, access is limited and the atmosphere is that of a rather sad building site. The fact that entrance is free, rather indicates their embarrassment at the situation.

Two new gems we discovered on this visit, were **Megalochori** (Μεγαλοχώρι) and **Messaria** (Μεσσαριά). Lying just off the main road to Akrotiri (impossible to drive through), Megalochori was tourist free except for us. It appears to have escaped the destruction wrought by the earthquake elsewhere and retained its original character. It also had an excellent restaurant serving modern Greek cuisine.

Megalochori

In Messaria (off the Fira to Kamari road) the town house of the wealthy 19th century wine producing Argyros family has been restored and opened to the public, giving a vivid insight into the life of the island when its prosperity was based on its wine trade. We arrived at 1.45pm, only to find that it closed at 2pm for siesta, but the custodian was happy to take us round, giving a commentary in Greek, carefully and slowly enunciated for Mary's benefit. It made her Greek studies well worthwhile. The guide's enthusiasm and concern for his two visitors brought back that feeling that Greece is a rather special place.

From the Greek point of view Santorini is a success story. With the decline of the wine trade and the catastrophe of the 1956 earthquake leading to depopulation, the history of the people has been tragic. Now tourism has given it a new prosperity and vitality, and the wine trade has revived too. The simplicity of life that we so appreciated on our first visit of course implied certain material deprivations for those who lived there, so it would be selfish of us to regret those changes when it is only our own material prosperity which enables us to spend time there. But, as in our own society, this also leads to us losing much that is of value in personal relationships and uniquely national characteristics.

We try to profile a mix of Greek areas and styles in each Greek-o-File book - but are obviously limited by what we receive or are able to research ourselves. Sometimes it seems that everyone has been to the same place! Last year it was the Cyclades, including <u>three</u> contributions for Santorini - all with something to add. Here are highlights from two more.

Theatrical Thira *by Terry Burton*

Reports of over-commercialism, black ash beaches and a reputation for being expensive had acted as a deterrent, but the draw of the largest caldera in the world, documentaries on TV and a WebCam site we found, finally prompted a visit to Thira. It was then we wished we had done this long ago.

The island is quite small and from a vantage point on Profitis Ilias a fine view can be had from **Oia** in the north to **Akrotiri** in the south and from west to east is a mere 4 miles or so.

We stayed at **Perivolos** (Περιβόλος) a quieter resort that merges with **Perissa** (Περίσσα) and shares the same beach which is several kilometres long and, from the profusion of sun beds, must be popular in high season. The first myth dispelled - the sand is grey not black and other than colour no different in consistency from the yellow variety.

So to the highlights. The town of **Fira** is a must - even with cappuccino at €6 a cup! But ... it is worth sitting and watching the hustle and bustle of the town as it deals with the hundreds of tourists disgorged by the tour ships.

They seem to spend a disproportionate amount of the time queuing for the cable car that brings them up from the harbour some 180m below and repeating the exercise in reverse a few hours later. The only thing that I envy them is the spectacular views they must have when entering the caldera.

Just a few kilometres to the North is **Oia**, with a similar magnificent setting, but without the cruise ships the atmosphere is chilled. There even remain some inhabited troglodyte dwellings in the cliffside. About an hour before sunset a ritual takes place that is not to be missed. You sense people on the move, at first slowly in one direction but as the numbers grow so does the pace. The narrow alleyways become full. Now there is an urgency to get to the destination. This turns out to be the end of the village that faces the caldera and the sunset. There is a party atmosphere now, which then quietens and as the last rays of the sun disappear there is a ripple of applause

in appreciation for the close of another day.

We visited the site of **Akrotiri** early in the morning and had almost exclusive access. However there was a degree of disappointment that the fine frescos have all been removed to Athens. No human remains were ever found and it is thought that the population would have made their way to the local beaches to await rescue, which it is believed never arrived. Pumice stone of varying size can be found everywhere on the island, providing evidence of the power nature unleashed all that time ago.

We loved Thira. I think you will too.

Santorini for the Sedentary *by Don Henderson*

My wife and I have enjoyed a variety of Greek Island destinations for the last twentyfour years or so. Our activities, however, have had to be restricted by age, and a double hip replacement for my wife - so no ferries, no swimming in the sea, and limitations on walking. We now have to look for accommodation with a lift, ideally a swimming pool and preferably not on a hilltop. In the past, we enjoyed the pleasures of '*domatia*', negotiated at the quayside, and had been able to avoid the worst effects of so-called 'civilisation'.

We knew of the volcanic catastrophe and had heard the modern day scenery was spectacular, so we decided to give it a go. A nice American website (www.greektravel.com), pointed out that if you get away from Fira, and Oia, you could get decent accommodation for the price of a hovel in Fira. On browsing the web we found a really promising place in **Akrotiri** which seemed to meet our needs. (www.vmathios.gr)

The whole establishment is run by a Greek family, with 'Momma' cooking excellent Greek meals in the restaurant, one son running the office and travel agency with car hire, another son running the poolside bar plus a small jewellery and souvenir shop, while their wives, and a few friendly staff, do every thing else and 'Pappa' benevolently supervises the whole thing. Everything is on one site and most of the accommodation is in bungalows at ground level. We returned for a second visit, now firm friends of the folks at Villa Mathios, and enjoyed it every bit as much as the first time. We were able to share the family's delight when their first grandson arrived safely, and duly celebrated the event. It is difficult to describe the atmosphere, I suppose 'staying with friends' comes somewhere near. Above all, it really is Greek and we are able to use our smattering of the language to good effect.

We were delighted to find a bus stop near the hotel entrance, with buses to **Fira** twice an hour, from whence buses run to all other places on the island. The journey from end to end of the island takes under an hour. It seems that there is no place on Santorini without a view worth looking at, even the eastern coastal plain where there are several beach resorts and the airport. However, the two towns of Thira and Oia, clinging to the rim of the caldera, with a drop of hundreds of feet below are probably unique, and barely believable. A trip down in the cable car to sea level provides an upwards view that induces a total admiration for the builders of these incredible vistas.

View across caldera from Oia

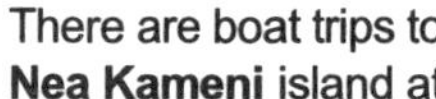

There are boat trips to **Nea Kameni** island at the centre of the caldera (still active!), and to **Thirassia** (Θηρασία), the island on the other side, plus so many walks which we wish we could still enjoy. Then, of course, there are the ruins (Akrotiri and ancient Thira). As one would expect, there is also an excellent museum, which tells the whole story.

It was so pleasant to visit the towns of Fira and Oia, enjoy the spectacular (sorry, but there is no other word) views of the caldera, with the cruise liners below looking like Dinky toys, and then retreat from the traffic, noise and hassle to our peaceful haven in Akrotiri, where you can almost hear the grass grow. Elsewhere we would seek a backstreet or water's edge taverna to enjoy the evening meal, with maybe an ouzo at a kafenεion on the way home. Here our evening finds us up in the hotel restaurant, watching the sunset, enjoying a good Greek meal, and then an amble to the poolside bar for a quiet drink and a chat. A bit sedentary perhaps, but ...

How to get to Santorini

By Air - Scheduled flights via Athens to Santorini, Domestic flight also from/to Mykonos, Charter Flights direct from UK

By Ferry - links with Anafi, Folegandros, Ios, Kimolos, Kythnos, Milos, Naxos, Paros, Piraeus, Serifos, Sifnos, Sikinos, Syros

Tour Operators - Actual Hols, ATG, Amathus, Archers, Argo, Best of Greece, Elysian, Excel Hols, Explore Worldwide, First Choice, Freedom of Greece, Greece & Cyprus Travel, Greek Islands Club, Greek Sun Holidays, Hidden Greece, Island Wandering, Islands of Greece, ITC Classics, Kosmar, Libra, Manos, Med. Experience, Olympic, Planet, Rosemary Barron (cooking), Seasons in Style, Simply Travel, Sunvil, Thomas Cook, Travel Lounge

Around the Peloponnese in a Week *by Peter Reynolds*

Back in 1992 when we purchased our tumble down cottage in the hillside village of **Exochori** (Εξοχώρι) we were the first 'foreigners' in a population of just 300. I had visited the ancient sites and driven part of the coastal routes whilst working as a trek leader in the 1970's. We were keen to discover how this area of outstanding natural beauty had changed and were intrigued to find out how far it is all the way round the Peloponnese on the coastal road.

From our maps we could see there would be sections where we would not always be able to keep the sea on our right hand side. For those of you who haven't ventured there, the Peloponnese is a big area, roughly the size of Wales measuring around 220kms x 220kms.

One fine May morning we loaded 'Rusty', our old Peugeot 505 estate with a week's supplies, sleeping bags and tent and set off in high spirits from the cottage 8kms above the working fishing village of **Kardamili** (Καρδαμύλη). First stop was the largest group of underground caves in Europe at **Diros** (Δυρός) - an amazing, truly visual experience.

Githio

After reaching the southernmost point of the Peloponnese at **Cape Tenaro** (Ταίναρο) we explored the fascinating Mani village of **Vathia** (Βάθεια), before a short drive on to **Githio** (Γύθειο), which in ancient times was the main port for the Spartan empire and harbour for access to the Mani. Tall colonial buildings lined the waterfront. Githio today remains a harbour city for Crete and the tiny island of Kithira. We found a quiet seashore campsite and rested up after day one's travel of 180 kms. We slept well to the gentle rhythmic sound of the sea lapping.

Saturday morning dawned bright and beautiful, wild flowers in abundance decking the ground like a carpet. We set off for **Monemvassia** (Μονεμβασιά), the Gibraltar of Greece. The Byzantine city was built around 600-700BC with a 1 km long causeway linking the old part with the new. The narrow cobbled streets ascend and weave through the mediaeval town like a snake.

Monemvassia

In the Middle Ages, Monemvassia was a strategic military location. The lush orange groves along the way reminded us it was still only springtime.

From here we really put the road map through its paces as we ran out of coastal road. Aiming for our favourite Greek city, **Nafplio** (Ναύπλιο), we followed small roads (some tarmac, some dirt) over the hills getting more and more lost. My travel log reminds me that we shouldn't automatically take the beaten path - wrong signs, wrong directions and then mountain mist before we finally descended to rejoin the coastal road at **Leonidio** (Λεωνίδιο).

Nafplio is truly cosmopolitan and vibrating with life. The Byzantines started the restoration of this war-ravaged town around 1200 AD. The Venetians built the stronghold Palamidi fortress around 1710 only for the Turks to retake control five years later. It was the fledgling capital of modern Greece 1829-1834 and is remembered for where the first Prime Minister of Greece, Kapodistrias, was executed by vengeful Maniot clansmen.

We sat in Syntagma Square admiring the Georgian and Victorian buildings all around, and wondered where we were going to stay that night. There are no campsites, so, after a day of driving almost 300 kms we settled for comfortable rooms overlooking the harbour and Bourtzi islet. This tiny castle at the mouth of the harbour was built by the Venetians to help protect the city from potential marauders.

We awoke on Sunday with a short drive ahead of 50kms to the ancient theatre at **Epidavros** (Έπιδαυρος), a 6th century BC religious and healing centre. Everyone should visit Epidavros at some time to stand in the middle of the amphitheatre and listen to the awesome acoustics. Construction started in the 3rd century BC and the open-air theatre (still used every July and August) was designed to seat an audience of up to 12,000 on 55 stone rows. We camped that night at **Palea Epidavros** right on the sea edge at one of Greece's premier 'Sunshine Sites'. Once again, the orange groves were in full blossom producing a wonderful scent.

Monday dawned grey and overcast; our drive of 60 kms took us first to **Corinth** (Κόρινθος). No one can visit without stopping to admire the engineering feat of the Corinth canal. Started in the 6th century BC and eventu-

ally completed in the 1880's (after many war years interruption), this magnificent feat of human endeavour is 6.5 kms long, the height of the cutting is 90 metres, width 30 metres, depth of water 7.5 metres and there are now no less than five bridges spanning the Gulf of Corinth and the Saronic Gulf. Shipping traffic is able to cut through from Europe to Africa without having to circumnavigate the Peloponnese. The ancient city is no less daunting perched high on a hill overlooking the modern city. We carried on as far as **Egio** (Αίγιο) where you can catch a ferry to **Aghios Nicholas** (Αγ.Νικόλαος), from which **Delphi** (Δελφοί) is only a short drive away.

Next day we prayed for, and were rewarded with, good weather for a detour to inland **Kalavrita** (Καλάβρυτα) on the rack and pinion railway built by the Italians in the 1890's. The 75 minute journey from **Diakofto** (Διακοφτό) rose about 700 metres and we were greeted with fog and rain, but the Second World War cemetery and town hall clocks remain particularly memorable. From here a road takes you to an alpine centre complete with rarefied atmosphere and ski-hire shops at about 2300m on Mount Helmos.

We caught the last bus of the day back down to the coast and drove on to **Patra** (Πάτρα), the third largest city in Greece and largest port on the Peloponnese. It has a colourful past being rebuilt in 1821 after the Turks had razed it to the ground. We continued, passing the Achaia Claus winery nearby, famous for its Demestica and Mavrodaphne nectar, to camp the night at **Kato Achaia** (Κάτω Αχαία) with a panoramic view to the north across the gulf towards **Messolongi** (Μεσολόγγι).

After the previous day's journey of 250 kms, we planned a shorter route for Wednesday - 180 kms to include Pirgos, Olympia, Kiparissia, Filiatra, Nestor's Palace, Pilos, Methoni, Finikounda and Koroni. I always return to **Olympia** (Ολυμπία) with fond memories of the Judas trees. As with Delphi, there is a spiritual feel about the tranquillity and sacred peace of Olympia. The original settlement dates back to 2800 BC as a place of worship and occasional athletic games. The official Olympic Games were first hosted in 776 BC and then four yearly, bringing together all Greeks in peace. Later the Romans took over and introduced 'professionalism', bribery and corruption. The demise of the Games finally came when the Roman Emperor Theodosius was converted to Christianity and as a result forbade most pagan festivities in 393 AD. The village is now very European with German signs in abundance.

My well-thumbed copy of The Rough Guide had intrigued me - it talked of a ludicrous folly at **Filiatra** (Φιλιατρά), which we were keen to find. As we rolled into the sleepy village we were not disappointed, being presented first of all with a 15 metre tall metal fretwork model of the Eiffel Tower and, a little further on, an equally ridiculous Disney-like model of the globe. Apparently, back in the 1960's, Harry Fournier, a local doctor returned to the village after

Filiatra

making his money in Chicago and decided to build these 'fantastic tributes' to make his mark.

We were now travelling down the western side of the first of the three spindly fingers that hang off the main body of the Peloponnese like cows udders, hoping to reach Methoni or Koroni before nightfall. **Methoni** (Μεθώνη) is a large village with a well-restored and impressive castle displaying a number of prominent Lion of St Mark carvings. From the Venetian octagonal fortified tower you can see the sea on three sides. **Koroni** (Κορώνη) is almost directly opposite on the other side of the finger. The Italianate terra-cotta roofed fishing village was reminiscent of Tuscany with similar coloured soil and terrain. The narrow streets gave the feel of being in Malta, very chic. We camped that night overlooking the bay and enjoyed the delight of a fresh water pool on site.

Thursday, our final day on the road and around 225 kms drive back to our starting point. First stop, was the capital of Messinia, **Kalamata** (Καλαμάτα), the first city to be liberated at the outset of the Greek War of Independence (1821-1829). After Patra, it is the second largest city on the Peloponnese and is sadly remembered for its earthquakes, the latest of which in 1986 claimed the lives of 20 people and made some 12,000 homeless. Today, the town is largely rebuilt and acts as the chief hub in the area for olive oil production and distribution.

The single-track railway terminates in Kalamata from Athens 'B' station with a choice of seven hours over the mountains via **Tripoli** (Τρίπολι) or eleven hours around the coast via **Patra**. This is one train journey you must try to make at some time in your life. The pretty small Victorian stations and gaily painted rolling stock all conjure up a picture of a bygone age.

Finally, after a highly enjoyable week of filoxenia, we returned to **Kardamili** near our Maniot home. Enough of time for the mind, now time for the body - a swim and muse on the outcome of the quest. Our journey around the Peloponnese coast had been a total of some 1250 kms.

(See Peloponnese map p.117 for places visited)

On The Piste in Greece *by Fiona Collingwood*

It was January and there had been heavy snowfall in the **Pindos Mountains**. The conditions were perfect for skiing. My fellow teachers and I sat on a bus destined for Metsovo, where I was to have my first experience on snow skis - in Greece of all places!

I had arrived in Greece with a case full of t-shirts and sunny weather wear as I had not imagined vast mountains covered in snow from December to March and temperatures in some of the highest mountain villages dropping to -20°C. Epirus was to change my perceptions and it was where my love for Greece began.

There are 14 well established ski resorts. The most famous and modern is at **Parnassos** (1600-2300m), the closest to Athens, hence its popularity. It has 16 slopes, 8 ski schools and skiing for all levels. According to my students it is the place to be seen, with plenty of trendy bars and clubs frequented by famous celebrities. It's also a good place for 'designer' shopping.

We were headed for somewhere much simpler, the Karakoli ski centre 2 km from Metsovo at an altitude of 1350m. Our journey started in **Arta**, (near Preveza) famous for its orange trees and 18th century stone bridge. From there we headed by bus to **Ioannina**, the capital of Epirus, where we made a short stop. There is plenty to see and you need days not the few hours we had to explore the town. We got back on the bus and continued our journey through breathtaking mountain passes, reaching **Metsovo** 58km on.

The village lies below the pass and clings majestically to the mountainside in a stunning setting. As the bus began its descent through the village we could understand why the EOT have made it a protected area. Our hotel had been pre-booked thinking it would be busy, but on arrival it seemed very quiet (€28 dble per night 2000, €60 in 2005 but with an amazing breakfast). Metsovo is busiest in the summer months when busloads of tourists often create a bottleneck on village roads. Spring and winter are better times to visit.

The hotel was Alpine style, a slate roof, lots of timber and fireplaces in each room along with lovely 'flokati' rugs, traditional to the area. After unpacking we went exploring. It didn't take long as Metsovo isn't as big as most other European ski resorts. There isn't the 'apns-ski' scene to be found in France, Austria or even at Greece's Parnassos. It was low key with just a few bars, cafes and tavernas. In the platia is the Church of Aghia Paraskevi, a folklore museum (Tossitsa mansion), a small art gallery, some fine 18th century mansions and a mixture of small shops.

We headed for one of the excellent *'psistaria'* (meat tavernas) that evening and tucked into mouthwatering spit roasted mountain lamb from the pastures around Metsovo, local *'hilopites'* (similar to tagliatelle), Metsovella smoked cheese (a nice change from feta) and lots of good red wine (Katoyi Averof) produced in the village. It was worth the trip just for the meal and an added bonus was live folk music.

Walking back across the cobbled platia we were taken aback by the clarity of the night sky, more stars than we had ever seen before. However, we could not stand around gazing for too long. It was freezing and the warm raki feeling from the shot we'd had after our meal was wearing off.

Next morning the sun was shining brightly and the air was crisp. Whilst waiting for our taxi to take us up to the ski centre we saw several of the older villagers wearing traditional costume, many of the men carried intricately carved shepherds' crooks and wore pompommed shoes. We contrasted sharply in our gaudy ski gear.

The slopes were quiet with no queues and we found a van hiring skis quite cheaply (still reasonable in 2005 at €8 per day). There were 2 downhill runs and a 5km cross country run. There was also a taverna/shop which was the stopping point for buses crossing the Katara pass. Katara means 'curse' so I dreaded to imagine what the route beyond Metsovo was like.

There was no tuition nor organised beginners' slopes, so I set off on my own. It was great fun, although I spent most of the day on my bottom. The next day I could hardly get out of bed, proving how unfit I was.

My friends were more experienced skiers so they took the ski lift and tried out the pistes. On meeting up for a much needed break we heard there is another ski centre at Metsovo, a further 6km away (Profitis Ilias 1420-1650m) with more challenging skiing - maybe not for me yet!

At the end of the weekend we all agreed the trip had been a real success. Metsovo had been delightful and there was so much we had not managed to do - several hikes, a visit to the Metsovella dairy, a few more tavernas we would have liked to try - we promised to return.

I've since visited other Greek ski centres - **Argyrolefkes** at Pelion 27km from Volos for skiing and snowboarding, **Dirfi** on Evia 7km from Steni, Pigathia Centre at **Tria-pente** 17km from Naousa and **Vermio Seli** 22 km from Veria, west of Thessaloniki. I must be hooked.

Profile of Tinos *by George Kennedy*

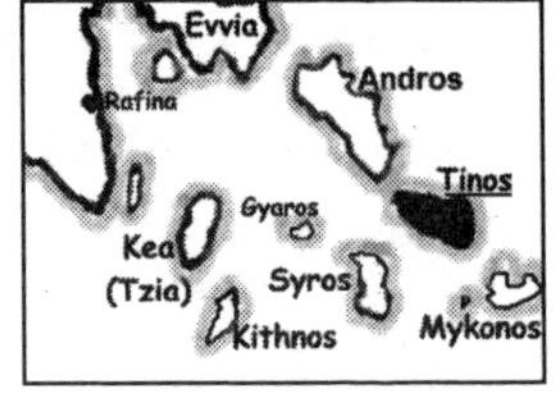

Tinos (Τήνος) is the third largest island in the Cyclades (after Naxos and Andros) being 195 sq. km with a population of around 9500. About half live in Tinos town and the rest in 50 villages. It is a hilly place, although the highest peak is only 727m (Mt Tsiknias) and the peak of the ancient capital **Exombourgo** (Εξώμπουργο) towers impressively over the town at about 587m.

The *peristeriones* (pigeon houses), of which there are over 1,000, are masterpieces - two storey buildings elaborately decorated and all unique. Many date back several hundred years. There are also some 800 pretty family churches and the magnificent marble Church of the Panagia Evangelistra which dominates the town.

Tinos is largely undiscovered by foreign tourists but is popular with Greeks since being designated Greece's holy island in the 1960s.

The island boasts some of the best safe sandy beaches in the Cyclades - **Aghios Fokas**, **Ormos Isterniou**, **Kolymbithra**, and **Panormos**, to name just a few - and the finest walking on ancient Roman roads and mule tracks.

Most accommodation is centred round Tinos town, however, the areas of **Kionia** (Κιόνια) 3km to the west and **Porto** (Πόρτο) 8km east are being developed and now offer a wide range of accommodation. Tinos also has a lovely camp site close to the town.

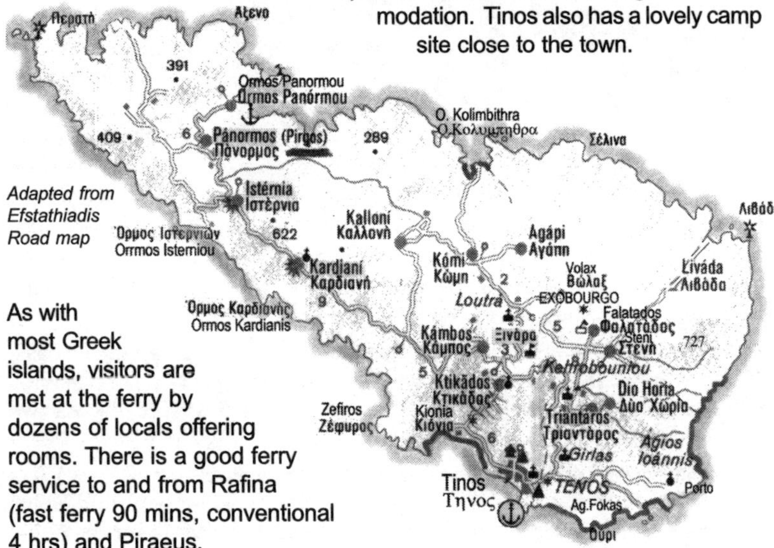

Adapted from Efstathiadis Road map

As with most Greek islands, visitors are met at the ferry by dozens of locals offering rooms. There is a good ferry service to and from Rafina (fast ferry 90 mins, conventional 4 hrs) and Piraeus.

Tinos Background *by Sylvia Cook*

- ❐ *Called **Ophiousa** in ancient times as it was full of snakes (φίδι) until they were driven out by Poseidon, the Sanctuary of Poseidon and Amphitrite, discovered in 1902 near Kionia, was a major religious centre from 3rd century BC.*
- ❐ *Tinos was ruled from Venice 1207 to 1714. It was one of the last to fall to the Turks. Because of the long Venetian rule about a third of the population are Catholic - in spite of Tinos now being the Greek Orthodox Holy Island.*
- ❐ *After the Greek War of Independence (1823) an elderly nun, Pelagia, had a vision leading her to a miracle working icon of the Virgin Mary in a field. This is where the white marble Panayia Evangelistra church was built to house the icon and Orthodox pilgrims visit all year round, but especially when it is carried in procession on 15th August.*
- ❐ *Two months before Mussolini declared war the Greek ship 'Elli' was torpedoed by the Italians on 15th August 1940 - arousing much anger.*

The Joys of Walking Tinos *by George Kennedy*

You must know the feeling - it's Monday morning and whilst you don't actually dread having to go into work neither can you say it is something you are looking forward to. You have some good days, and some pretty lousy ones but in the main they are just average and the months and years drift by as you work to pay the bills.

Well that all changed for me just over 2 years ago. The long established company I had worked for virtually all my adult life was taken over by a large American organisation and boy did they want to make changes. Redundancies were inevitable and at first voluntary termination was offered to those over 50, to be followed by compulsory lay offs. It would have suited me to have stayed on for a couple more years, but after some deliberation I decided to take the money and run.

This was a decision I certainly didn't regret! Jane and I discussed buying a holiday home in France and I went on a couple of trips to look at property where we had been many times over the years. We also visited the Cycladic island of Tinos to stay with Jane's sister who has lived there all of her married life. We had been before, but this was our first opportunity to explore the island in depth and we both fell in love with the place and its people.

Before we left we found a small apartment, ideal for holidays. Our offer was accepted and we left for Ireland excited about developments. This was short lived because when we arrived home there was a message to say the owner had decided to increase the price. It seems he learned we were foreigners

and as such thought we could afford more! Things have a habit of turning out for the best though. Shortly after (November 2002) we heard about a much larger apartment which we bought on the strength of a few photographs. It is on the seafront and plenty big enough to live in permanently. In 2003 I made seven trips to Tinos spending most of my time searching out walks on the many '*monopati*' which crisscross the island.

An idea was forming in my head to offer walking holidays to ramblers from Great Britain and Ireland. Tinos has so much going for it - largely undiscovered by foreigners and the Greeks cannot understand why anyone should choose to walk when there are cars and public transport available. It means that you can walk the paths all day without seeing anyone, save for the odd farmer on his mule. The scenery looking out over the Aegean is stunning. The hundreds of family churches, the numerous elaborate dovecotes every one different, the quaint white washed villages and generous hospitality of the locals is something everyone should experience.

Throughout the winter we worked on our brochure, advertising and circulating walking clubs with information. If the walking holidays were to take off, it would be necessary to be there during the cooler walking months of spring and autumn, so we left in time to be on Tinos for Greek Easter and to stay until the end of October. This would be a good test of whether or not we could live here on a permanent basis.

Fortunately a booking for 15 people turned up, from a rambling club in Ireland. Whilst this was very welcome I would have preferred a smaller group to cut my teeth on. As things turned out it was a great success with the group enjoying the walking and we loving their company. Lasting friendships were established and I look forward to more people coming to share with us the magic of Tinos.

Friends in Ireland often ask how I fill my days, or am I not bored? I can honestly say this has never been the case. Aside from finding new walks and the thrill of walking on an interesting path for the first time, I find I can spend hours watching people arriving by ferry. It never ceases to amaze me how a family of four can arrive, complete with camping gear, luggage, cool box and dog all on a 50cc step-through moped.

On the subject of mopeds the local fish market has a resident pelican which has a tendency to roam. Often it can be seen looking out of a cardboard box on the back of a moped as it is returned home. Also there is a large dog which travels on the pillion of its owner's moped, sitting with its front paws on his shoulders. He has been known to sport old fashioned goggles - the dog that is! One day we had a rather large piece of furniture delivered to the apartment and as we saw the man off we were amazed to see him climb onto a motor cycle. He told us he managed this feat by resting the base on his knee with his arm over the top. He did not explain how he started or stopped or what he would have done in an emergency. I think it would be worth ordering another piece just to witness the delivery.

Another day I was walking along the seafront at dusk when something flew past my face, it seemed like a football. Then several things happened simultaneously - the object landed in the road with a splat, there was a huge splash accompanied by oaths coming from the rocks and a car drove over the object (by now identified as a big octopus) with both its nearside wheels. It seems that Yiorgos, had managed to prise the creature from the rocks and scoop it out. In doing this he had lost his balance and gone into the harbour. Meanwhile the road was stained with black ink and gore. I went to look at the octopus and got the fright of my life when it opened its eyes, shook itself and took off down the road with a dripping Yiorgos in pursuit.

The Irish walking group were due at the beginning of October. We had the first rain since April two weeks before then, the shower coinciding with my morning cycle ride. I was just coming down a hill into the town when it really started to pour and I came off badly on the greasy surface. As I slid across the road all I could think of was *'please don't let my legs be damaged'* aware of my visitors soon to arrive. As it turned out my shoulder, elbow and side took the brunt of the fall and after a couple of days I was OK.

The day they were due on Tinos dawned as most do, pleasant sun, yachts and fishing boats entering and leaving the harbour. We were nervous but excited as we knew the programme we had lined up couldn't fail to impress. Imagine our dismay when we received a text from their leader to say they

were stuck at Rafina - no ferries running due to high winds. What could I suggest? Once I had spoken to the Port Police on Tinos it was obvious that no ferries would go that day so I suggested they spend a day seeing Athens and book into a Rafina hotel to be convenient for the ferry next morning.

The following morning started a bit mixed with some dark clouds over the hills and some sunshine between. As we watched the ferry approach the sky got darker and darker and we prayed that the cloud would pass quickly. As it backed in to the quay and its ramp landed the heavens opened right on cue. Our visitors struggled off and one was heard to remark that it was just like being back at home in the Mournes. Fortunately the rain was short lived and after lunch we were able to go on a short walk to break them in for the next few days. Since they were a mixed ability bunch Jane acted as sweeper in the car as the paths were never that far from a road. This gave the novices a degree of reassurance and she was only called on once to pick someone up. The walks included a swim during or after and proved to be very popular, as was the dinner on the last evening.

On one of the walks we experienced hospitality and friendliness so typical of Tinians. We had stopped for a break in the village square of **Ktikados** (Κτικάδος) and as we sat there several young people arrived each carrying trays with delicious cakes which they offered round to our party. The walkers took some convincing that I had not prearranged this surprise.

We may have been spoiled by having such a friendly happy bunch in our first group and can only hope that in 2005 we are as lucky. Can't wait to find out.

See p.177 for details of Walking Tinos holidays.

How to get to Tinos

By Air - Scheduled or charter flights to Athens then ferry (Rafina quickest)

By Ferry - links with Andros, Chios, Lesvos, Mykonos, Piraeus, Rafina, Syros.

Tour Operators - Actual Hols, Explore Worldwide, Freedom of Greece, Greece & Cyprus Travel, Greek Sun, Island Wandering, Travel Lounge, Walking Tinos.

Greec[illegible] Wheels *by Ivan Calderwood*

After twen[illegible]ing various Greek islands I still had an unfulfilled dream to [illegible]rland, preferably by motorcycle, and explore the country ou[illegible]ourist resorts. As I had sold my bike ten years previously [illegible] remaining just that, a dream. However an impulse purch[illegible]00 and a 'Bike and Sun Tours' brochure, brought the dream i[illegible]us. Five weeks after seeing the website I had booked my [illegible]he bike, psyched myself up, and ridden from N.Ireland to [illegible]he rest of the group - a mixed bunch of people and machine[illegible]d bike travellers to first-timers like myself.

Three days la[illegible]n through France, Germany, Austria and Italy we sat on a ve[illegible]lock waiting to board the Minoan Line ferry to **Igoumenitsa** ([illegible] Tuesday, we disembarked after a pleasant passage down [illegible]d ten miles down the road we celebrated the start of our holi[illegible] Greek salad and retsina at a roadside taverna. Our first [illegible] in Greece was at **Nafpaktos** (Ναύπακτος), 170 miles from Ig[illegible] The Plaza Hotel overlooking the beach.

Having up to now [illegible] miles I felt no guilt whatsoever in spending the next day slippi[illegible]mode, lazing on the beach and catching up on my laundry. Th[illegible]g however I was up and away by 6.00 am to try one of Stua[illegible]d runs. I headed east towards **Eratini** (Ερατεινή), along th[illegible]ia breakfast at the Greek version of roadside fast food where[illegible] ter for coffee was he[illegible] the cupful on a little [illegible] stove. At this time of m[illegible]ning the sea was calm, the sun pleasant, and the day's traffic not really started. At Eratini, just as the traffic was thickening I turned north-west and inland onto much smaller roads. This was more like what I had imagined, narrow roads which could turn to gravel without warning and stunning scenery through the 'Sea of Olives', the largest olive grove in the world, all the way to **Lidoriki** (Λιδορίκι) on the shore of **Lake Mornou** (Λ.Μόρνου) where I enjoyed a *tiropita* (cheese pie) hot from the village bakery. Just as I was feeling like an intrepid explorer my *tiropita* was served by a young girl who in response to my halting Greek replied in perfect English! From here I looped back to the hotel, lunch and the beach for the rest of the day. Our last day in Nafpaktos, I

explored the picturesque port in the morning before retiring to the beach.

New Rio/Andirio Bridge before opening

Next morning we caught the ferry south to **Rio** (Pίο), soon to be replaced by the amazing new bridge. After 30 miles of main road we headed south for **Kalavrita** (Καλάβρυτα) through more gloriously barren scenery. After Kalavrita it was mostly fast main road until we passed through **Sparti** (Σπάρτη) and on to our **Mystras** (Μυστράς) hotel - 160 miles that day. Arriving hot and dusty it was heaven to discover the hotel had a lovely cool pool hidden at the back among fruit laden orange trees. Sunday morning I went up the winding road to the castle above the village and on along some very dramatic single track roads towards the **Taigetos** (Ταΰγετος) Pass. Here, clinging to the side of a hill I found the 'Mystras Bistrot' with the most breath-taking views from its terrace. I can still feel the strengthening morning sun on my face and taste the coffee I lingered over for the best part of an hour.

On Monday morning I left early to cross the switchback Taigetos Pass into **Kalamata** (Καλαμάτα) in the morning coolness. This is one of the most spectacular roads I have ever ridden and the absence of crash barriers in places and the odd gravel covered bend, usually above a massive drop, certainly concentrated the mind! After passing through Kalamata (urban and ugly) I headed south down the coast of the Mani peninsula with sea views most of the way to **Itilo** (Οίτιλο), our next stop. The Hotel Itilio sits just across the coast road from the beach and I spent a very quiet and enjoyable afternoon there with only a good book for company. On Tuesday morning, two of us decided to go and see the **Diros caves** (Σπήλαιο Δυρού) just a few miles away. The boat journey through them was enjoyable, the change in temperature and brightness when we emerged at the other end was almost as dramatic as the caves themselves. That afternoon, impressed by the peacefulness and scenery of the Mani I gave up an afternoon on the beach to do some house-hunting. There are some beautiful stone houses being built in stunning locations, unfortunately none within my budget.

Next morning it was main road as far as **Geraki** (Γεράκι) and then another switchback road to rival the Taigetos into **Leonidio** (Λεωνίδιο) and then up the coast to our next stop in **Nafplio** (Ναύπλιο), about 140 miles total. Nafplio is a very characterful old town, full of narrow winding streets, a beautiful square and lots of pavement tavernas all overlooked by the castle. After a day exploring the castle and town on Thursday I went on Friday to the amphitheatre at **Epidavros** (Επίδαυρος) which has the most perfect acoustics

of any outdoor theatre. It was incredible to sit at the top of the theatre and hear people on the stage below talking normally without any electronic assistance.

Saturday morning was a 125 mile hop to our last stop in Greece and a touch of luxury at the Best Western in **Olympia** (Ολυμπία). Here I have to confess I spent the next three days lying beside the pool and didn't visit the ruins at all. My excuse, apart from scenery and ruin overload, was that I must leave something to justify returning, as I fully intend to do.

Aside from the 80 mile run up the main coast road to **Patra** (Πάτρα) on Tuesday evening to catch the ferry back to Venice our Greek odyssey was at an end. I had travelled around 1300 miles in Greece on roads from single track to four lane motorway. I'd rate Greek drivers no worse than any others but I would, especially in rural areas, recommend expecting the unexpected. Also be aware that some roads, especially older ones, are surfaced with limestone chippings which can polish to a lovely shine. This combined with rain and/or the residue from trees can make life very interesting indeed. The big GSX did very well, returning over 45mpg for the trip overall, including some high speed motorway work. Would I do it again? Yes. Will I do it again? I hope so, only next time with my wife on the pillion.

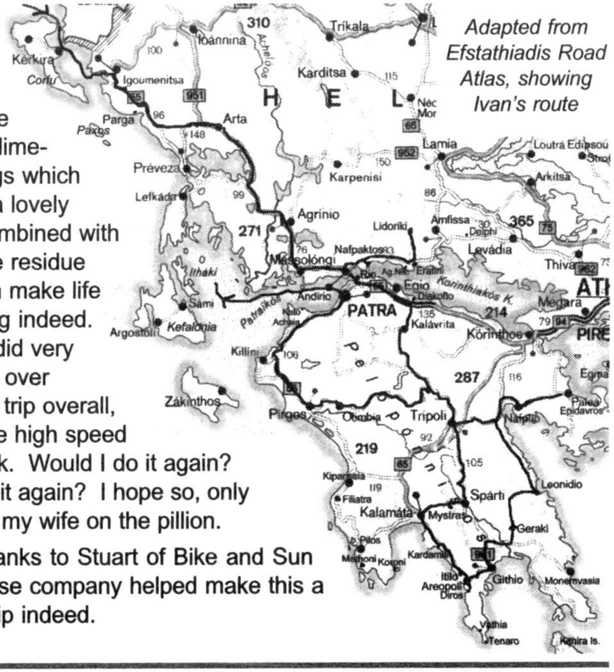

Adapted from Efstathiadis Road Atlas, showing Ivan's route

My sincere thanks to Stuart of Bike and Sun and to all whose company helped make this a very special trip indeed.

Spotty Legs & Ratty *by Janet Unsworth*

Our Greek initiation was on the Sporades island of **Alonissos**, staying in the town of **Patitiri** (Πατητήρι) in October 1989. We fell in love with Greece and Alonissos although we had dreadful weather some of the time. We had no car but an excellent walking map which my husband, David, studied very carefully (he's a 'map' person).

On a bright day we packed our bags for the day; picnic, swim gear and of course the map. Our chosen destination was a beach off the road to **Marpounda** (Μαρπούντα). We walked up the hill out of Patitiri. Six dogs came to greet us (David is also a 'doggie' person). We said hello to all of them and continued on our way. One doggie followed us. We called him Spotty Legs for obvious reasons.

The map came up trumps and we found the path down to our beach. The three of us scrambled through scrub and soon came to the end of the pathway. Unfortunately we were at least 10 to 12 feet above the beach. Spotty Legs jumped this with no problem. We took a bit longer. We threw our bags onto the beach and scrambled down, using overhanging branches and a small ledge part way down as a foothold. It was a delightful little cove, full of Greek charm and character.

We swam, ate a bar of chocolate shared with Spotty Legs and ate our lunch. Spotty Legs didn't expect any lunch and settled into a cool patch of seaweed. Around 3 o'clock the sun left the cove so we decided to leave too. We threw our bags up and looked at the height wondering how Spotty Legs would manage it. He jumped so far, then started to cry. David had to push his bottom the rest of the way, trusting he would not turn round and bite him. He didn't. We struggled up after him and headed towards Marpunto, with Spotty Legs showing us a short cut to the beach. David read his book, I had a swim and gazed at the views and Spotty Legs stayed too. When we later returned to Patitiri, Spotty Legs....

just trotted off home, no doubt to tell his doggie chums what he'd been up to. We felt privileged to have had his company.

We've visited other islands since then, but still have a soft spot for Alonissos. Five years later we returned, but this time hired a car so that we could stay in one of the smaller villages. We chose 'Beach House' from our holiday brochure, right on the shore in **Barbakis**, {known also as **Vamvakies**} *(Βαμβακιές)*. It was wonderful and peaceful. We even saw dolphins one morning. We loved it, then...

"Did you hear something?" I whisper as we settle in bed. We both held our breath. *"Yes, it's coming from the next door bedroom, a sort of gnawing sound!"* Eventually we drop off to sleep.

Next morning we inspect the other bedroom. The door jamb had chunks gnawed out of it and there was a hole in the mozzie netting on the window. A rat of course. So pleased we had closed that bedroom door.

The next night we were suddenly woken by a clattering sound, this time from the kitchen. I made David get up to investigate, making sure he shut our bedroom door first! I heard an even louder clatter and David yelling at something. He'd grabbed the nearest weapon available, the pole from the sun umbrella, and waved it furiously at the intruders - this time two rats. They had been eating their way through our plate of tomatoes. At the sight of my husband and stick they flew across the room and out through a hole, this time in the kitchen window netting.

The next night we shut all the windows and doors, but worried that there was still the chimney.

We mentioned our visitors to the rep and the following day she brought a rat trap and a cube of feta cheese. That night we heard the trap spring go off. In the morning we found ratty number one (or was it number two?) looking rather fed up. He didn't seem to appreciate his lump of feta - a bit salty I expect.

He sat in his trap on the balcony all day whilst we went out. Nobody came to check the trap and we felt sorry for him. We let him go that evening. He set off into the hills as we went off to the taverna.

No more visits, but a twist in the tale. I'd mislaid a necklace during the time of the nightly visits. Later, for some reason I decided to look up the chimney. There was my half eaten necklace - naughty ratty!

BZ

Profile of Southern West Crete *by Sylvia Cook*

Possibly the most barren, least touristy part of the Cretan coastline, there are still a few gems to be found and marvellous walking through some of the lesser known gorges that run north to south between the Cretan mountains.

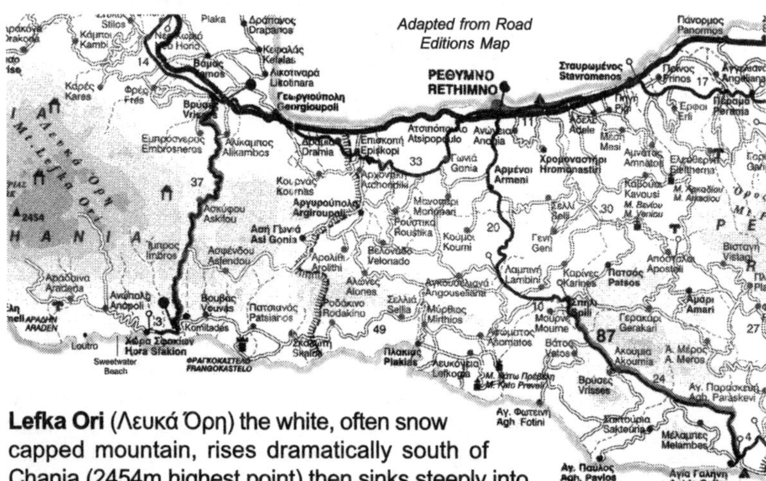

Lefka Ori (Λευκά Όρη) the white, often snow capped mountain, rises dramatically south of Chania (2454m highest point) then sinks steeply into the Libyan Sea with no roadway linking the south east of Chania province to the south west - except via the north. The harbour villages of **Ag. Roumeli** (Αγ. Ρουμέλη) at the base of the Samaria Gorge and **Loutro** (Λουτρό) along this south coast depend on the sea for transport and supplies. The road north to south beside and above the **Imbros** (Ιμπρός) Gorge is a fairly recent improvement, so the **Sfakia** (Σφακιά) region with its administrative centre **Chora Sfakion** (Χώρα Σφακίων) has not surprisingly remained somewhat apart from the rest of Crete.

Along the coast to the east of Sfakion, however, the terrain is less rugged and farming is possible, although the mountains still loom large until you reach the south of **Rethymnon** province. Now you start to notice more trees on the hillsides, more agricultural villages and on the coast more tourist development, principally at **Plakias** (Πλακιάς), although nothing like the scale of development on the north coast. Visitors to this area almost always arrive from the more accessible ports or airports in northern Crete.

Southern West Crete Background

❒ *The area was inhabited in ancient times and Sfakian archers represented the area in Alexander The Great's army.*

❒ *During Byzantine times Sfakians were renowned ship builders for Vene-*

tian merchants. In 1371 the Venetian rulers built ***Frangokastello*** *(Φραγκοκάστελο) to protect themselves against pirates and Cretan rebels. Local legend says that the strange shadows (Drossoulites) that appear at dawn in May and September are the long dead people from these times.*

- ❑ *The inhospitable region of Sfakia could be easily defended, so has always spawned many freedom fighters. It was largely ignored by the Turks of the Ottoman era. In 1770 the Russians, who were looking for diversion tactics, encouraged Daskaloyiannis of Anopolis to start an unsuccessful rebellion against the Turks from Sfakia.*
- ❑ *Sfakia played a key role in WW2, when allied forces were escaping from German attacks during the Battle of Crete. Very few gunmen were needed to guard the narrow Imbros gorge which was the only path to Sfakia until the 1960's.*

Sfakion Villages, Gorges & Plains *by Sylvia Cook*

Crete is an ideal destination for independent travel, so last September we booked an 11 day return on scheduled flights via Athens to explore Southern Crete and visit a friend who now lives near Chania. Trying to prearrange overnight stays in advance seems unnecessary outside high season - either time consuming to find prices in advance, or more expensive than the reality when you get there. However a little advance planning with a couple of pre-booked nights gave us a sense of security, a few ideas and allowed us to remain flexible.

Graham met us early morning at **Chania** (Χανιά) airport and took us to see his wonderful villa in the village of **Plaka** *(Πλάκα)*. After a relaxing breakfast and chat we set off at midday in a hire car from **Almirida** *(Αλμυρίδα)*, heading south through farming villages sprinkled with *ex-pat* villas in the Apokoronas region, through **Vrises** (Βρύσες) towards the bleak hills and small plain between **Lefka Ori** and the lesser peaks of **Angathes** and **Tripali**.

After the small farming villages of the plain we were back on winding roads, heading downhill roughly alongside the **Imbros Gorge**, with spectacular views from above. The final descent laid out before us, snaking over barren hills towards the coast hiding our destination, **Hora Sfakion** but over-

looking a flat coastal plain and **Frangokastello** to the east.

The final few kilometres west to Sfakion were through barren land. I say barren, but on closer inspection these lower brown hillsides were covered in seasquill flowers, the leaves long ago dead but with single stems thrusting up from bulbs which had found a pocket of soil, each topped with a sphere of white flower heads.

We found The Panorama outside the village where we had prebooked a room at €20 per night from details found on the internet. It was VERY basic, no drawers or even ledges to put things on, one tatty chair outside and no hot water. We went down the stairs 2 floors to report the lack of hot water, were assured the water just needed switching on, so we changed the outside switch to the other position, unpacked what we could, but an hour later still no hot water ... so down the stairs again we finally persuaded the young girl to come to check, then eventually to give us another room. It was smaller, no better storage but at least the water ran hot. We came across this indifference of reluctant teenagers several times on this trip - a marked contrast to the *filoxenia* of their parents' generation, who were more welcoming when we stopped at the downstairs taverna for beer later.

Although not particularly picturesque, Sfakion was a friendly, charismatic place with good food, local specialities and reasonable prices in spite of primarily serving people who are just passing through, departing or arriving on boats to Loutro, Agia Roumeli at the base of the Samaria Gorge or Gavdos, or maybe on a stopover on a walking holiday. It only had a small pebbly beach, but with good harbourside tavernas, a shopping street behind and a selection of basic hotels to choose from.

On our second afternoon we found much nicer rooms nearer the centre at the Tria Adelfia (not many studios here, but we had a travel kettle) and moved there the next morning for the rest of our stay. They quoted more at first, but as we walked away we were offered the same €20 rate. I don't really like packing and unpacking every few days and find that if you don't have a base you miss out on finding regular haunts and getting to know people. We found a few favourite tavernas and a regular kafeneion style

Sfakion and mountain backdrop

bar outside the Stavris hotel for early evening beers. Every taverna served complimentary raki - not just a small glass, but (especially if you drank it the first time) a little carafe each!

Komitades (Κομιτάδες) was the nearest village to the east with about 6 tavernas and rooms at the base of the Imbros Gorge - ideal for pre or post walking. Our first day we had stopped there en route, to sit at a pretty taverna sheltered from the high winds that day, overlooking the blue **Libyan Sea** and island of **Gavdos**, enjoying a beer and sampling the local mizithra cheese pies and honey. Passing through the next day we were detained about 15 minutes on the narrow road through the village whilst the driver of a tall sided delivery truck we were following had to dismantle the high sides in order to pass between close buildings. This main route across the south is certainly no motorway!

The **Imbros Gorge** we had seen from above was a must to visit. Many say this ravine is a more appealing walk than Samaria, being relatively short (2.5 hours walk) and not crowded, yet still with impressive scenery, steep rock sides, an archway, caves, trees and much green vegetation in the higher parts. The path starts near a collection of tavernas outside Imbros village and you could take the early morning bus from Sfakion to Hania getting off at Imbros, or take a taxi up leaving your car at a Komitades taverna for the day. We asked a few walkers we met whether the top or bottom was better. They said 'the middle'. As the lower part was less steep we decided to park at Komitades, have a leisurely coffee and cheese breakfast then walk up until we'd had enough, then down again. Not a bad plan for the less energetic and we enjoyed a very pleasant 1.5 hour walk finishing with fresh orange

juice at a taverna near the bottom. The front cover 3rd picture 2nd row shows Terry taking a rest in the Imbros gorge.

We headed east on a few of our explorations and found a quiet beach with a taverna (**Cafe Stavros**) before Frangokastello which we returned to several times as it was a relaxing spot with friendly service. **Frangokastello** had been investigated early on to decide if we wanted to move our base there. It is well worth visiting for its imposing castle ruins and sandy beaches, but with only a few tavernas, studios and rooms scattered around, rather than a village centre it was not our kind of place to stay. After Frangokastello we stopped to see what was going on when we saw many cars parked at the roadside. Perhaps inspired by the recent Athens Olympics, the Sfakion *Demos* seemed to be looking for potential athletes. Men and boys were all 'having a go' at the shot put and a running track was also marked out and there were a few sidestalls.

The nearby mountain plateau village of **Anopoli** (Ανώπολη) was a surprising find on another day. An extraordinary unexpected green oasis hidden in the midst of barren hillsides at a height of about 600 metres, but not far at all as the eagle flies. The 180° hairpin bends up the hillside afforded amazing views in all directions, but without crash barriers I wouldn't want to drive it at night. There were a few rooms to let and tavernas along the straight road as we approached the main platia and its statue of Daskaloyiannis who was from this village. We strolled around the back streets looking into small gardens where vegetables and fruits flourished, chatting with some building workers we passed. From here the more adventurous could continue walking the track through inland hamlets, then pathways to eventually reach **Aghia Roumeli** at the base of the Samaria Gorge, or (closer) descend from **Livaniana** (Λιβανιανά) to **Loutro** which is inaccessible by road.

We took the easier route to **Loutro** (Λουτρό), just a 20 minute journey on the boat to Aghia Roumelli, with day trippers who had arrived at Sfakion by coach that morning to visit the bottom of the Samaria Gorge. We looked across to **Sweetwater beach** halfway - a large mountain backed beach with a small jetty and taverna hut, accessed by sea or on the bleak path across steep hills either side. We had met a couple of our fellow travellers

Sweetwater Beach

on the ferry who were part of a jolly 'Happy Walker' international party. Not content with walking 3 gorges in the previous 2 days they were spending their day off walking back from Loutro to Hora Sfakion via this beach. It wore us out just thinking about it. Our destination village looked more welcoming - tavernas, 'rooms', small hotels and houses all in two shades of blue with white, behind a narrow pebble beach at one end - a bit touristy perhaps, but no noise (not even Greek music), just somewhere to laze, eat and drink. We had a late breakfast at the far end taverna then explored the ruined lookout on the headland at the other end. We sat on the beach a while with beers from the little grocery shop, checked out prices where displayed (rather more expensive than Sfakion) and had a light lunch before returning across the blue water on an afternoon ferry.

One sunny morning we set off early. There was a mist out to sea and ominous clouds over the mountains as we headed east through familiar territory at first. As we approached the Rethymnon province the terrain changed; olive and fruit trees on the plains to the south, then hillside villages amongst trees, but still the bare hillsides above. The recently surfaced road with crash barriers wound high up through **Ano** and **Kato Rodakino** (Ροδάκινο), on to **Sellia** (Σελλιά) from where we could see the bay of **Plakias** (Πλακιάς) spread out below. We chose not to take the small road just 4 km down, but to visit **Myrthios** (Μύρθιος) first where there was once a Youth Hostel, a regular backpackers haunt, I had read about. The village seems quite large with old and new houses, but we saw just one minimarket, a few tourist shops and tavernas. From here the drive down to Plakias was picturesque - a fertile valley, then a long sandy beach with the many resort hotels, tavernas and shops at one end. If you like a resort with a good choice of things to do, you could do worse, although I guess it has its noisy areas in the evening. We stopped for a very pleasant breakfast.

We continued on our way via **Assomatos** and **Frati** near another impressive gorge, the **Kourtaliotiko Canyon**, turning right onto the main road and through **Spili** (Σπήλι), whose herb, soaps, honey and linen shops (expensive) and waterfall and springs we visited on our return. You could sense the age of the majestic countryside around, although we were on a top quality new road, that has made this area far more accessible than when I used to visit 20 years ago and we gave up on a drive from Galini to Rethymnon.

Finally we arrived at **Ag Galini** (Αγ. Γαλήνη) - my old haunt from those days, although I could not recognise the approaches. Its traffic free taverna streets

and harbour front still have a certain charm, but it is definitely a very touristy resort these days with far more hotels than the narrow beach can handle. We walked around the cliffside, now made safer, to the increasingly taverna backed beach. We looked for and found 'Stochos' where Terry and I had stayed a couple of nights 9 years ago when looking for my old friends. The owner Manolis was sadly not there, but his daughter Eva who served us had the same friendly outgoing manner as her father - and raki chasers seemed the norm even at lunchtime. We squeezed between other sun-bathers for a short beach rest before setting off back to quiet Sfakion.

Varying our route slightly after Spili, to see different scenery, we headed north of **Mt Kouroupa** (Κουρούπα) rejoining the previous route before Selia. We stopped off for coffee at a kafeneion cum butchers, cum general store in **Ano Rodakino**, just 3 young men inside. An elderly gent (80-years old he said) came in and sat next to Terry. We chatted in simple Greek, saying we were staying at Hora Sfakion. He asked what we thought of it. We said "not as green as here" which seemed to amuse them. The young lad who had made our coffee would not let us pay anything - perhaps we had entertained his grandfather. It was good to be off the tourist track with friendly locals and tinkling sheep along the roadside.

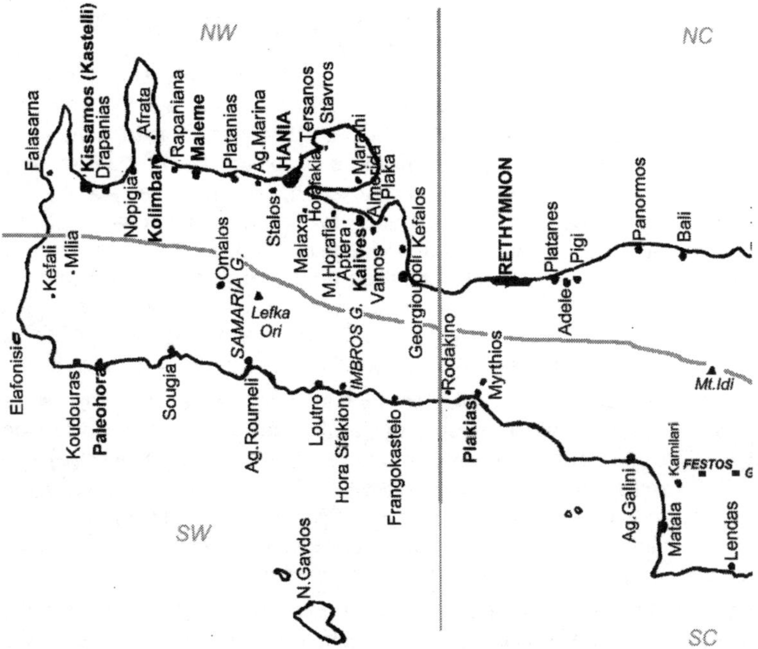

Guide to Who Goes Where in Crete *by Sylvia Cook*

As anyone who has been there knows, Crete is the largest island in Greece with diverse natural and man-made characteristics. Holiday destinations range from quiet inland villages where tourists are few and far between, small coastal villages where fishing and farming coexist with tourism, to lively noisy touristy resorts (that most Grecophiles prefer to avoid) and out of town luxury hotel complexes - with many more styles in between.

Overleaf you will find a clarification of not only who goes to which part of the island, but also the type of accommodation and services offered to help you to decide which companies to consider for your next Cretan holiday. Some of the larger companies cater to all tastes, whilst some of the smaller specialists may offer exactly what you are looking for. The map shows the principal resorts catered for.

Crete's varying natural characteristics and its interesting history, provide an ideal setting for specialist activity holidays too. Many travellers choose Crete for walks along the coast or inland - especially the famous gorges. A number of companies offer guided walking holidays, some specifically to observe nature (Cretan spring flowers are a must to see alone or with a guide), others will guide you through the lesser known gorges and mountain hikes off the beaten track, or set you off on your own with instructions and accommodation en route. With several ancient Minoan sites, other companies invite those interested in archaeology to join their study tours. The long coastline means it is also ideal for watersports holidays, or how about painting, Cretan cookery or more spiritual pursuits.

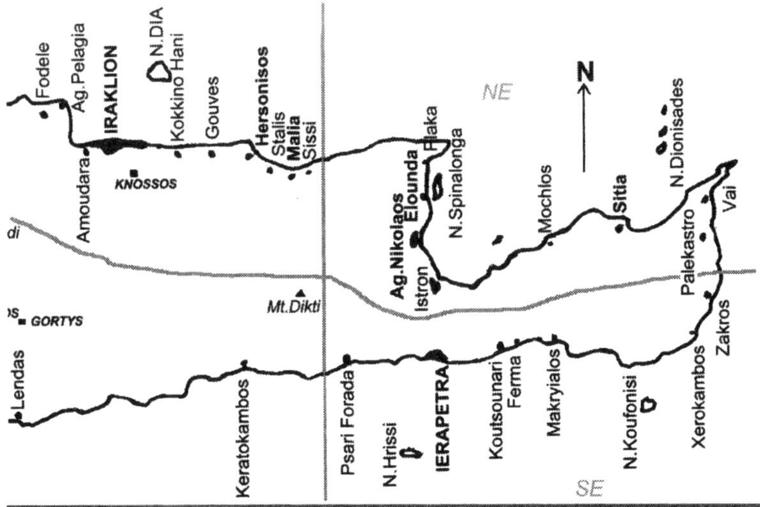

Tour Operators	Supporter details Page no.	North West	North Central	North East	South West	South Central	South East	Studios / Rooms	Villas / Houses/ Apartments	Villas with pool	Small Hotels	Hotels with Pool	Flights to Heraklion	Flights to Hania	Flight Only	Accommodation Only	Flight & Accomm.	Half or Full Board Option	Walking Holidays	Other Special Interest	U=Unescorted, R=Rep
Actual Holidays	178	Y	Y	Y	Y	Y	Y	Y	Y	Y	Y	Y	Y	Y	Y	Y	Y	Y	Y	Y	R
Airtours Group			Y	Y				Y	Y			Y	Y		Y		Y	Y			R
Amathus Holidays		Y	Y	Y								Y	Y				Y				R
Archers Direct/ Cosmos		Y	Y	Y					Y			Y	Y	Y	Y	Y	Y	Y		Y	R
Argo Holidays	182	Y	Y	Y				Y	Y		Y	Y	Y	Y	Y	Y	Y	Y		Y	R
Best of Greece/ Seafarer	182	Y	Y	Y	Y	Y	Y	Y	Y	Y	Y	Y	Y	Y		Y	Y	Y		Y	R
CV Travel				Y								Y	Y		Y	Y	Y	Y			U
Cyplon Holidays		Y	Y	Y					Y	Y		Y	Y	Y		Y	Y	Y			R
Direct Greece	178	Y						Y	Y				Y	Y	Y		Y				R
Elegant Resorts				Y						Y		Y	Y				Y	Y			R
Elysian Holidays	180			Y						Y						Y		Y			U
Excel Holidays		Y	Y	Y				Y				Y	Y	Y	Y		Y	Y			R
Filoxenia		Y	Y	Y	Y			Y	Y	Y	Y	Y	Y	Y		Y	Y	Y	Y		U
First Choice Group		Y	Y	Y			Y	Y	Y	Y	Y	Y	Y	Y	Y	Y	Y	Y			R
Freedom of Greece		Y	Y	Y	Y	Y	Y	Y	Y	Y	Y	Y	Y	Y	Y	Y	Y	Y			R
GB / British Airways													Y		Y						U
Greece & Cyprus Travel		Y	Y	Y	Y	Y	Y														U
Greece Rediscovered	182	Y	Y	Y	Y	Y	Y	Y	Y	Y	Y	Y	Y	Y		Y	Y	Y			U
Greek Islands Club	177	Y	Y							Y				Y	Y	Y	Y				R
Greek Options		Y							Y	Y				Y			Y				R
Greek Sun Holidays				Y				Y	Y		Y		Y				Y				U
Hidden Greece	179	Y		Y	Y	Y	Y	Y			Y	Y	Y	Y			Y				U
Island Wandering	179	Y	Y	Y		Y		Y			Y	Y	Y	Y	Y	Y	Y				U
Islands of Greece	183	Y	Y	Y			Y		Y	Y		Y	Y	Y			Y				U
ITC Classics				Y						Y		Y	Y			Y	Y	Y			U
James Villa Holidays		Y	Y							Y			Y	Y		Y	Y				R
Kosmar		Y	Y	Y	Y		Y	Y			Y	Y	Y	Y			Y	Y			R
Libra / Priceright		Y	Y	Y				Y	Y			Y	Y	Y	Y	Y	Y	Y			R
Manos	182	Y	Y	Y				Y	Y	Y	Y	Y	Y	Y	Y		Y	Y		Y	R
Mastersun			Y										Y				Y	Y			R
Mediterranean Chapters/ A & K		Y		Y						Y		Y	Y			Y	Y				U
Olympic Holidays	180	Y	Y	Y		Y		Y	Y	Y	Y	Y	Y	Y	Y	Y	Y	Y			R
Planet	181	Y	Y	Y					Y	Y		Y	Y	Y	Y	Y	Y	Y			R
Saga			Y									Y	Y				Y	Y		Y	R
Simply Travel	180	Y	Y	Y	Y	Y	Y	Y	Y	Y	Y	Y	Y	Y		Y	Y	Y			R
Simpson Travel	179	Y		Y	Y			Y	Y	Y	Y	Y	Y	Y		Y	Y	Y	Y	Y	R
Solo's		Y										Y		Y			Y	Y	Y	Y	R
Sunvil	177	Y		Y	Y			Y	Y		Y	Y		Y	Y	Y	Y	Y			R
Thomas Cook	182		Y	Y				Y	Y	Y	Y	Y	Y		Y	Y	Y	Y		Y	R
Thomson Holidays		Y	Y	Y				Y	Y	Y	Y	Y	Y	Y	Y	Y	Y	Y			R
Travel Club of Upminster		Y						Y	Y		Y	Y	Y	Y		Y	Y	Y			R
The Travel Lounge		Y	Y	Y	Y	Y	Y	Y	Y	Y	Y	Y	Y	Y	Y	Y	Y	Y			R

Tour Operators	Supporter details Page no.	North West	North Central	North East	South West	South Central	South East	Studios / Rooms	Villas / Apartments	Villas with pool	Small Hotels	Hotels with Pool	Flights to Heraklion	Flights to Hania	Flight Only	Accommodation Only	Flight & Accomm.	Half or Full Board	**Walking Holidays**	**Other Special Interest**	**U=Unescorted, R=Rep**
CRETE ONLY SPECIALISTS																					
Brake to Crete		Y						Y	Y		Y			Y			Y				U
Cachet Travel		Y	Y	Y	Y	Y	Y	Y	Y	Y	Y	Y	Y	Y	Y	Y	Y	Y			R
Catherine Secker's Crete		Y							Y	Y			Y	Y			Y				R
Cretan Ambience		Y	Y	Y	Y	Y	Y	Y	Y	Y	Y	Y	Y	Y		Y	Y	Y	Y	Y	R
Crete Escapes	185	Y						Y	Y	Y						Y					U
Freelance Holidays	178	Y	Y		Y	Y		Y	Y	Y	Y		Y	Y		Y	Y		Y	Y	R
Meltemi Travel	178	Y						Y	Y	Y	Y	Y	Y	Y		Y	Y	Y			R
Mistral Singles Holidays	178	Y										Y				Y		Y	Y	Y	R
Prestige Holidays				Y						Y		Y	Y			Y	Y	Y			R
Pure Crete	182	Y	Y		Y				Y	Y			Y	Y		Y	Y		Y	Y	R
Smart Holidays		Y	Y		Y	Y	Y	Y	Y	Y	Y					Y			Y	Y	U
SPECIALIST HOLIDAYS																					
Alternative Travel Group		Y									Y			Y			Y	Y	Y		R
Andante Travels			Y	Y								Y	Y			Y	Y	Y		Y	R
Erna Low Body & Soul				Y								Y	Y				Y			Y	U
Explore Worldwide		Y	Y		Y			Y			Y		Y	Y			Y		Y		R
Happy Walker	178	Y	Y	Y	Y		Y	Y			Y					Y			Y		R
Headwater Holidays		Y		Y	Y						Y	Y	Y	Y		Y	Y	Y	Y	Y	R
InnTravel		Y	Y	Y					Y	Y	Y	Y	Y	Y			Y	S	Y		U
Midas Historic Tours			Y									Y	Y				Y	Y		Y	R
Naturetrek		Y	Y								Y	Y	Y	Y			Y	Y	Y	Y	R
Page & Moy		Y									Y			Y		Y	Y	Y		Y	R
Ramblers Holidays		Y	Y	Y	Y						Y								Y		R
Sherpa Expeditions					Y			Y			Y	Y		Y			Y	S	Y		R
The Travelling Naturalist		Y	Y								Y	Y	Y				Y	Y	Y	Y	R
The Traveller		Y	Y	Y	Y	Y	Y				Y	Y	Y				Y	Y		Y	R
Walks Worldwide	180	Y	Y		Y	Y					Y	Y	Y	Y		Y	Y	Y	Y		R
Waymark		Y			Y						Y			Y				Y	Y		R
World Walks		Y			Y						Y			Y		Y			Y		U

Contact Tour Operators for further details. See page number in 2nd column for sponsor adverts in this issue. Please say you saw their details in The Greek-o-File.

Photo - Taverna at Komitades

Winter Musings *by Marian Cropper*

Now the winter months are here I find it's a good time to get out all my 'Greek-o-Files' and dream of past and future holidays. As soon as I start to read I go off into a little world of my own - I'm back there totally. It's wonderful to be able to transport myself to Greece in this way.

My husband Dave and myself have been twice a year visitors to Greece for some years now. **Parga** is our favourite. We've been there four times, compared with no more than twice to anywhere else. It really has a magical attraction and we have some wonderful memories.

One wedding anniversary in Parga our Manos rep brought flowers to our room and booked us the best table at the Kastro restaurant, at the edge of the balcony overlooking the whole of Parga. Needless to say we were 'over the moon', which incidentally was full, making it even more romantic shining on the calm waters in the bay and lighting up the little islands like jewels in this precious place.

Another evening I like to remember was a trip high up in the hills. First stop was Ali Pasha's fortress, which we had been longing to visit after unsuccessfully trying to reach it on foot on a previous occasion. It was further than we thought, sitting on a high hill above the pretty village of **Anthousa** (Ανθούσα) above the Valtos Valley. The coach trip was easier. At dusk the sky was a pretty pink, shining through the arched doorways of the fortress, with spectacular views down to Parga.

After strolling around and taking photographs we gathered at the Oasis Taverna, in the nearby mountain village of **Agia** (Αγιά), for a meal and a Pub Quiz! *"Oh no"* you say *"a Pub Quiz in Greece!"* Well it turned out to be rather special. After eating we were invited inside, to a room that went back in time. The walls were covered with old Greek tin-plate advertising signs, old black and white photos of film stars and tourists long gone. There were shelves full of old ouzo bottles and cans, etc. Old sewing machines, clocks and magazines completed the picture. To me it was magic. I was enthralled - tears came to my eyes. I'm like that, I can't help it. Who could! It just wasn't what I'd expected.

We took more photos and eventually settled. Armed with a drink (ouzo, Metaxa, Mythos and suchlike) the quiz commenced. It was a bit like any Pub Quiz back home, but in these surroundings and with a few drinks we

did a lot of laughing, but were on top form. Dave and I even won a bottle of Ouzo 12 complete with glass. We took our trophy home to England, a reminder of a lovely evening, back in time in a village miles from anywhere, amongst wonderful people.

We've been to **Plomari** (Πλωμάρι) in Lesvos twice and found it a very interesting place. We love the old plateia with the big plane tree, and the walk along the winding road from Plomari to nearby **Ag. Isidoros** (Αγ. Ισίδωρος). Now, if I can't get to sleep, I don't count sheep, I count the bends on the road and try to picture what was at each turning. We walked it so many times it has become infused in our minds.

Oh the simple pleasures of a Greek holiday. Wonderful!

My Kitchen

I love my Greek-style kitchen, painted white with blue,
Old ouzo bottles on a shelf, a few gold icons too.
A Greek *pithoi* painting hangs, resplendent on the wall,
Lace cloth on the table, wine jugs large and small.
Taverna sign above the door, bright plates, an 'eye' or two,
I feel as if on holiday, but sadly no sea view.
I play bouzouki music to recreate the mood,
Whilst drinking ouzo slowly and savouring the food.
There's gigantes and stifado, Greek salad and meatballs,
Tzatziki with black olives, then, my favourite dish of all,
'Lamb baked in the oven', oregano fills the air,
Memories of Greek holidays make me feel a millionaire.

Old Wine in New Bottles *by Mary Lambell*

On a recent holiday to Ikaria we were reminded that Dionysos was said to have been born on this island and introduced the first wine here. Their ancient capital was called Oenoe (linked to the word for wine). Certainly the local wine, named Pramnian after the local mountain range, was famous, and is referred to by Homer in the Iliad and the Odyssey.

Wine was produced throughout Greece in ancient times as the climate and soil favoured the growing of vines. Dionysos, the god of wine, was highly honoured.

A bottle of wine in Greece today has on its label the Greek word 'οίνος' (eenos) which is the ancient Greek word for wine, only used now in writing, but the 'οινοπωλείον' (eenopoleon) is still the wine shop. The modern word used for wine 'κρασί' (krasi) is also an old word, linked with the verb to mix.

In ancient Greece wine was thick and sweet, and invariably mixed, typically three parts water to one of wine. Other things were often added, such as herbs and honey. The storage jars, (amphorae) were probably lined with resin to prevent them leaking (one theory for the origin of retsina). As one writer said *"Mix half and half and you get madness, unmixed, total collapse"*.

This is what happened to Polyphemos, the Cyclops in The Odyssey. On a previous raid on his return from Troy, Odysseus had acquired some very potent wine which required diluting with twenty parts of water. He took some with him into Polyphemos' cave, and offered him some, neat. After three cups the Cyclops passed out! Thus Odysseus and his companions were able to blind him and escape his clutches (Odyssey *Book 9*).

The enchantress Circe welcomed Odysseus' companions with *'a potion.... mulled in Pramnian wine'* (from Ikaria) before turning them into pigs. (*Odyssey Book 10*). In the Iliad, in Nestor's tent *'A woman ... mixed them a strong drink with Pramnian wine.'* (*Iliad Book 11*). Other specific areas were particularly famous for their wines, notably Samos (whose wine is still highly thought of), Chios and Thassos where some fifth century BC inscriptions containing laws on the wine trade have been discovered, forbidding among other things the dilution of wine before sale.

In the eighth century BC the poet Hesiod, who lived in Boeotia in central Greece, wrote a poem giving instructions to farmers. Regarding the grape harvest he wrote: *'When Orion and Sirius come into mid-heaven and rose-fingered dawn meets Arcturus* [ie early September], *then set about cutting off all the grape clusters for home. Expose them to the sun for ten days and nights, cover them over for five, and on the sixth draw merry Dionysos' gift off into jars.'* (Hesiod, *Works and Days*) The first half of his instructions for enjoying the product in high summer could be followed today: *'You want to drink gleaming wine, sitting in the shade, having had the heart's fill of food, facing into the fresh westerly breeze. From a perennial spring that runs away and is unclouded pour three measures of water, and the fourth of wine.'*

Wine played an important part in daily life. There was an annual festival in Athens called the *Anthesteria*, which celebrated the new vintage. Jars were opened and serious drinking contests were held. Before any sacrifice a libation was offered of wine poured on the ground. The *symposion* (cf συμπόσιο / banquet), drinking party, was a regular event in the life of Athenian men, held in the *andron*, or men's quarters of the house. Wives would not attend, although lower class women, like dancers and flute girls would be invited to provide entertainment. The drinking would begin after the food was eaten, and sometimes more serious discussions took place, as described by Xenophon in his *Symposion,* when Socrates was present. A game called *kottabos* was often played, where wine was flicked at a target (not unlike the modern antics of public school boys!). This and other activities are well illustrated on numerous vessels used at such parties.

The variety of wine related pottery found is proof of its importance in the

A kylix cup showing reclining male guests drinking, playing kottabos and listening to music - from Cambridge Illustrated History of Ancient Greece

ancient Greek world. The *amphora* was used for storage, the *hydria* for water, *krater* for mixing the wine and water (cf κρασί), the *oinochoe* was the jug for pouring (cf οίνος), *kylix* and *skyphos* were cups for drinking.

Finally, if further proof were needed, an extract from the World Atlas of Wine *'Greek wine's reputation is built not on imported grapes but on indigenous grapes which may well be able to trace their lineage back to ancient Greece,* ***the cradle of modern wine*** *as we know it.'*

Wine Making, Naturally *by Sylvia Cook*

Reading Mary's article I was struck by Hesiod's winemaking poem and thought it sounded pretty much the same recipe as used to make village wines today, except that the grapes are not left in the sun so long for today's preferred taste and strength. Our friend Alekos makes superb natural wines - clear, bright, delicious dry style and noted by many to be 'hangover free'.

He says that most of the work is in growing the grapes - keeping them well watered, bugs and flies away, weeds removed so the grapes get all the nutrients the soil has to offer (we've helped with this bit so can vouch for the back breaking effort needed). He does spray with sulphur as otherwise he would lose his grapes to insects, but there are no other additives and his wine is made pretty much as the ancients made it.

His recipe could be followed by anyone who has a crop of ripe grapes.

Method

- ❒ Spread ripe grape bunches out in the sun for 2-4 days. This increases the sugar content and timing varies depending on the grapes used.
- ❒ Squash or break the grape skins and leave in a loosely covered barrel or plastic bin, in a dark room (21-22°) for 4-8 days. Only fill barrel to 80% to leave room for fermentation. Stir several times a day.
- ❒ When fermentation slows, press grapes, strain juice from skins, pips and stalks. Return juice to barel covered loosely. Gradually tighten lid down over the next 2 days.
- ❒ After 1 week siphon the wine off the sediment. Close barrel/bin firmly and fit an airlock water filter to allow gases to escape.
- ❒ After 40 days taste the wine. Siphon into bottles, cork or seal. Some wines improve with keeping (in a cool shaded place), but your wine is now ready - so drink, enjoy and be merry.

If you want some natural wine vinegar too - just put some of the skins and pips after pressing back into a barrel or bin with 2-5 litres of warm water. Cool. Add a little vinegar. Close and leave to mature, then siphon off into bottles. It's just like making wine.

A Slippery Slant on Moussaka *by Miles Lambert-Gócs*

Heading south from Thessaloniki to the Thessalian capital of Larissa, I stopped off at the cooperative winery of Tyrnavos to try out their wines, and afterward found myself with an appetite. I asked the winery manager if he could recommend a place to eat in Larissa and he recommended *'Godis'* at least that was how I heard and jotted down the name. His decisiveness was encouraging, because I presumed I was being sent to a place known for local specialities that foreign tourists typically miss. I could have slapped myself on the forehead when Godis turned out to be the Larissa branch of the Goody's chain of fast-food hamburger houses that had begun a Trojan horse invasion of the age-old olive oil based Greek diet.

Profoundly dismayed by the winery boss's presumption that I would prefer Goody's, I beat a retreat and a few blocks away found a taverna where several generously lacquered specials were on display. Mostly they were *'ladera'* dishes. The name denotes 'oiled ones' and to an English-accustomed ear it sounds enough like 'lathered' to grease the funny bone. The theory behind the *ladera* is that they should cook until the watery part of the ingredients have evaporated, so that the food is left standing, if not sliding, on its oil. But the *ladera* are not to be glossed over, because they have formed the basis of Greek culinary efforts since at least Hippocrates' time. In Greece where the olive tree has always been profuse, the olive's ooze naturally became a major source of calories for poor people, not just a cooking medium.

Photo by Sylvia Cook

Two workmen were both eating gleaming green okra and I was sorely tempted to follow suit, but these dishes can take an unaccustomed intestinal tract by surprise, and so I passed up in favour of a viscous and resplendent moussaka.

To my way of thinking, a proper moussaka is an olive oil dish par excellence, though for strict constructionists it does not belong to the genus *ladera*. The exact classification of moussaka is a bit of a head-scratcher and probably depends mostly on how one can best slice it. Moussaka certainly cannot lay with the en croûte delicacies; but on the other hand it does not sink with the fluid casseroles, either. Sometimes it seems to slide in between the terrines and pâtés: it leans towards terrines if it is of the high-built kind and served at Mediterranean room temperature when several days old; and towards pâtés if it is also crusty and baked with a lining of aubergine skins. However, the rarer low-built moussaka, with its slim strata, cuts nicely on

the bias and, if highly flavoured with sweet spices, can seem a soft, nonstick baklava.

Moussaka has never been a fixed edifice. To slosh under the umbrella of *moussaka* a dish need only consist of at least two separately pre-cooked parts, usually fried, that subsequently have been baked together. Its most constant constituent over time and territory has been aubergine (eggplant, as we call it in America), whose affinity for olive oil is as celebrated in the East as it has been notorious in the West. Indeed eggplant is the obvious protagonist in the genesis of moussaka.

Originally, moussaka had no structure at all. Its name is Arabic, and in Arab lands moussaka usually is not a layered dish, but rather a sort of vegetarian baked 'wet' chilli: aubergine and onions are fried in olive oil, and then chickpeas and more oil are added before baking. Truly its place is with the amorphous *ladera*. Greeks of the eastern Aegean islands make a dish along those unstructured lines, but it is not baked - and not called moussaka, either. Baking is a fundamental requirement of any sort of moussaka.

Architecture came to moussaka with ground meat, whose introduction suggested layering the dish before baking. This must have happened by around 1800 since Ami Boué, an early 19th century explorer of Ottoman Europe, mentioned moussakou (sic) as *"a ragout of chopped mutton with sorrel, and sometimes currants and aromatic herbs."* Layering also opened the sluice for improvisation, and variations can still be encountered in Greece, especially in the north, but in almost any region seasonally, though never in kitchens catering to tourists seeking authenticity.

The familiar custard cap is a mark of O Megas Moussakas (Le Grand Moussaka). This superstructure also corroborates those who maintain that moussaka could reflect elements of Byzantine cuisine that were preserved by monastic communities and the wealthy classes. White sauce, after all, was invented by the ancient Greeks; and the possession of such lush skills is only reinforced by an early 19th century notation that *"the blanc manger [sic], in Greek 'thiason', is not much known [in the Balkans] outside the refined Greek kitchen."*

This is not to suggest that Hippocrates would recognize moussaka. But neither is a classical lineage out of the question. For in addition to white sauce the ancient Greeks also knew the frying pan, ground meat and sweet spices. What is more, according to one of Plutarch's dining companions (in Table-talk) the ancient Greeks had become rather undemocratically clever at concocting sloppy dishes: *"The custom of distributing portions of meat was abandoned when dinners became extravagant; for it was not possible, I suppose, to divide fancy cakes and Lydian puddings and rich sauces and all sorts of other dishes made of ground and grated delicacies."* In none of its manifestations is moussaka a finger-food.

Olive oil puddles are natural to moussaka. Aficionados advise taking to them with bread even before piercing the custard cap with a fork. In its puddles may be read the entire history of a moussaka. As this history can span upwards of a week, the reward is greater than in the case of the true *ladera* dishes, which as a rule neither improve with age nor have any shelf life. It is no small irony that now, just when olive oil is waxing in the world, a movement is underway among some less unctuous Greek chefs to see to the mopping up of the puddles before the plate ever reaches the table, or even to forestall a drip by eschewing extravagance in the early stages of assembling aubergine moussaka. Avid bread-eaters will be sent diving for their butter or margarine.

Adapted from Miles' book, Greek Salad: A Dionysian Travelogue (Reviewed Vol.3)

The Taste of Greece Back Home *by Anne Richardson*

Those of you who have read previous Greek-o-File books will know that my husband and I spend time each year on the island of Samos. Our landlady is a superb cook, who speaks no English, but who has a natural flair as a teacher. She and I have spent hours sweating over a tiny two-ring, integral oven, holiday accommodation cooker, producing 'authentic' Samiot food fit for kings and queens.

I have written down and adapted many recipes so that we can continue to produce the 'taste of Greece' when we return to England and have identified a number of 'musts' to bring home in order to recreate that authentic Greek taste to recapture memories of your Greek holidays.

TOMATO PASTE - to pep up the flavour of those (mostly) insipid supermarket tomatoes, I have discovered an ingredient that puts back some of the Greek sun-ripened 'zing'! It is a very concentrated tomato paste from KYKNOS, sold in red-labelled tins about €1.20 for 410g, €0.70 for 200g. Once the tin is opened the contents only keep 2-3 weeks in a fridge so I store small polythene bags of 2-3 tablespoons in the freezer to use as required.

Picture from Kyknos.
UK wholesaler NATCO supply many UK 'ethnic' shops

RICE FOR STUFFING MEAT AND VEGETABLES - My landlady always uses 'Agrino' rice, in a white and brown packet, labelled 'for stuffing' in Greek. I have tried various other brands in Greece and the UK, but have to agree that this rice best absorbs and maximises the other flavours in the dishes we have cooked.

SEASONING FOR FISH - We eat quite a lot of fish in England and in Greece, such as bass and bream, cooked as simply as possible. 'Captain's mix for grilled fish', sold in blue capped spice jars in Greece, is a perfect ready-made Greek seasoning that compliments fish splendidly. According to the label it contains garlic, onion, spices, salt, pepper, rosemary and lemon aroma. I use it for pan-fried, barbecued, grilled and baked fish.

'YELLOW FLOUR' FOR FRYING MEAT & VEGETABLE DISHES - This flour, made from very finely ground semolina, is the 'secret' ingredient for fried dishes that need a crisp outer coating. It ensures that 'Keftedes' have that extra dimension and do not merely fry up like common or garden beef-burgers! NB Do remember to pack the flour inside a polythene bag in your suitcase. A burst yellow flour bag is not welcome when you unpack!

AVGOLEMONO SAUCE - Knorr prepare a wonderful dry sauce mix in packets for the Greek market which can be used with chicken, pork and fish. It is very easy to make, the instructions are in English on the packet, which shows a picture of stuffed vine leaves coated in the sauce. The sauce is so popular with friends and family here that I have to buy massive amounts to meet demand. You can add lettuce or uncooked spinach to the sauce just before serving for a very presentable 'Greek (meat) Fricasse'. Furthermore, all the children in our family love the sauce and will eat all manner of previously 'unliked' foods disguised in it. A boon for any mother!

FRESH VINE LEAVES - Vine leaves are 'in season' in Greece during May, June and July. Having been offered copious numbers of vine leaves to bring home over the years and ending up with broken, chewy results I have finally perfected the 'Greece to England' process. Although the preparation is a bit tedious, believe me, the results are superb and worth the trouble.

From England, in preparation, I bring medium sized (approx. 8 inches wide) 'Zip and Seal' bags to pack the leaves into. To ensure good results, prepare the leaves no more than one day before you leave for home.

Decide how many leaves you are realistically likely to use when you get home. Harvest the leaves from the vines, choosing leaves that have a wide centre area, about 4½ - 5 inches across the middle. Pick about 10 more than the number you require, to allow for 'discards'.

Carefully blanch the leaves, in batches of about 20, in a large saucepan. To do this, fill the saucepan with water, add a tablespoon of olive oil and bring to the boil. Gently add no more than 20 leaves to the saucepan, making sure they are not bent or folded and boil for about 5 minutes. Drain the hot water from the saucepan, fill with cold water and allow the leaves to cool before you drain and handle them, (or carefully lift the pile of leaves and place in bowl of cold water). Drain when cooled.

Place paper kitchen towel or a large clean tea towel, on a large plate or clean worktop. Gently lift the leaves INDIVIDUALLY and place them flat, vein side up on the towel. Make sure they are not bent or folded or they may not survive the freezing process. Discard any torn leaves. Move to one side and deal with the next batch of leaves.

Repeat the boiling/cooling process until all the leaves have been blanched, cooled, drained and stacked on the towel. (If you are doing large numbers, it is easier to have a couple of large saucepans on the go at once!)

The packing stage is very important. The leaves are going to be frozen when you get home, so label the 'Zip and Seal' bags with the contents, quantity and date, before you pack the leaves into them.

To pack the leaves:

First inspect each leaf and discard any that are torn or too big to fit FLAT into the bags. Decide how many you would want to use at one time for each pack (say 20-40). Lay that number of leaves, CAREFULLY, vein side up, on top of each other in very neat piles. Slide the pile gently into the bag and seal. Place the sealed bag into another polythene bag and pack FLAT, in your suitcase, between clothing.

As soon as you get home, place the 'Zip and Seal' bags into the freezer. Store flat otherwise the leaves will break.

When you want to use the vine leaves, take them from the freezer and defrost slowly. Ensure they are completely defrosted, before using them for your chosen recipe, treating as if they were fresh or prepacked.

MY GREEK RECIPES - Of course, I also bring back any new recipes I have discovered to recreate the taste of Greece back home. The vegetable omelette recipe on the next page is just one example of Samiot cooking from my personal recipe collection.

Spinach & Spring Bean 'Omelette' *by Anne Richardson*

We have discovered that 'Omelette' is a term used by Greeks to cover most dishes containing one or two main ingredients that then have several eggs added to them, before serving. The result looks nothing like the conventional 'omelette', but is tasty none-the-less. Quantities given below are enough for 4 people.

1 kilo broad beans in pods, plus their tender leafy tops and leaves

500 g spinach, roughly chop large leaves

2 onions, finely chopped

2 cloves of garlic, finely chopped

4 tabsp chopped fresh fennel tops

Optional : mint, celery or parsley chopped, quantity to taste

Salt, to taste

Pepper, to taste

3 tabsp olive oil

6 eggs

Method

❒ Thoroughly wash the herbs and vegetables. Leave to drain.

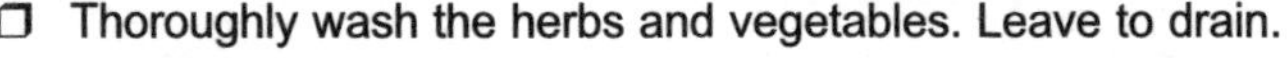

❒ Chop the drained bean shoots, leaves and whole bean pods into ½ inch pieces. Partially cook for 5 minutes in boiling, salted water until nearly tender. Drain. (Broad beans in pods without leaves are fine. For fresh or frozen beans without pods, use 750g and increase the quantity of spinach to 750g.)

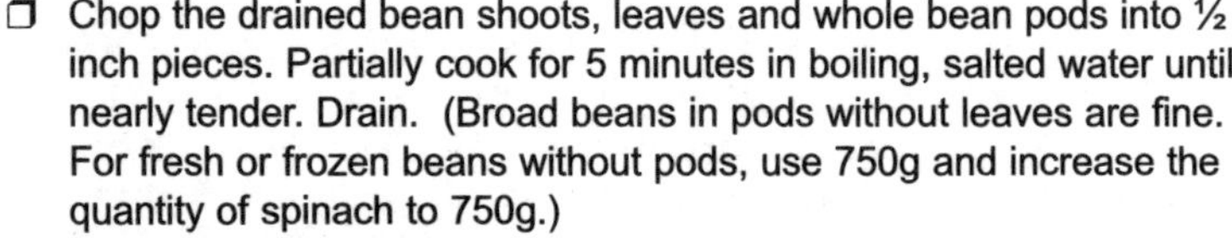

❒ Transfer the partially cooked bean mixture into an open frying pan with the spinach, herbs, onions, garlic and olive oil. Cook gently together until everything is soft.

❒ Add salt and pepper to taste.

❒ Beat the eggs in a bowl until they are well mixed.

❒ Add eggs to the frying pan and cook for a minute or two until they are set, stirring the egg mixture well into the vegetables. (NB The eggs will have turned a pale green colour!)

❒ Serve immediately with fresh, crusty bread.

Melitzanasalata (Aubergine Dip) by Sylvia Cook

We love the smoky flavoured version of this light and tasty starter - great for sharing, with crusty Greek bread to dip (for the beer, ouzo or wine) or with a selection of other appetisers at meal time.

My first attempt at this from a Greek recipe book many years ago was fairly tasteless as I didn't burn the aubergine skins, so I asked around and tried a few methods before coming up with this tried and tested version.

Without the mayonnaise or yoghourt (or with low calorie versions) and with vegetable sticks to dip (carrot, celery) instead of bread, this is also a good dish for those watching calories or on low carb diets.

2-3 large aubergines

1 onion finely chopped

2-3 garlic cloves to taste

1 tabsp lemon juice (or white wine vinegar)

4 tabsp virgin olive oil

salt & fresh ground pepper to taste

(optional 2 tabsp mayonnaise or Greek yoghourt)

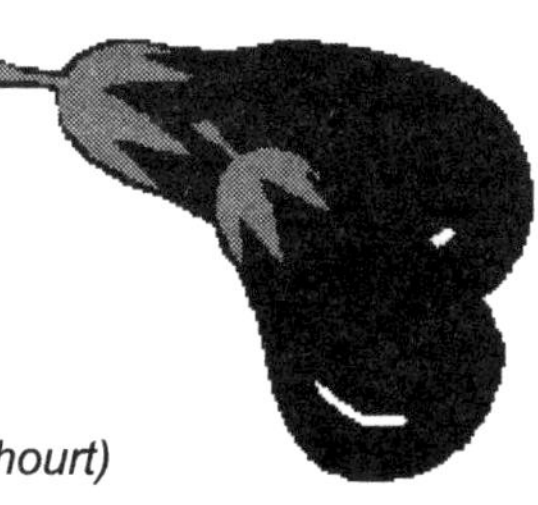

Method

- ❒ Cut the green end off aubergines and place them above a glowing barbecue, turning until all sides are blackened (slightly burnt, not just browned, to achieve the smoky taste) and the aubergine is soft. Alternatively place under grill, turning until all sides are blackened. About 15 mins under a high grill, maybe longer on a barbecue which is the preferred method. Leave to cool.
- ❒ Scoop aubergine flesh out from skins when cool enough to handle. Cut across a few times and drain the juices off. Dab with paper kitchen towels to remove the excess liquid.
- ❒ Blend chopped onion, garlic, lemon juice, oil, seasoning (plus mayonnaise or yoghourt) if desired. Add aubergine and blend again, but not too smooth. Adjust seasoning to taste.
- ❒ Chill for at least 1 hour.
- ❒ Serve sprinkled with chopped parsley and/or a few olives, with crusty bread or vegetable sticks to dip.

Jars of Aubergine Paste found recently (Greek Lyttos brand in Aldi) make an almost as good melitzanasalata in a fraction of the time. They have wine vinegar in as a preservative, so omit the lemon juice.

Fresh Marinated Gavros by Theodore Kyriakou

Reproduced from The Real Greek at Home (see book reviews) with permission.

"On a sailing holiday, moored at Kythira, the chugging of a fishing boat returning to the harbour could be heard early one morning. Fresh anchovies* were the catch. A swimmer was despatched with money rolled inside a plastic film case to intercept the fisherman.

We used sea salt, collected from the deck over the previous 2 weeks of sailing, to cure the anchovies with some good local red wine vinegar and plenty of sliced garlic. After putting the fish aside to marinate, the difficult part was waiting until dinner time to taste them. That's what I love about eating back home: we eat first with our imagination and the anticipation is all." (*Anchovies are preserved gavros or similar small fish, but you will often find 'gavros' translated as 'anchovies' in Greece when they mean fresh fish. Ed.)

Γαύρος Μαρινάτος - Gavros Marinatos (serves 4)

These little fish taste great and teach us the valuable lesson that the dishes that taste best are not necessarily those that require the most skills.

500g (18oz) fresh gavros or substitute small sardines

4 garlic cloves, thinly sliced

250ml (9 fl oz) aged Corinthian red wine vinegar

2 tabsp sea salt

50ml (2 fl oz) extra virgin olive oil

1 bunch flat leaf parsley, finely chopped

Method

- ❒ Behead all the fish. Grasp the top of each backbone, then give it a sharp jerk away from the meat and it will come free bringing the little bones with it. This should leave two fillets of meat linked at the tail end.
- ❒ Wash the fish and place in a single layer in a shallow dish. Arrange the garlic on top. Add enough vinegar to cover and sprinkle with the sea salt.
- ❒ Marinate for 6-24 hours, or until the fillets have turned white and firmed up - this shows that they have been 'cooked' by the vinegar. Personally I don't leave them in the marinade for more than 6 hours, as I like them less vinegary than some.
- ❒ Drain the fish. Rinse in cold water and arrange on a serving plate. Dress with the olive oil and parsley.

Saganaki (Fried Cheese) *by Sylvia Cook*

Saganaki is the name for a particular kind of heavy based skillet, but used alone on menus it usually denotes fried yellow cheese. You will also find 'saganaki prawns' or other 'saganaki' cheeses such as feta on Greek menus.

Different areas have different favourite cheeses for this dish. You will find kefalotyri, ladhotyri, kolios and other local hard yellow cheeses which also grate well for Greek cooking. (We've found kolios in supermarket prepacks of two slices labelled 'for saganaki'.) Try any of these you can find at home, or fresh parmesan or other hard mature cheeses (not cheddar as its high fat content melts too much).

Usually served as a meze dish or appetiser. Coating quantities are approximate, vary according to size of cheese.

2 x ½ cm thick slices of hard Greek cheese (kefalotyri, ladhotyri, etc)

lemon juice

1 tabsp flour

½ teasp oregano

½ teasp paprika

fresh ground black pepper

2 tabsp olive oil

lemon wedges to serve

Method

- ❒ Sprinkle cheese slices with lemon juice
- ❒ Mix flour with rubbed oregano, paprika, fresh ground black pepper on a small plate (to fit cheese size)
- ❒ Heat olive oil in saganaki pan or skillet
- ❒ Place cheese on flour mix and turn over to lightly coat both sides.
- ❒ When oil is hot, fry cheese slices until golden brown, turning once.
- ❒ Serve hot with lemon wedges to squeeze over the saganaki cheese.

Revithia Yiahni (Chick Peas) *by Sylvia Cook*

Typically a Lenten dish when meat is not traditionally eaten, this substantial dish is ideal for vegetarians, but also tastes delicious cooked with pork pieces added. Yiahni (Yιαχνι) is not Yianni as some translations suggest, but the kind of casserole pan it is cooked in.

500 g dried chick peas

2 onions, quartered & sliced

4 spring onions, sliced

3-4 garlic cloves, crushed

400g / 14oz tin tomatoes

small can tomato paste or 4 tabsp tomato puree

4 tabsp olive oil

chopped mint, selino (celery tops), parsley or dill

salt & pepper

(optional 500g diced casserole pork)

Method

- ❒ Soak chick peas in plenty of water overnight or up to 24 hours.
- ❒ Drain and put in tea towel. Rub back & forth to simplify removal of skins.
- ❒ Put peas in large saucepan with plenty of water. Bring to boil & simmer for 2 hours. Top up with hot water if peas become uncovered.
- ❒ When nearly ready, in a separate pan sauté the onions and spring onions until soft. (Add pork pieces if making meat dish and fry until coloured).
- ❒ Add onion (and meat) to chick peas in water, with crushed garlic, chopped tomatoes, tomato puree, seasoning & generous quantity of fresh chopped herbs of your choice.
- ❒ Return to boil & continue simmering 30 mins (1 hour if pork used).
- ❒ Serve sprinkled with fresh chopped flat leaf parsley.

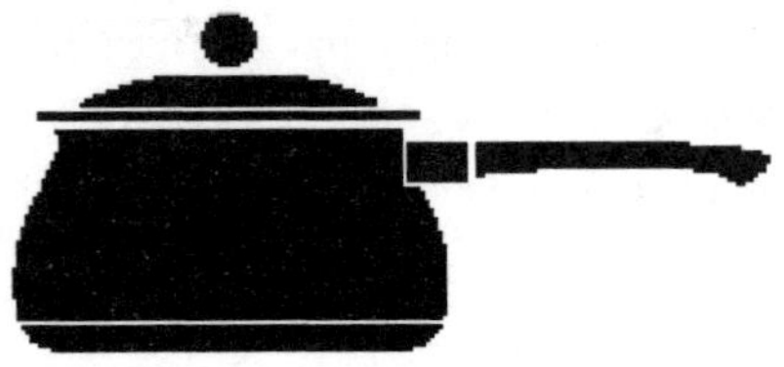

Rizogalo - Greek Rice Pudding by Vivien Eliades

Ριζόγαλο

This is Greek rice pudding, but doesn't really resemble what we know as rice pudding – it's a wonderful rose-flower water flavoured cold dessert that's really refreshing on a hot summer's day. This recipe makes 8 generous servings.

¾ cup ((6oz/170g) white (round grain) rice

4 cups (2 pints/1.2l) milk

½ cup (4oz/110g) sugar

¼ cup (2oz/55g) rice flour or ground rice

1 tbsp rosewater

Method

- ❒ Bring 1½ cups water to a boil in a tightly lidded pot.
- ❒ Add the rice, return to a boil, lower the heat and simmer, covered, for 20 minutes. Turn off the heat.
- ❒ Transfer the rice to a larger cooking pot and gradually stir in the milk and sugar.
- ❒ Slake the rice flour with enough water to make a smooth, creamy liquid and add to the pot. Mix together well, then bring to a boil and simmer for 15 to 20 minutes over a medium heat, stirring frequently to prevent sticking.
- ❒ Once the mixture has thickened, turn off the heat and add the rosewater.
- ❒ Pour into a large dish or individual small dishes and chill completely before serving; it will thicken further as it cools.
- ❒ You can sprinkle chopped nuts on the top (walnuts are good), or serve with fresh or dried fruits.

(Ed - also often made without the rosewater and sprinkled with cinnamon before chilling. Vivien used cows' milk, but rizogalo is often made with goats' milk too.)

Christopher Columbus - A Greek? *by Matt Barrett*

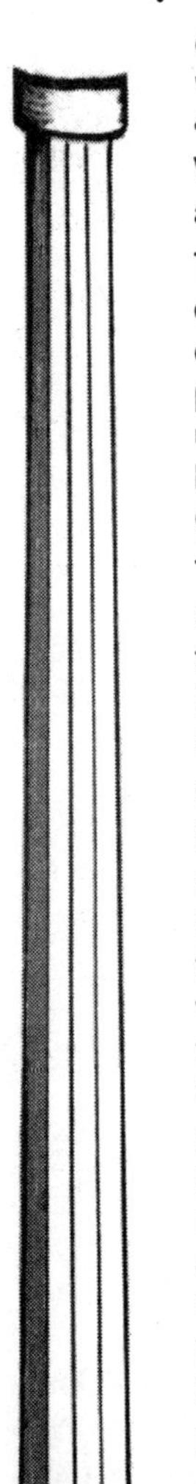

Offered and adapted from Matt Barrett's website history pages, www.ahistoryofgreece.com, where you will find more Greek history articles, or see www.greecetravel.com for all things Greek.

Was Columbus a woolworker from Genoa or a Byzantine Prince and sailor from the island of Chios?

Travelling from Lesvos to Athens by ferry there is time to jump off in Chios where the ship stays for an hour - enough time to eat a souvlaki, have a coffee, wander around a few shops and perhaps buy some mastika (the gum that comes from trees unique to Chios), or visit one of the bookstores. It was here I bought a small book that changed my mind about the origins of Christopher Columbus, the man who discovered America.

The book *'A New Theory Clarifying the Identity of Christopher Columbus: A Byzantine Prince from Chios, Greece'*, was written by Ruth G Durlacher-Wolper, founder and director of the New World Museum and the New World Foundation in San Salvador, Bahamas, where Columbus' ships first landed in 1492.

Much has been written about Christopher Columbus, and yet his past is still shrouded in mystery. We have been told that he came from the Italian city of Genoa and sailed for Isabella and Ferdinand, the king and queen of Spain, after many years of trying to convince them that the world was round (a belief that was uncommon despite the fact that Aristotle had said it over a thousand years before). But most of what we know about Columbus is conjecture and much of his history was written by people who never knew him or had reasons of their own for presenting as a truth something that was just a theory. The story of his being the son of a woolworker from Genoa for example only came from the fact that there was someone named Columbus from Genoa who was a woolworker. In Genoa today you will see monuments and a show of pride in it being the birthplace of Columbus.

But I have been convinced Columbus was from Chios.

The book is carefully researched and even if it does not convince, you will certainly be less sure that all you knew before was the truth. For those who know Byzantine history, you may recall that the Paleologos Dynasty were the Byzantine Emperors who traced their descendants to the Royal House of David and fled to the west after the fall of Constantinople. According to the book, Columbus and his kinsman Colon-the-Younger came to France with the Paleologi and mixed with the royalty of the period, which would make sense. Why would the King and Queen of Spain give him three ships and a lot of money if he was the son of a Genoese woolworker?

Columbus did not say he was from Genoa, but 'from the Republic of Genoa', something much different. The island of Chios was part of the Republic of Genoa in his time. The name Columbus is carved above many doors in the villages of Pirgi and Cimbori and a priest with that name traces his ancestry on the island back over 600 years. There are also many Genoese families who trace their ancestry back to Chios. Also Columbus wrote about gum-mastic (mastika) which comes only from Chios.

The book presents many convincing arguments and in the end summarises them with 22 'facts contributing to the clarification of Columbus' identity'. Among the most interesting:

Columbus signature *'Xro-Ferens'* Christophoros is Greek-Latin or Byzantine, and he spelled Chios with a Greek 'X'.

Columbus named Cape Maysi, Cuba using the Greek words for the first and last letters of the Greek alphabet - Alpha and Omega.

Columbus never asked Italy for ships, or aid for food and shelter when he needed help. If he was from Genoa then why not? Nor does he ever mention the Columbo family of Genoa to whom historians say he was related. He neither spoke nor read Italian. In his favourite book 'Imago Mundi' by Cardinal Pierre d'Ailly he wrote in the margins in Greek.

Columbus was called Genoese because he dressed in the Genoese fashion, as would other wealthy Chiots. He signed his name 'Columbus de terra Rubra' which means of the red earth. The Mastic area of Chios was known for its red coloured earth. He banked at St. George in Genoa along with others from colonies such as Chios.

Columbus kept two logs on his journey, one real and one false. The true log used the measurements in Greek leagues and the false in Roman. The author used the real logs and measurements to reconstruct Columbus' dis-

covery of the island of San Salvador, which cleared up many discrepancies in the geography of the area.

The Colombo family of Genoa were illiterate and the Genoese Christophoro was a woolweaver. For this person to acquire the learning, experience and spirituality that Columbus had to convince a foreign king and queen to entrust a small navy and a fortune to him doesn't seem probable. Maybe in today's America a poor son of a common garment worker can grow up to become president but in the Europe of the 15th century it is unlikely he could make Captain, much less Admiral in command of a fleet. It is more likely that for Columbus to have an audience with a king and queen he would have been royal himself or have some pretty good connections.

Columbus' son Ferdinand wrote that his ancestors always followed the sea. Unless the Columbo family of Genoa had a long history of being ships tailors then they were not related. Although living in Genoa at the time that Ferdinand was writing about his father, they are not even mentioned, nor are they mentioned in Columbus' Will.

I am convinced that Columbus was not a woolworker struck by God like Joan of Arc and instantly filled with knowledge of navigation, philosophy, astronomy, psychology, languages and the power to convince kings to give him whatever he wanted. This was a man with a lifetime of education, culture, experience and inspiration who had a sense of his own destiny and the drive to fulfil it.

In the book we discover that not only was Columbus connected with the Paleologos family but many of his friends were Greek too. Perhaps this is the most convincing argument for me. Anyone knowing Greeks in exile will be aware that they are a tight group that trust each other and spend much time together, bound by that thread of Hellenism. As convincing as all the other arguments, (and there are many in this small book), the fact that his peer group was Greek, proves to me that Christopher Columbus was not the son of an itinerant Genoese woolworker, but a Byzantine prince from Chios who came from a life of enlightened education and spiritual aspirations, and as an islander, combined it with his love of the sea.

The islanders from Chios have long been known for their sea skills and the high number of sea-captains and ship owners from there. If Columbus was Greek then Chios is the most likely island he would be from. With its Genoese architecture still in evidence, its seafaring history, the heroic exploits of the people of Chios and evidence that Chios was the birthplace of Homer, where else would he be from?

Are you convinced? I am. Columbus was a Greek.

Gortys - A Tale of Two Millennia *by Terry Cook*

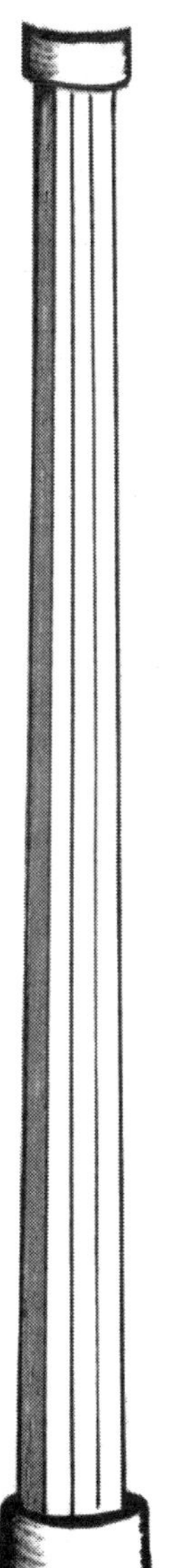

Crete boasts many interesting places to visit and glimpse into the ancient history of the island, notably Knossos, Phaistos, Zakros and Malia. The period of Minoan civilisation is well documented. It is held by some that for much of the (approx) 3,500 years after the demise of the Minoans and the destruction of what many considered the first great civilisation of the Aegean, Crete was in a back-water of Hellenic history.

Certainly, many of the city-states spent more time feuding with each other rather than cultivating a place in the development of Hellenic culture. The only occasions when they came together and acted as one people were in the face of a larger threat from outside forces. Many feel there is, however, still a single Cretan 'persona' despite the disparate peoples each vying for their own destiny on this, the largest island of Greece.

There is a place, however, in the southern part of Central Crete nearly 50 km below Iraklion and Knossos, and 10 km east of Phaestos, which seems to have carved out its very own and quite unique chapter in the annals of history. Ancient Gortys (also known as Gortyn or Gortyna) developed, flourished, adapted to changing times, and then disappeared - all but some monuments in stone, part excavated but many still waiting to give up their story of a colourful past.

Mythology stakes a claim to this area as the love-nest of Zeus and Europa *(see next article)*, and there are traces of habitation from the end of the Neolithic or Stone Age, about 3,000 BC. The name Gortys comes from a grandson of Zeus, a hero and nephew of King Minos. For an as yet undiscovered reason, Gortyna is also the name of a genus of the moth species, commonly known as the Artichoke Moth because it particularly likes to devastate artichokes. Perhaps the clue is in the way Gortys learned to adapt itself to changing times and environment to make the most of its chances. Albeit, in the end it was snuffed out almost without trace.

Gortys appears to have started to flourish in the late Minoan period or Bronze Age, and apparently because it was on the south side of the island, it was not as devastated by the Thira explosion which annihilated much of Crete. Remains of a villa and shrine have been found at Kamia near the town of Metropolis in the south-west and from about 950 BC the an-

cient city was growing on an acropolis further north up the Litheos River. Walled and fortified, it also enclosed the site of an Archaic Temple to Athena built in the 7th century BC. Whether the Dorian invasions from the north of Greece were the catalyst for this development, or the result of new settlers choosing the land least destroyed by recent events, we cannot tell. The Spartan-like Dorian influence, however, played an important role in Gortys' capacity to survive and grow.

At first, joining forces with mighty Knossos, the rest of Crete was subdued under their power, but once unity was achieved, the allies became enemies and spent their time fighting each other in order to gain supremacy over the whole area. As Gortys grew in power and influence, cultivating trade with mainland Greece and Egypt, the city began to spread eastwards from the valley – a theatre was built on the banks of the Litheos and another Temple erected, this time to Pythian Apollo on the eastern side. No doubt life in 'Classical Age' Gortys was good – if you were a member of the Dorian citizen class that is. Probably housed in some kind of Public Assembly Building, the famous Gortyn Law Code, discovered engraved on stones dated to early 5th century BC, described much of what life was like in family, property, inheritance, marriage and divorce rights. The laws show a marked difference in the way you were dealt with according to your position in society. The serfs (probably the indigenous Minoans) came off worse than the ruling Dorians, but if you were a slave, you really got a raw deal.

Estimates as to the population of the city at this time vary anything from 30,000 to 300,000 people, as do the thoughts on where the main sources of their wealth and prosperity were. It would appear that they were not farmers, but traders they certainly were, and accomplished commercial entrepreneurs. But like many 'successful' businessmen, maybe not all their profits came from legal activities! Piracy from their base harbour on the coast at Levin (modern day Lendas), was a common supplement to the wealth of Gortynians. The 600 lines or so of the Law Code which survive deal mostly with civil law. Apart from 'rape', for which, rather disturbingly, the rapist would just be fined, there is little on criminal law. Maybe other crime was unheard of, or maybe it was summarily dealt with by the authorities without recourse to the niceties of a judicial system. Or maybe those in charge were the biggest criminals of all!

Perhaps though, a more probable explanation is that they were lost in an earthquake which destroyed the Hellenistic structure, The Forum, used for the purpose of a courtroom. Those tablets covering criminal law and other civil matters not included in the surviving specimens may have been either broken beyond recognition or buried under tons of rubble. When the Roman emperor Trajan ordered the Odeion music school to be built on the same site around 100 AD, parts of the old building were re-used, or at least those stones containing the Law Code, to preserve something of the history of the city.

During the third century BC at a time when Gortys was friends with Knossos, the city of Phaistos was conquered and later destroyed, as was the town of Lyttos to the east, but as time went on the tide of prosperity began to turn for all of Crete. The new world power of the Romans was looming on the horizon, and after one abortive attempt, Crete eventually fell around 68 BC. Unlike many of their neighbours, however, the wily Gortynians could see the inevitable writing on the wall, and instead of opposing the conquering armies, made a pact with them and fought with them against the more rebellious elements elsewhere on the island. Thus they ensured not only that Gortys was not destroyed as were many other cities, but also its future was established as the capital of the Roman province which included Crete and Cyrene, part of North Africa.

Prosperity and security grasped with both hands, the new era brought with it massive development which included many public works any modern-day city would be proud of. In the two hundred years that followed a grand Praetorium was built, with an administrative centre and private quarters for the Roman Proconsul. An aqueduct was constructed to bring water from Zaros up in the hills to provide not only for the drinking requirements of the growing city, but also a public baths and courtyard with fountains, together with the Nymphaeum where statues of nymphs were housed. The Odeion mentioned above was part of the Romans' desire to promote art and music of the highest quality, and a new amphitheatre and sports stadium in the south-east and yet another theatre completed the municipal facilities, now second to none in the whole of Greece. In addition to all this, there was a new temple area immediately to the north of the Praetorium dedicated to the cults of the Egyptian deities such as Isis, Serapis and

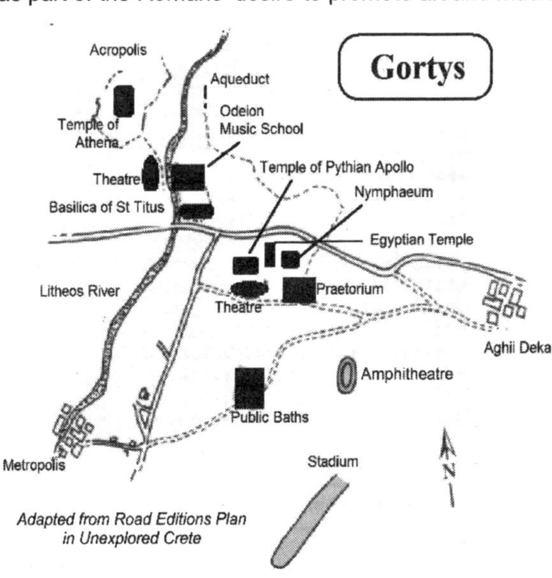

Adapted from Road Editions Plan in Unexplored Crete

Anubis. The rectangular enclosure included a short stairway down to the 'Nilometer' – a symbolic area where the flooding of the River Nile in Egypt was simulated for local worshippers.

The hustle and bustle of modern city life in cosmopolitan Gortys drew people like a magnet from all over this part of the Roman Empire and from overseas, and made this the most important town in all of Crete at this time. And so the next phase of Gortys' metaphorsis took place, although slowly at first. A sizeable Jewish population had become established in the city, and it is recorded that on a return visit to Jerusalem for a Passover Feast, a number of them were converted to a new religion, later known as Christianity. The Apostle Paul was enticed to visit Gortys on a missionary journey and left his disciple Titus, behind to develop the growing church there.

It would appear the evangelical zeal of these early converts was quite infectious, and Gortys became the main centre for the growth of the Christian Church in Crete. The Roman authorities, as elsewhere in their domains, were not in favour of this departure from the religious traditions their empire had been built on. So ferocious was their opposition on occasions that under the persecution of Emperor Decius around 250 AD, 10 prominent Cretan Christians were martyred at a spot to the west where the village of Ag. Deka stands today. The new religious movement could not be stopped by this, and by 500 AD the most important Christian basilica in Crete was built not far from the Odeion on the banks of the river – it was dedicated to the first bishop and named Ag. Titus in his honour. The remains of the building can be seen today, as can the influence of the church in the development of Cretan life beyond the Romans, and into the Byzantine era.

Many influential Bishops followed in the path of Titus and in the early 9th century AD when the island was taken by the Arabs, Archbishop Cyril was slain for refusing to apostatise. Maybe the Christian influence was too entrenched to accept life under Muslim control and this time Gortys' ability to adapt with the times came to an abrupt halt. Gortys was so completely destroyed that it never rose from its ruins. One commentator suggests that it was Zeus who was angry that the worship of his gods had been overturned in favour of another god. He was so displeased that the place of his love-affair with Europa had been desecrated that he cast one almighty Thunderbolt (in the form of the Saracen invaders) to destroy the city forever – as only Zeus knew how!

From its earliest beginnings and two millennia of prosperity and influence, changing and adapting with the passing times, Gortys is now no more than another archaeological treasure trove, waiting for someone to lift the lid, interpret what they find and fill in the gaps in our knowledge of this ancient city.

Zeus & The Naming of Europe *by Terry Cook*

An interesting thing about Greek mythology and the Greek gods is that the stories are always practical and simple. The myths explained what the ancient Greeks saw around them in a way everyone could understand. If someone had a question about life or the universe, there would be a ready explanation in language even the children could relate to. Sometimes, one story seemed to wrap up the answers to several problems all in one go. Possibly because with the constant telling of each myth, they rolled into mega-myths, solving life's queries at a stroke. If only it was that easy!

Take Zeus for example, the daddy of all the gods, but he had to work hard at it - all those wives and all those mistresses, both mortal and divine. He also had to keep everything in the skies in order, check that his subjects and the lesser gods were all behaving themselves and doing what had to be done .... AND he had to try and keep on the good side of his main wife (and sister) Hera, who really knew how to give him a hard time.

You wouldn't have thought he had much time to just sit around enjoying himself, but maybe he would have said it was work anyway, keeping a watchful eye on everything and everyone. That is where one of those mega-myths started one day. It explains in one story the origin of the people of Crete, how Europe got its name, why certain stars are in the heavens, etc, etc - and why he was so good at his job and deserving of the benefits and perks he seemed to constantly enjoy.

It started with a dream. The beautiful young princess Europa (Εύροπε) was the daughter of Agenor, king of Sidon in Phoenicia (now part of Lebanon). One night just before dawn, she dreamt that two continents in the shape of women were fighting over her. Asia claimed the maiden should be hers, since that was where she was born and lived. The other (as yet without a name) argued that birthplace didn't count for a lot and as Zeus needed to establish his domain he would give Europa to her continent.

So troubled by this dream was the young princess that when she awoke she gathered her dearest friends around her and made for the peaceful meadow by the seashore to calm her spirit. The girls picked the beautiful flowers and inhaled the sweet scent of the blooms, and soon began to relax in the early morning stillness. But Zeus was up early too, and saw this enchanting

group from his heavenly bed - at once falling madly in love with the beautiful Europa.

Some say Aphrodite had stirred Cupid to practise with his arrows and caught old Zeus unawares, but who knows?

Anyway, aware he couldn't just show up as himself on this distant shore and use one of his famous chat-up lines, he changed himself into a very handsome white bull, and strolled across the meadow to mingle with his prey. So gentle, smelling so sweet and lowing so melodiously, the girls were soon caressing him, tying garlands around his neck, and eventually decided to climb on his back to let him take them for a ride. First up was Europa, and take her for a ride is exactly what Zeus did. He bounded off towards the sea, before any of the others could mount him, and plunged into the waves, his precious cargo screaming with dread.

Once swimming out into the depths of the ocean, he was joined by the strange sea-gods, the Nereids on dolphins' backs, Tritons blowing their horns and even Poseidon himself, to guide the abductor and his prize to a safe haven far away. But not too far. It was the shores of the island of Crete where Zeus landed with his catch, and having changed back into his normal image, Europa actually breathed a sigh of relief, for she knew only a god could have made so daring and difficult a journey as they had just experienced. It would seem she was quite happy with her new lot, and the couple wasted no time in producing three fine sons - Minos, Rhadamanthus and Aeacus (or Sarpedon).

Legend has it that the place chosen for consummation of this affair was an arbour of platanos trees by a spring close to Gortys. It is said they never lost their leaves and one of the plane trees is still thriving today. Others say the affair was conducted near Diktaion in the mountains where Zeus was reared. In any event, it was soon time for Zeus to resume his other duties and left Europa with three gifts to remember him by: a Talos to protect the island of Crete, a golden dog and a quiver of arrows which never missed their mark. He also placed an image of the bull (Tauros) in the heavens as a constant reminder of his love, and of course that second continent from Europa's dream got its name as a lasting memorial.

Finally to combine the myth with history, king Asterius of Crete kind-heartedly took on the gentle Phoenician damsel with her three strapping babies, and the Minoan dynasty was born. That infusion of Phoenician blood, they say, was the beginning of the early Cretan people.

Certainly the imagery has found itself a lasting place in our culture. There are many famous paintings of the 'Abduction of Europa' and statues too, even outside the European Council building in Brussels. The pair also feature on the Greek two Euro coin, a German phone-card and a British stamp commemorating the European Parliament in 1984. Perhaps it really was Zeus who was responsible for founding the Cretan people and the continent of Europe.

Mythology in Modern Language *by Terry Cook*

Pan, whose name gave rise to 'panic' and the prefix 'pan' meaning 'all', wasn't the only mythological character to give his name to modern words in every day Greek and English. (See Mythology in The Greek-o-File Volume 3). These other mythological characters have also found a place in modern English.

Aphrodite – the goddess of erotic love and marriage – gives us ***aphrodisiac***, a food or drug that excites erotic desires.

Chronus – the Greek god of time, in whose honour an annual festival was held called 'chronia', (χρόνια - modern Greek for years), and from which we get all the time-related words beginning with chron- such as ***chronology***, a list of things in the order of their happening.

Gordius – a mythological peasant who was chosen by the Phrygians to be their king on the instruction of an oracle. In gratitude he dedicated his ox-cart to Zeus, securing it with a knot no one could undo. To prove his supremacy over all Asia, Alexander the Great cut it with his sword, giving us the expression to 'cut the ***Gordian knot***' meaning to solve a problem or end a dispute in a very direct manner.

Helios – Greek god of the sun, gave us words like ***heliotherapy*** for all you sun-bathers, or ***heliograph***, an instrument for sending messages (***heliograms***) by flashes of light.

Muse – (modern Greek μούσα) a goddess who inspired learning or the arts. There were nine muses, the daughters of Zeus and Mnemosyne, and today we ***muse*** upon something when we meditate or think reflectively to gain inspiration, and a ***museum*** (from the Greek μουσέιον – the Temple of the Muses) is a place to reflect upon the history of life in all its forms.

Nemesis – the goddess of justice and vengeance gives us an identical word meaning retribution or punishment for deeds of evil.

Sirens – mythological sea nymphs who by their enchanting song lured sailors onto the rocks around their island, thus destroying them. Today a ***siren*** gives out a loud wailing noise to warn of imminent danger.

It's Well Worth Trying *by Sylvia Hodges*

I was tucking into a plate of 'payeethakia' (παϊδάκια - lamb chops) when the waiter brought a plate of prawns. *"Garethes"* he said as he put them in the middle of the table. We both looked at him in surprise. As he walked off my husband asked me if I had ordered these. I was as amazed as he was but as I had ordered in Greek anything could happen - and often does.

I had learned, I thought, the word for 'portion' (μερίδα) - had I confused it with shrimps (γαρίδες)? Things like this are always happening. We just put it down to another Greek experience, like the time a bacardi and coke arrived whilst we were halfway through our 'kotopoulo' (κοτόπουλο - chicken) - I had actually asked for a 'boukali' (μποκάλι - bottle) of coke but perhaps my Yorkshire accent had confused proceedings.

I have been interested in 'trying' to speak Greek for many years, ever since the BBC Greek Language and People programme was shown on TV and I watched every episode and bought the accompanying book. If only they would show it again, or do something similar.

On Kefalonia some time back, our guidebook had said that if we wanted to look at the English Cemetery we should knock on the cottage door next to the locked gates. When we did this an old man emerged. We did the appropriate gesture for 'open the gate please' but as he was having his lunch he invited us in to wait for him. He introduced his wife and gestured for us to sit at his table. His wife brought cloudy red wine and he cut off slabs of cheese for us to share. It seemed a very poor household so we didn't like to take his food, but he insisted. During the next half hour we learned that he had made the wine from the fruit of the vine shading his patio and their children lived in 'Americana' and 'Avstralia' (his wife said as she showed us photographs). We felt quite sad for the old couple living in simple circumstances with their children abroad, but I suppose this has happened to many parents in Greece. They were so proud of their family. All in all a lovely experience but unfortunately the best we could say in Greek was *"efharisto"* (ευχαριστώ - thankyou) for the hospitality. As I left their cottage that day I decided I would find an evening class and really try to learn more.

I was fortunate to find a class locally and enjoyed talking to my classmates about holidays in Greece as much as actually learning the language. I won't say it was easy but we were not made to feel stupid if we didn't understand the words and the homework wasn't too hard. Twenty of us started but at the end of the first year just 12 of us were left. We were all still keen so we joined for year two, after which our teacher returned to her hometown in Cyprus - so that was that.

I really like the reaction we get in Greece, mostly astonishment that we try to speak their language - even though we don't always get it right. The funniest experience of getting it WRONG was when we entered an old Greek cafébar on Naxos. It was very small, very dark, and full of locals. Being Greeks they all stared at us when we entered. The owner shouted over to us *"Hello, where are you from?"* (in English). My husband Paul (6ft and 15 stone) said in a very loud voice *"Imai Angleetha"* to which the locals roared with laughter. Paul looked at me and asked if he said it wrong. *"Yes"* I said *"you actually said you were an English WOMAN".* We all laughed together. He should have said *"Imai Anglos"* (I'm an English man). Somebody sent over a carafe of wine and we made many friends. Much later we stumbled bleary eyed outside so pleased that we had had such an experience - and all because we had tried.

I can recommend having a go at learning Greek to anyone who hasn't tried it yet. The phrases I found most useful at the beginning were:-

What is your name? *Posas lene?* Πως σας λένε;

Where are you from? *Apo poo esastay?* Από πού είσαστε;

What do you call this in Greek? *Pos legetay sta elinika?* Πως λέγεται στα Ελληνικά;

I'm still interested in learning more, now on Year 3 with another group. It will all come in useful when I retire and move to Greece - in my dreams!!!

There's Always a Way *by David Brooker*

Staying at Skala Mystegna, Lesvos on holiday a few years back, we decided to go to the village to get some supplies. As we turned up through the olive groves there was a loud *"KALIMERA!"* from the other side of a metal gate into a garden. We returned the greeting and continued on our way.

When we went into the grocery shop the lady there indicated that her husband had gone to market to get more stock, and that she did not speak much English, but as we did not speak much Greek we couldn't understand why she was apologising to us. Anyway, by sign language we managed to order what we wanted, including a piece of cheese, the size of which was communicated by moving the knife around until we got the required size wedge. Order completed, we waited while the lady calculated the total cost, which she wrote on a piece of paper.

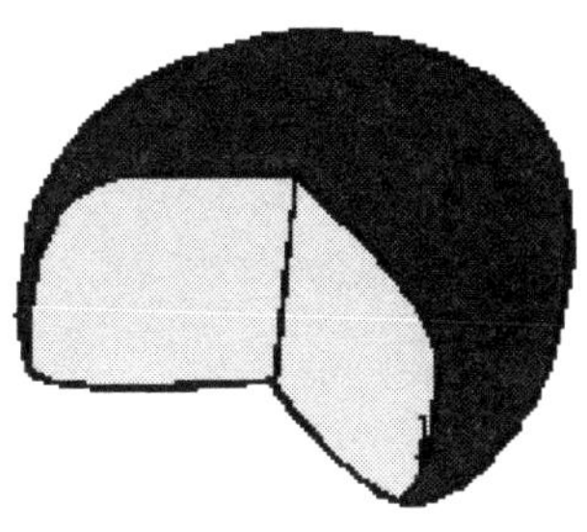

OUCH! A quick conversion of Drachmae to Pounds Sterling, indicated that we had probably purchased their entire stock of cheese. Well it was a lot of money anyway. We said it was too much, and a look of complete bafflement crossed her face. Neither of us was in a position to go into the intricacies of the mathematics involved, so - *impasse*.

At this moment a man passed by (maybe the postman). He was immediately called in to give assistance. The conversation started amicably enough, but gradually the voices got louder until we were not sure whether they were going to come to blows or whether they were just emphasising various points to each other. We were completely ignored. This went on for about five minutes, then the postman leaned out of the shop door and called in another lady from the road outside - to act as arbitrator, or maybe to apply her mathematical knowledge! However in a short time, the cacophony of the three voices shouting in Greek was horrendous.

By now we were cowering in the corner, wondering if we should creep out and leave them to it. At this point a young lad of about 10 yrs came into the shop and quietly sat down on the chair provided for customers. He didn't say a word, just sat there quietly waiting. A few minutes later the shouting suddenly stopped and everyone looked at him. The lady behind the counter produced the piece of paper and presumably explained the problem to him. With pencil in hand and tongue sticking out of the corner of his mouth he quickly solved the problem. We thanked him profusely, paid our bill (roughly 10% of the previous charge) and staggered out of the shop clutching our sides. Out of earshot, we collapsed, laughing.

Later we reached the point near the beach where we had received the morning greeting. There was a bang on the gate and a hand gestured at us through an open panel. We walked over. The gate didn't open, nothing was said, but the hands appeared again offering a large pile of fruit, including a small melon. We thanked the donor very much. We didn't see his face, just his hands, and although we passed that way many times during the holiday we never heard or saw anyone in the garden again.

Greek Delights *by Jackie Bott*

In search of Daphne - We went into a backstreet shop (very much a back-street, nearly in the back of beyond) in search of some bay leaves to take home. Herbs bought in Greece are always so much bigger, better, and cheaper than in UK. We started having an unsuccessful look around when a lady appeared from the bowels of the shop. We hopefully said *"Bay Leaves?" "Eh?"'* she replied. *"Bay Leaves?"* we said again. *"Ah, ne"'* she said, and disappeared back into the depths, returning a minute later, proudly clutching a bottle of Baileys. "*Ohi, efharisto*" we said, "*Bay Leaves*".

Fumbling in my handbag, I found a biro and an old till receipt, on which I did my best attempt at a sketch of a bay leaf. *"'Ah, ne, ne, ne"'* she said, and hotfooted out again, returning with a huge grin and a small box of bay leaves. *"Daphne, Daphne"'* she said, which turned out to be Greek for bay leaves. So excited was I at finding a new supply, we promptly bought several boxes of huge *daphne*s, for which we paid the princely sum of €1 each.

Dining out - Fancying something different from salad to start our meal one night, we ordered *'Taramasalata'* - a large plate of tomato salad arrived. Never mind, pleasantly replete, but we decided to finish the meal with some macaroons. We were presented with a large bowl of macaroni.

We invariably study each menu in great depth before ordering, as we like to sample as many different things as possible, and local specialities. Some translations are mildly amusing, others have had us a bit stumped :

Spagetti with winced meat

Octapus vinegary

Lamp in earthen with vegetables and kind of hard cheese

Roasted entrails

Scrabbled eggs

Handburger with setchup / cetsup

Fried aborigine

We still ponder about *"All our fish is caught by local fishermen, except that which is frozen"*, which accounted for 7 out of 8 dishes offered.

And all to be accompanied by some *'bulked retsina'* or *'pubic wine'*.

More Greek Delights *from Janet Rodwell*

Here are a couple of photographs taken on our travels recently which may amuse you. The 'inkstand' is on offer at a little café bar in Andissa, Lesvos. Next time you are passing you may like to try one. I'm afraid we weren't able to pluck up the courage to sample it, thinking we might go 'blue in the face'.

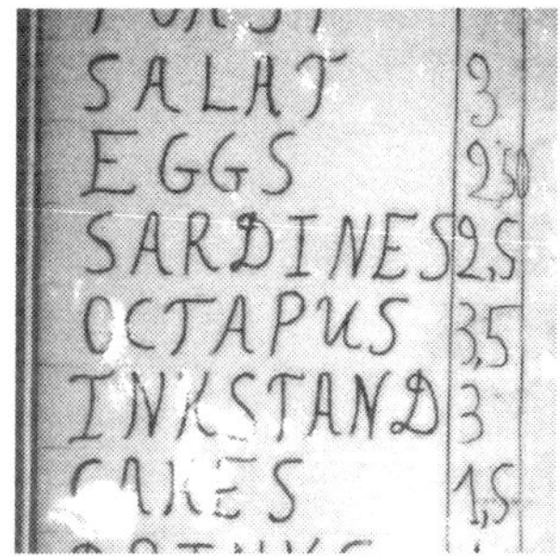

Sawed fish
Red snapper
Perch
Cod
Calamari

The other 'gaff' - *sawed* fish - may have amused you before. It is a fairly common error, along with *lamp* for lamb. Unfortunately I don't have a photograph of another amusing item on a menu seen in Argos on the Peloponnese a couple of years ago. In Greek you had to pay a 'κούβερ' (cover) charge, in English you were charged a 'bedspread'!

As other readers have pointed out, it's not all one-sided. I've made a few blunders myself whilst trying out the Greek language. In Sarando's kafeneion in Anaxos, Lesvos I tried to tell them about my mule trek that day. I couldn't get my tongue round a way to say mule-trekking and I tried to tell them, much to their amusement, that I had been riding a mule ... or so I thought. Μουλάρι (moo-la-ri) is the Greek word for mule, but I told them I had been riding a lettuce 'μαρούλι' (ma-roo-li). Can you image what a Greek waiter would have thought if I had ordered a dish of mule!

And finally ....

Beach only available on Sundays? gambling on good weather? or what?

photographed by Vivien Eliades

Book Reviews

Reviews by Sylvia Cook (except where indicated)

Farewell to Salonica by Leon Sciaky

Publisher: Paul Dry Books Inc ISBN 1-58988-002-1 £12.99*

Leon Sciaky was brought up in the Salonika (Thessalonika) of the Ottoman Empire at the turn of the 20th century. In his early years it was a happy place for a 'Spanish Jewish' merchant's son, where people of different national and religious backgrounds lived side by side. As more modern western ways influenced the people and political tensions started to boil, it marked the beginning of the end of an era. Leon's story is very personal, painting an endearing picture of his family life, and yet in explaining the historical backdrop it also brings alive a period of Macedonian history before it was reunited with Greece. Leon moved with his father to America in 1915 and first published this book, subtitled 'City at the Crossroads' in 1946. This edition published 2003 is just as fascinating and readable today.

Aristo's Family by Raymond Nickford

Publisher: Haunted Books ISBN 0-9546963-0-1 £8.99*

Pavlos lives with and is schooled by his father, Aristos, in a Cyprus museum - an unusual atmosphere for a strange upbringing that has already caused his English mother to walk out. Aristos is obsessed by tracing and belonging to his family, even though told they were all burnt and left unidentifiable during the Turkish invasion. As Pavlos tries to get closer to his own father he gets embroiled in the sinister research into his 'family'. Quite spooky at times.

The Leaden-Sky Years of World War II by Kimon Farantakis

Publisher: Efstathiadis ISBN960-226-609-0 £5.50*

The original notes for this book were a diary of the personal experiences of a 13 year old boy living in NW Crete during the German occupation, written up nearly 50 years later and published first in Greek. Translated by P Davis Seaman, his memories of poverty and atrocities are tempered with personal anecdotes, even some humour and the optimism of a young boy living in a strong social environment.

*above books marked * available from Gazelle*

The Late Night News by Petros Markaris

Publisher: Harvill Press ISBN 1-843-43169-6, £10.99

I really enjoyed reading this lively detective story set in Athens, translated well from the Greek by David Connolly. Detective Inspector Haritos (a kind of Greek version of David Jason's Frost) investigates a string of murders - an Albanian couple, then two TV journalists - coping with the media, battling against authority and corrupt influences, risking suspension from his job as he investigates 'important' people to finally solve the mystery, save his good name and expose other crimes along the way. It shows some interesting insights to public and private life in Athens.

Vignettes of Modern Greece by Melissa Orme-Marmarelis

Publisher: Cosmos Publishing Co Inc. ISBN 1-932455-09-4 •15.60 available from www.greeceinprint.com

This book of anecdotes, observations and personal experiences over 15 years of visits to Eresos, Lesvos and Athens was of particular interest to me. It shows a different side of the Greek village we know. The American author met and married one of the Greek 'diaspora' whose family originally came from Eresos and who visit in the summer along with other former Eresians who now live in Athens and return annually to their summer playground at Skala Eresou. She is adopted into a circle of family and Greek friends, joining in family parties, learning about traditions and life on Lesvos in harder times. Even though her mother-in-law's family were rich in comparison to most villagers, the men often squandered their money leaving their wives to struggle, or political views led to imprisonment or even execution. In the final year of the book they are able to spend a longer period in Greece, mostly in Athens, with their twin 4 year old sons who have inherited a love of Greece, but who also seem to eat vast numbers of ice creams! There must be similar communities of emigrants from many Greek island villages who left for a better life or education in Athens or around the world, but who keep in touch and return regularly to their roots.

Suggested by subscriber Carolyn Hadden

Greece - A Traveller's Literary Companion Edited by Artemis Leontis

Publisher: Whereabouts Press ISBN 1-883513-04-9 £12.50*

This collection of 24 short stories and essays translated from 20th century Greek writers is organised by region, allowing you to explore Greece through the eyes of its people. Some are travellers' musings, most are works of fiction, but the settings are real and the editor's selections give a varied insight to the cultural background of mainland and island Greeks. Some are a little heavy, others delightful or thought provoking.

A few of my favourites: A short story of a young Symi girl's experience on her first day at an Athens School, comparing it with her small island school; A youth cuts corners when writing letters for their illiterate maid to her family and discovers the impact of his omisssions when he later meets them;

A Thracian family tend a Turkish youth's grave for as long as they are able and keep in touch with his family after they must move out in the1920's. In another story was an alternative explanation for a Five F's taverna name *(Arthur Deeks article p.81)* - **Φ**ίλος, **φ**έρει **φ**ίλοι, **φ**άγουν και **φ**εύγουν (friend, brings friends, they eat and leave).

Good Beach Guides - Ionian Islands by Mike Arran

Publisher: Efstathiadis ISBN 960-22661-04 (Corfu/Paxos/Parga) -12 (Zakynthos) -20 (Cephalonia/Ithaca/Lefkas/Meganissi) £7.50 ea*

If visiting beaches is an essential part of your Greek holiday then these could be the most approriate guide books for you. They include a short background, location style and facilities of the main resorts plus clearly laid out, comprehensive details of island beaches (description, location guide, good colour photographs, food & beach facilities, shade, parking, mooring, even suitability for disabled visitors) to help you ensure your planned destination suits your style of holiday. The points system used may not award most stars to your kind of beach, but the descriptions and photographs tell you enough to know which are right for you. Beaches are listed alphabetically with no map showing those included, so you need to look at them all to see which are near to your destination.

The Real Greek at Home *by Theodore Kyriakou & Charles Campion*

Publisher: Mitchell Beazley ISBM 1-8400-851-2 £20

More than just a cookbook of dishes that real Greeks eat at home, this is a wonderful colourful insight to the role of food in a Greek home, seen through the eyes of a Greek lad who now lives in London and is chef/proprietor of The Real Greek restaurant. The anecdotes and background comments at the start of each chapter and before each recipe add to the enjoyment - and show that mum's cooking and words of wisdom reigned supreme in the Kyriakou household! It is a delight to read with mouthwatering colour pictures of food and Greek scenes that make you itch to recreate the simple pleasures of the Greek food Theodore enjoyed as a child. Recipes are clearly explained and those I have tested to date have certainly not dissappointed. A simple example in the recipe section explains clearly how to prepare marinated 'gavros' - it's easy when you know how!

Beginner's Greek *by Elizabeth G. Uhlig*

Publisher: Hippocrene ISBN 0-7818-101-9 £12.99*

Greek evening class teacher Margy Gulland had a quick look at this book for me and declared it passed her initial checks for pet hates. Its structure with grammar and practical examples offers a sensible approach for beginners who want to get started learning Greek. As always, you need to combine this with practice speaking with Greek natives to really learn Greek - but that's the best part.

Greek-English/English Greek Dictionary *by Michael O Kambas*

Publisher: Hippocrene ISBN 0-7818-1002-7 £12.99*

Well laid out with, unusually, both English and Greek pronunciation phonetics for words and their translations (useful when looking up words with Greek speakers) in both sections, and masculine, feminine and neuter endings this pocket dictionary could be useful to both Greek and English speakers. Just 8,000 words (each end) selected for the traveller to Greece, but there were often times when the words I searched for were not included.

** Books available from Gazelle*

The Summer of My Greek Taverna *by Tom Stone*

Publisher: Simon & Schuster ISBN *074324771X* £7.99

After visiting the beautiful island of Patmos last September I finally managed to track down a copy of this book. It started off on a slightly disappointing note, with an air of melancholy about it, (a business problem due to a Greek friend) however it soon emerged into a fascinating book about Greece, with some evocative descriptions of Patmos island (and many other similar Greek islands) and finally became one of the "must read constantly 'til finished" books. Highly recommended, especially to past and future visitors to Patmos. *(Review by **Kathy Boyce**)*

(Another review received later from Dave Evans, so doubly recommended!)

The Mani *by Bob Barrow*

Publisher: Antonis Thomeas Services, Distributed in the UK by Portfolio ISBN 09537517-08 £8.99

My wife and I have completed the Mani 'circuit' on two occasions and can recommend this slim volume (112 pages) written, illustrated and self published by Bob Barrow of Thomeas Travel in Stoupa. It is well worth the few euros, especially to any would be 'deep Mani' explorer. *(Review by **Eric Ball**)*

Plato: Meno & Other Dialogues *translation by Robin Waterfield*

Publisher: Oxford University Press ISBN 019-280425-1 £7.99

Although I have read *about* Greek philosophers before, I confess this is the first book of a more studious nature that I have read on this subject. It is a new translation (with notes) of some of Plato's work after the execution of his revered master, Socrates. I have to say that as a person who enjoys a good discussion I really enjoyed these lively dialogues. They are on the subject of virtue - self control, courage, friendship and the concept of virtue as a whole. Socrates debates, with agile questioning and arguments, the moral concepts, often baffling those he speaks with. This translation was surprisingly fun to read and thought provoking.

Events

Public Holidays in Greece 2006 to 2008

To help you plan ahead, the following dates are Public Holidays in Greece, when banks and public offices are shut. Tourist services tend to stay open 7 days a week. An exception is Easter Sunday when there are very few bars and tavernas open and definitely no shops. Town and village shops are closed by law on Sundays, but tourist shops may be open.

Easter Sunday - Sylvia Cook

Many Public Holiday dates are the same every year, but those in italics marked separately for 2007 and 2008 are moveable feasts, related to the Greek Orthodox Easter dates, which are based on a different calculation to our Easter dates.

	Year 2006	Year 2007	Year 2008
New Year's Day	1 January		
Epiphany	6 January		
Clean (Ash) Monday	*6 March*	*21 February*	*10 March*
Independence Day	25 March		
Good Friday	*21 April*	*6 April*	*25 April*
Easter Sunday	*23 April*	*8 April*	*27 April*
Easter Monday	*24 April*	*9 April*	*28 April*
Labour Day	1 May		
Pentecost	*11 June*	*27 May*	*15 June*
Whit Monday	*12 June*	*28 May*	*16 June*
Assumption Day	15 August		
Ochi Day	28 October		
Christmas Day	25 December		
Second Day of Christmas	26 December		

In addition to the above public holidays there will be local festivals commemorating local events or the name day celebrations for the patron saint of local churches. If you see festivities in progress, do ask around. You will often be encouraged to join in.

For those with internet access, many Greek festivals are listed on Matt Barrett's site - **http://greecetravel.com/holidays/index.html** - worth looking to see what may be happening while you are in Greece.

To find your name day or that of a Greek friend, try The Symi Visitor website: **http://www.symivisitor.com/greek_name_days.htm**

Homage to Vamvakaris *by Ed Emery*

Since 2005 year is the hundredth anniversary of the birth of Markos Vamvakaris, the 'father of Rebetiko' (1905-72), this is an ideal opportunity for a few words in his honour.

The *Autobiography of Vamvakaris* (Papazisi, Athens, 1978) is not universally approved of. He makes no secret of his dope-smoking, his time in prison, his anger at his first wife, and his love for his socially deviant companions in the low-life milieu of Athens and Piraeus.

In some places it reads almost like a religious confession: *"That started me on the steps that lead down into perdition..."* But the confessional aspect is not accompanied by any sense of rejection, who he is and what he has done. This is a man who stands by his life, who is proud of who he is and the music he has made.

Vamvakaris was born in Ano Chora of Syros in May 1905 and died in February 1972. He began his working life as a barefoot kid doing unskilled jobs wherever he could find them. On Syros he worked for butchers, and then for newspaper wholesalers, collecting and distributing newspapers. Later he worked for a fruit and vegetable wholesalers, and later still as a coal heaver – this was the age of steam ships that needed coal to stoke their boilers. It was a hard life, and it immediately took him into contact with all kinds of badness. The life of the *alitis*, the underworld, the dishonour, the card playing, "*kai ola ta kaka tis moiras"* (all the bad things of fate).

But he loved the society in which he lived and moved and this love was reflected in his songs. When he sings "*Oli i rebetes tou dounia, emena m'agapoune*" (all the rebetes in the neighbourhood love me), the sentiment is real and it is reciprocal.

It should be noted, by the way, that when he moves from Syros to Athens, to find work and to find the life of the big city, he often finds himself working in a community of fel-

A Young Markos with friends

low-countrymen ('sympatriotes') from Syros. A migrant community of workers from that same island working-class reality that he left behind him. And what about that other specific of low-life port socialising – the hashish? As Markos explains, "*Kai to chasisi apo tin Syra xekinise stin Palia Ellada*" (the hashish also came to Greece from Syros).

Anyway, as regards his working life, in the early years he turned his hand to many trades - a fact that is reflected in his song "*O Markos o Polytechnitis*" (Markos the Jack of All Trades).

> "*Oles tis technes pou ekana, akouste pou tis leo,*
>
> *tis grafo kai san thymytho, mou erchetai nai klaio.*"
>
> (Listen to me while I sing about all the jobs I have done;
>
> As I write them down, it makes me want to cry.)

In his description of his early years he also offers an insight into the discrimination that he experienced: like many Syrans he was Greek Catholic rather than Greek Orthodox. It is worth noting that the cosmopolitan society of his native Syros also had a measure of French culture and read French newspapers: "*O kosmos tis Syras ixerane gallika*" (the people of Syros knew French).

Before long the young Markos was in trouble. There is a story about him rolling a big rock down on top of someone's roof. It broke through the roof, smashed the tiles, and the police came to his mother's house looking for him. He decided to leave the island, stowed away on a ship and found his way to the port of Piraeus.

In Piraeus his working life was that of a manual labourer. As a heaver of coal, then again in the butchery trade. Working in the slaughterhouses of Piraeus and then moving on to the slaughterhouses of Athens. In between was a period in the army.

In the early 1930s two things happened that shaped his life. First, the boss of the slaughterhouse ordered him to slaughter a calf that Markos and a friend had reared themselves. As Markos tells us himself, the animal cried real tears.

Second, he heard the bouzouki player Nikos Aivaliotis, a one-time friend of his father's. When he heard the *taximia* played by this man he went crazy. He swore that either he would learn to play the instrument, or he would cut off his own hand with a butcher's chopper. He learned to play like a master in the very short space of six months – from listening to the old guys playing in the *tekkedes.* The rest is history.

Greeks are always saying *"Markos was a simple man. He was not a political man."* This is particularly said by Greek musicians who make a vocation

of being non-political. But for me Markos is political in the best sense of the word. From his *Autobiography* you get a tremendous sense of the power and the dignity of the working man. His descriptions of working conditions in the slaughterhouses are of great force, particularly because they are accompanied by a description of the wages and working conditions. These qualities come to the fore in one or two of Markos' own songs.

One in particular, "The Butcher", was written and recorded by Markos in 1935. If you like rebetiko, you may have heard it.

Χασάπη μου, με την ποδιά, που σαν τη δέσεις πίσω
Όταν σε δω, χασάπη μου, τώρα θα ξεψυχήσω
Χασάπη μου, όταν σε δω, τώρα θα ξεψυχήσω

Γυαλίζουν τα θηκάρια σου, στη μέση που τα βάνεις
Με την ποδιά την κόκκινη, εσύ θα με τρελάνεις
Με την ποδιά την κόκκινη, εσύ θα με τρελάνεις.

Αστράφτουν τα μαχαίρια σου, λάμπει και το μασάτι
Λάμπουν τα μαύρα μάτια σου, μαγκίτη μου χασάπη
Λάμπουν τα μαύρα μάτια σου, μαγκίτη μου χασάπη.

Παλεύεις με τα αίματα, μα δεν πονεί η καρδιά σου
Σε αγαπώ, χασάπη μου, μ' αυτή τη λεβεντιά σου
Χασάπη μου, σε αγαπώ, μ' αυτή τη λεβεντιά σου.

(Rhythm: 4/4: Hasapiko)

English Translation:

My butcher man, with your apron tied behind you,
When I see you, my butcher man, I feel like I'm about to faint.
When I see you, my butcher man, I feel like I'm about to faint.

Your knives shine and glisten in the sheaths at your waist.
With your red-stained apron, you'll drive me crazy.
With your red-stained apron, you'll drive me crazy.

Your knives glisten, and the whetstone flashes.
Your eyes flash too, my butcher man, my mangas.
Your eyes flash too, my butcher man, my mangas.

You struggle in blood, but your heart does not grieve.
I love you, my butcher man, in all your manhood.
My butcher man, I love you, in all your manhood.

The song has the familiar 15-syllable line with a mid-point *caesura* (pause)

(8+7). The second line is repeated, sometimes with phrasal reversals. It is a *hasapiko* – and this brings us closer to the truth of the statement that "*hasapiko* is a butcher's dance".

The butcher occupies a unique position in Greek culture. In villages he will be the person responsible for killing animals for meat. He may also operate as the local vet, having knowledge of animals. Inevitably, because he is armed with knives and choppers, he is a figure with social standing and authority. And since Greeks are so passionate about their meat-eating - think of the status associated with killing and roasting multiple lambs at Easter-time - the butcher fulfils an almost liturgical role. Not to mention theatrical, as anyone can attest who has walked through the central meat market in Athens, with the stall-holders shouting their wares and pushing great handfuls of tripes under your nose for you to admire.

In this song the dark and bloody realities of the meat trade contrast with a sparkling and a glistening - the glint of the butcher's knives, the gleam of his whetstone, and of course his flashing black eyes.

So Markos' song is a celebration of that figure, but it is also a big personal statement. He himself had worked for 13 long years in the trade, among the shit and the entrails and the stink. In writing the song he elevates the figure of the butcher to heroic status. A personification of Greek manhood - *leventia* - but more than that, it is a love song. How many love songs take you this close to the *viscera* of the matter? How many songs in the European tradition have their protagonist "struggling in blood" in this way?

These are themes we will be examining further at our 2005 Rebetiko Conference on the Greek island of Hyrdra (13-17 October) in a session entitled "Homage to Vamvakaris". www.geocities.com/HydraGathering.

For readers who know Markos' songs, I hope that this article has provided useful background material; for those who do not, I hope it encourages you to seek out his music.

For authentic Vamvakaris try : ΜΑΡΚΟΣ ΒΑΜΒΑΚΑΡΗΣ, ΦΡΑΓΚΟΣΥΡΙΑΝΗ (Markos Vamvakaris, Frangosyriani) Philips 526 351-2 £15.99. Recorded in 1960's and re-released on this CD in 1994.

Photos from "Rebetika Tragoudhia" by Elias Petropoulos

Music Recommendations *suggested by Trehantiri*

Στη Σκηνή - Οι Καλυτερες Ζωντανες Ηχογραφησεις

(*Sti Skinee* - On Stage) Lyra CD 4974 £15.99

A good mix of well known contemporary Greek singers (not the *'boom-boom'* kind) - 16 live recordings 1991-2000. The second track 'Ας Κρατησουν οι Χοροι' by Dionysis Savvopoulos is the same song he sang as the final number in the closing ceremony of the Athens Olympics where all the performers (and audience) joined in. If you enjoyed the music on that occasion you will enjoy this CD too.

Tribute στον Διονυση Σαββοπουλο - Τραγούδια έγραψα για φίλους

(Tribute to Dionysi Savvopoulo - Songs written for friends)

Polygram CD 538 671-2 £15.99

Prompted by the previous CD, Aki suggested this collection of modern Greek artists performing the songs of Savvopoulou. We certainly enjoyed listening to it. The mix of different artists' styles, all singing a favourite Savvopoulos number make it ideal music for any occasion when you want to feel you are in Greece.

Giorgos Dalaras sings the songs of Markos Vamvakare

Parlophone Minos - EMI 7243590014 £15.99 ***- review from Gordon Burns***

Coincidentally this recommendation and review was received for those who prefer a modern rendition of the old rebetika favourites.

Markos Vamvakaris was one of the best known, and loved, Rebetika singers in Greece. He was elderly, when he died in 1972, but was performing up to the end. Here Dalaras performs a selection of his songs in his own inimitable style, but giving them all the respect they undoubtedly deserve. For best atmosphere, listen with a bottle of your favourite Greek wine, and be transported back to Athens.

Yassou Spiti Cook by Janet Ellis

Photo by Sylvia Cook

"Which way do you think they will come from?" I ask Peter. There are paths and roads leading in from a variety of directions. We are sitting at Sam's Taverna in the Platia in Eresos village waiting to meet up with Sylvia and Terry.

As we lived near them in England, we met up with Sylvia and Terry soon after we joined Greek-o-File and they had been encouraging us to visit Lesvos for some time. Like so many other Grecophiles, we have a whole long list of 'must visits' and 'must go backs'. It's a problem trying to fit them all into our annual holiday entitlement.

They said that although Lesvos is a big island it is not reliant on tourism for its economy, so it is not all 'touristy', and they assured us we would enjoy the walking. So on their recommendation, we booked two weeks in early May, staying in Petra, in the North of the island. Once it was booked we obviously told them. The reaction was spontaneous, *"You must visit us in Eresos and come and see Spiti Cook"*. This was an offer not to be refused - I was thrilled - we were going to meet Spiti Cook. Yes, I know, a house is inanimate but after hearing and reading about Sylvia and Terry's Greek home, Spiti Cook seems more like a person. After all, the three of them have been through so much together.

"Here they come." Peter has spotted our hosts walking over from the opposite corner of the Platia. It's wonderful to see them again; especially looking so fit and well on this warm late Spring morning. After greeting, Sylvia suggests *"Beer?" "A cold beer will go down a treat"* answers Peter, *"Just one, as I need to find somewhere to park the car." "No problem"* replies Terry *"you can park not far from Spiti Cook."* So we sit back with our Mythos and Amstels - the introduction to Spiti Cook will have to wait just a little longer.

We relax and chat over our beers about our holiday so far. Terry and Peter drive off in our hire car to park up, while Sylvia and I walk across the Platia and head off through the narrow streets. We turn left, right, left, across here, left again and so on - gee am I confused.

"No wonder you suggested we met up at the Platia," I say as we pass a small shop with empty beer crates stacked outside, *"we never would have found our way to Spiti Cook, especially as there are no street names. The village is an absolute maze."* Sylvia chuckles, *"Well, when Terry brought me here for the first time I didn't dare venture out on my own in case I couldn't find my way back!"* I make a mental note, in case Peter and I go out for a walk around on our own, to take the GPS (satellite navigator) with us. (Those who have read previous editions of Greek-o-File, will note that we have now gone 'up market' from the coloured chalk we used to use to mark our routes. Mind you, I do still carry a piece when we are out walking about, just in case of battery failure or poor signal, etc. You probably think I am one of those sad people who carry around all sorts of bits and pieces just in case - well you've got it in one!)

One last left turn, a few more metres and here we are, standing outside the blue gate with 'Spiti Cook' painted on it. Great timing because along come Terry and Peter from the opposite direction, to join us. Terry pushes open the gate to reveal all that makes up Spiti Cook, the courtyard garden, the apothiki, the old stone privy and of course the newly built house with the old stone steps up to the double blue door. We make a fuss of the tiny foster kittens Pippa and Squeak, who have been asleep in their designer cardboard house out in the garden. Terry suggests *"How about a quick tour? Then we can sit out in the courtyard and have some lunch".* Excellent suggestion.

Photo by Sylvia Cook

We start by entering through the kitchen door. The kitchen is the only remaining room of the old Spiti Cook, retaining some of the original features, from here we go through a door into the new part of the house. To the right, stairs lead off to the first floor but first we go straight ahead and down a few stairs, pausing at the bathroom, complete with corner bath and shower, as well as the usual bathroom fittings and, true to typical Greek homes, the washing machine. Further along is Sylvia and Terry's bedroom, with its colour co-ordinated furnishings, set in the coolest part of the house with the original (re-rendered) half-metre thick stone walls around. From here we retrace our steps and go upstairs to a large versatile airy room open to the wooden ceiling under the tiled roof. This room is multifunctional, can be and is used as an office, living area and spare bedroom as required. Above the office end is Terry's recently constructed wooden platform, created to provide extra storage space. Back in the main room, the 'front' door opens out to the steps going down to the secluded courtyard garden. Another door up a few more stairs at the office end of the room, leads to a balcony terrace above the kitchen, which looks out over the village houses, surrounding hills and even the sea just 4 km away. *"The terrace is a great place to sit out in the early evening to dry my hair in the sun"* Sylvia informs me - looks like a good place to enjoy a pre-dinner ouzo too!

Impressed ? How could we be anything but! Sylvia and Terry have put so much careful thought into the design of the new Spiti Cook, from locating their bedroom in the coolest part of the house, to the large versatile main room, and the terrace where they can enjoy the evening sun and rooftop views.

It wasn't so long ago that Spiti Cook was a heartbreaking pile of charred wood, tiles, tumbled walls and frazzled remains of personal belongings. Just look at it now, truly risen from the ashes. Only the charred inside of one of the wooden gates gave any indication of what happened before. Anyone who has read previous Greek-o-File volumes will be aware that once the shell was complete the rest of the rebuild was completed by Terry and Sylvia, not forgetting assistance from friends. It wasn't until our visit that we fully appreciated the extent and diversity of the work they have both 'turned their hands' to. Hours of back aching grafting and finally the interior décor, influenced by Sylvia's artistic flair, have resulted in this welcoming and functional Greek village home.

So, with our introduction to Spiti Cook complete we settle down to an excellent lunch in the garden. *"We still have a lot more to do."* remarks Sylvia *"There's the terrace to be finished, more painting, the kitchen floor to be levelled, the gate ...."*

With lunch completed and the kittens relishing the last sardine we spent the rest of the weekend in the company of our hosts who took us out and about in Suzie the Suzuki, to places where we could walk around and get a taste of their Lesvos. We walked to a waterfall, were invited for an impromptu Greek coffee and freshly made mizithra cheese at a shepherd's house, saw

the local dam, lake and monastery and enjoyed an evening meal in the Platia.

We did go out for a walk on our own, part way up the old Sigri road early the next morning and, yes, we did remember the GPS - thank goodness! We would have been hard pushed to have found our way back to Spiti Cook without it.

Photo by Sylvia Cook

After another enjoyable walk, Sunday found us taking a late lunch in Tavari, sitting outside a fish taverna, at the end of the beach - most pleasant. Here we said our farewells before we headed back to Petra to continue our holiday, walking around the surrounding countryside. Sylvia and Terry drove off in the opposite direction, to their much loved village of Eresos and the winding streets that lead to Spiti Cook.

Sylvia was right, of course, Lesvos is a great island. We thoroughly enjoyed the walking, aided by Mike Maunder's excellent book (On Foot in North Lesvos). We loved our base in Petra, in particular eating at the Women's Co-Operative and enjoying a beer with George in the late afternoon. So Lesvos has moved from our list of 'must visits', to the other list of places we 'must visit again'.

Oh, just one other thing to mention. Terry makes a terrific bed - no I don't mean he is a dab hand at tucking in sheets, I mean the beds we slept in that he physically made from wood; with mattresses on top, then bedding, or covers and cushions to turn them into day couches. We both slept like logs, they were oh so comfy - looks like they could have a whole new business here!

P.S. Spiti Cook it was good to meet you.

See also inside front & back covers:
Flexicover Travel Insurance
Greek National Tourism Organisation in London
Ionian Island Holidays

Greek Island Specialists

One, Two Centre or Island Hopping Holidays

A selection of **over 60 islands** and a few mainland resorts, many unspoilt and off the beaten track. Tailor made holidays. Visit as many or as few as time and inclination will allow. Transfers & ferry tickets included. Flights optional.

Island Wandering Holidays *0870 777 99 44*

enquiries@islandwandering.com *www.islandwandering.com*

TAPESTRY

H O L I D A Y S

ABTA

The very best of uncommercial Greece

Tapestry Holidays take great pride in providing a specialist, knowledgeable and personalised service offering a variety of holidays to what we think of as the "real Greece". These exclusive holidays, to Pelion, Skopelos, Cephalonia, Ithaca, Corfu & Paxos, are uniquely to be found in our attractive and informative brochures. Please feel welcome to call for your copy on

020 8235 7888 or visit us at **www.tapestryholidays.com**

SIMPSON'S

Discover the clarity of light, the bluest of seas and the timelessness that is Greece with Simpson Travel.

Idyllic villas with private pool, character cottages, apartments and hotels in Crete, Corfu, Paxos and Meganissi.

Speak to someone who's been there! **0845 811 6502**

www.simpsontravel.com ATOL 5858 ABTA

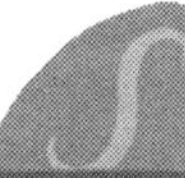

Colin Murison Small's

Hidden Greece with Simply Simon Holidays

Tailor-made holidays at package prices in over 70 unspoilt places in the Dodecanese, East Aegean, Cyclades, Crete and the Argolid peninsular. We offer scheduled flights via Athens as well as charters from regional UK airports direct to our island gateways.

Colin Murison Small and Simon Lanyon have been Greek specialist tour operators since 1961.

Tel: 020 7839 2553 Email: info@hidden-greece.co.uk

47 Whitcomb St. London WC2H 7DH Website: www.hidden-greece.co.uk

The leading tour operator to **24 Greek Islands & Cyprus**, flights from 16 UK airports

0870 429 4242 or visit

olympicholidays.com

ATOL Protected 4108 ABTA V8302

A fresh approach to the Greek Islands

With a choice of Greek islands and a range of villas with pools set in unspoilt locations, Sunisle clients benefit from flexible arrival days and flights from local airports. Our website has full details of all properties and shows up to the minute availability. Let our knowledgeable customer services team tailor make the perfect holiday for you this summer.

Web: www.sunisle.co.uk Tel: 0871 230 0588

Walks Worldwide

*Experience the **Corfu Trail** (self guided flexible walking holidays), the wonders of walking in the **Pindos Mts, Pelion, Mani, Naxos, Crete** or **Mt Olymbos.***

Tel **01524 242000** for brochure, or see **www.walksworldwide.com**

NASSOS GUEST HOUSE, Lesvos

Relax in the heart of characterful Molyvos.
Friendly atmosphere €20-35 double room p.n.
Tel / Fax +30 22530 71432
www.nassosguesthouse.com

Lovely villas on 16 islands, best personal service

Elysian Holidays

01580 766599

www.elysianholidays.co.uk & new **www.elysianpropertysales.com**

GREECE
villas, cottages and pensions

We had a surreal, but rivetting evening in Ithaca, when we happened across a poetry reading. As the only people in the restaurant, we were serenaded by Alexos the town's fireman, reading his own (but side-splittingly funny) verse.

Debby

Simply Travel www.simplytravel.com
020 8541 2222

Blue Bay Hotel, Haramida, Lesvos

Family run hotel/restaurant overlooking olive grove, fields & peaceful Haramida Bay. 9 km Mytilene airport. From €35 per day for dble low season.

George & Theano Gonidelli **Tel +30 22510 91000, www.bluebay-lesvos.com**

ISLANDS OF GREECE LIMITED

We have a large selection of villas, apts, character and luxury hotels with wonderful views overlooking the sea in **Skiathos, Skopelos, Alonissos, Milos, Naxos, Mykonos, Paros, Antiparos, Crete, Santorini.**

020 8940 5157 AITO, ATOL protected 1680 **www.islands-of-greece.co.uk**

Great **Car Rental** rates throughout **Greece** and its islands

SKYCARS 0870 789 7789

book online at www.skycars.com email sales@skycars.com

No. 1 SCHEDULED AIRLINE FROM UK TO GREECE

*FLIGHTS FROM **LONDON HEATHROW** TO **ATHENS***
LONDON GATWICK** TO **THESSALONIKI & ATHENS
MANCHESTER** TO **ATHENS

OLYMPIC AIRLINES S.A.
11 CONDUIT STREET, LONDON W1S 2LP
TEL: 0870 606 0460 FAX: 020 7629 9891
www.olympicairlines.com

Allsun Faraway Holidays, a subsidiary of Olympic Airlines, offer Greek-o-File readers **special prices on scheduled flights** from the UK (Heathrow, Gatwick & Manchester) to Greece and her islands. Book early for best rates.

Call Allsun for a quote 020 7399 1550
Fax 020 7399 1560, email info@allsun.co.uk,
or complete booking request form online www.allsun.co.uk

Don't forget to quote **Greek-o-File**

Are you paying too much for your travel insurance?

Columbus offer Greek-o-File contacts <u>10% off</u>
when you book via our website link - www.greekofile.co.uk - or telephone Columbus Direct on **0845 330 8518** and quote **Greek-o-File.**

<u>Europe</u> - <u>Single trip</u> from :			<u>Annual multi-trip</u> **from:**		
10d/15d	~~£9.95~~	**£8.96**	Adult	~~£45~~	**£40.50**
31d	~~£24.75~~	**£22.28**	Couple	~~£68.88~~	**£61.99**
90d	~~£49.35~~	**£44.42**	Family	~~£82.95~~	**£74.66** at 8/05

NB. No discount on annual insurance for over 65s. You do not have to take insurance with your tour operator, but may be asked for details to prove you are covered.

Index

*In this index main article subjects are in **bold**, reference only items in plain text and place names are listed after their island or region name.*

The Greek-o-File Volumes 1, 2 & 3

If you have not read our first 3 volumes, you can still buy them direct from Greek-o-File (or from retail outlets) to build your File on all things Greek.

Volume 1 ISBN 0-9543593-0-5 Ret £8.50
Volume 2 ISBN 0-9543593-1-3 Ret. £9.50
Volume 3 ISBN 0-9543593-2-1 Ret. £9.50

OFFER PRICES just **£8** Individually direct from Greek-o-File inc. UK P&P

or

£15 for 2 different volumes, £21 for 3 inc UK P&P.

All volumes are192 pages, approx 50 illustrated articles in each book. Similar style to this book - reader experiences, anecdotes and researched articles from ourselves and fellow Grecophiles. (Details of content and extracts on website www.greekofile.co.uk)

Back Issues of our former **Quarterly Magazines** are also available - published Autumn 1998 to June 2002, A4 prepunched pages build into a file of information and anecdotes. Some **Stock Clearance issues just £1**, others at **£3 each** (inc UK p&p) or all **15** with a **FREE** white 4 ring Greek-o-**FILE** and dividers for just **£35.**

Greek-o-File™

Greek-o-File Logos to personalise your T-shirt, sweatshirt, vest, shorts, sundress, or other cotton item - **Iron-on** Greek-o-File registered trade mark logos **cyan & black** (colour as book front) seagull silhouette & name or just use the seagull **3 logos 6x4cm** for **£1.95** or larger **2 logos 9x6cm** for **£2.50** inc VAT & UK P&P.

Notecards - Sets of Images of Greece, Animals, Cats, Flowers, Lesvos or Eresos available. Watercolour impressions from photographs by Sylvia Cook. Each set 9 cards 148 x 105mm with envelopes for **£4.20**, **3 sets £11** inc VAT & UK P&P.

Plus additional offers for direct subscribers

Contact Greek-o-File 01225 709907 or mail@greekofile.co.uk for latest information, or see website **www.greekofile.co.uk** for more content detail of books, magazine extracts & notecards.

Reply Form

If you would like to be **notified when future issues** are to be published, **order offer items**, or **send an article** for consideration in future books, please complete this form (or a copy) where appropriate and post with relevant additional details or payment to our new address:

Greek-o-File, 29 Littlejohn Ave, Melksham, Wilts, SN12 7AW, UK

Name Mr/Mrs/Ms/Miss ______________________

Address ______________________

______________________ **Post Code** ____________

Tel (Day / Eve) ______________________

Email address ______________________

Where did you buy/find this book? ______________________

I would like:

To be notified when future Greek-o-File volumes will be available ___

If you purchased this book direct you will automatically be notified - let us know if you move.

Circle or underline as appropriate or send separate letter where clarification is needed. Prices quoted **inc UK P&P** on all items and **VAT** on logos and notecards.

To purchase more Greek-o-File Paperback Books

Set of **all 4** volumes **£27** __ Any **3** different volumes **£21** __

Any **2** different volumes **£15** __ **Individually** Vol **1, 2** or **3** @ **£8** each __

Specify which volumes required ______________________

(For overseas add per book: Rest of EU £1, Rest of World £2)

To purchase ALL 15 Greek-o-File loose leaf magazine back issues, now **£35** ___ includes UK P&P AND a **FREE Greek-o-FILE** (4-ring A4 white file with dividers).

Individual issues available @ **£3** each, some stock clearance @ **£1** each.

To purchase Greek-o-File Notecards 1 set of 9 for **£4.20**, 3 sets **£11** ___

- specify sets: Images of Greece, Animals, Cats, Flowers, Lesvos, Eresos

To purchase Greek-o-File logos inc VAT, P&P 2 large (9x6cm) for **£2.50** ___

3 small (6x4cm) for **£1.95** ___

I enclose an article/ item for consideration (max 3 x A4 pages, 2,000 words) ___

(Free copy of book supplied to contributors of articles printed of at least 1 page)

Under the terms of the Data Protection Act we do NOT supply names & addresses to others, but may send mailings about appropriate products from our offices.

Optional Additional Information:

Favourite Greek destination(s) (max 3) ______________________

Age Group Less than 30 ☐ 31-45 ☐ 46-60 ☐ 61+ ☐

Greek-o-File™ Company Reg. 3620858, VAT Reg GB 711 1751 75